NEGOTIATION

Theories, Strategies and Skills

NEGOTIATION
Theories, Strategies and Skills

WYNAND D. PIENAAR

Professor Emeritus
Graduate School of Business Leadership
University of South Africa

H.I.J. SPOELSTRA

Management Consultant
Formerly Professor in Organisational Behaviour
Graduate School of Business Leadership
University of South Africa

JUTA & CO, LTD

First published in 1991
Second edition 1996

Copyright © Juta & Co, Ltd
PO Box 14373, Kenwyn 7790

ISBN 0 7021 3578 X

Typesetting: Zebra Publications, Cape Town
Cover concept: Tania Spoelstra, Pretoria
Cover design: Joy Wrench, Cape Town
Subediting: Julia Krone, Mike Golby, Cape Town

Printed and bound in the Republic of South Africa
by Creda Press, Eliot Avenue, Epping 2

Preface

Over the last few years South Africa has emerged as a world leader in the field of practical negotiation. 'It's a miracle', were the words President Bill Clinton of the United States of America used to endorse South Africa's achievement of a historic political agreement, after decades of conflict, through the proper application of the principles of negotiation. Through an understanding of the processes and skills of negotiation, our political leaders were able to negotiate agreements from extreme positions — emphasising the enormous potential of negotiation as a method whereby many of the problems and challenges of human relationships can effectively be addressed.

Today, everyone negotiates. Negotiation is the only really effective tool to ensure that all individuals in our society have equal rights and opportunities. Managers, for example, are essentially negotiators. They have to influence and motivate, as part of their daily activities, a diversity of people, often of different language groups and cultures, and have to balance the conflicting aspirations of individuals and groups. The remarkable progress achieved through negotiation in the political and social arena has stimulated demand from commerce and industry for knowledge of negotiation processes and practical negotiation skills.

The new, second edition of *Negotiation—Theories, Strategies and Skills* is published with this in mind. The book can be used as a guide for detailed planning and training and to improve interpersonal relationships. Above all, it is a book that marries academic and practical knowledge of ways to reduce human conflict and enhance co-operation between people. It is the authors' sincere hope that it will help establish a culture of negotiation.

Contents

CHAPTER 1

Introduction to Negotiation

In this Chapter

❏ *Negotiation:* What is it?
❏ *Key Concepts* in negotiation:
  - Integrative
  - Distributive
  - Destructive
❏ *Negotiation Relationships:*
  - Continuous
  - Intermittent
  - Crisis
❏ *Negotiation Styles:*
  - Direct
  - Indirect
❏ *Negotiation Content:*
  - Packaging
  - Progressive Summarisation

THE NATURE OF NEGOTIATION

We are living in the era of negotiation. Around us the world has changed and is still changing rapidly because of and by means of negotiation. Negotiation is a fact of life: just as we cannot exist without communicating, so we can barely exist without negotiating.

Through negotiation great progress is made that previously could only take place through military action. A decade ago South Africa was still at war in Angola, world sanctions were in full force, terrorist bombings were virtually daily phenomena, and a fully fledged state of emergency was in force — a country under siege. Within the last few years dramatic changes have taken place. Peace in Angola; Namibian independence; the state of emergency lifted; the ANC and the National Party members of an interim government, and President Mandela leading all South Africans to a new democratic era. The unthinkable has happened and is still happening!

It has been realised that because the price of conflict can only be paid afterwards, the price of peace must be paid beforehand.

How did this new thinking come about? Only through a worldwide realisation that, forty years after World War II, great changes can take place when people **face** each other across a table instead of **avoiding** each other. Leaders in all spheres of life have now realised the potential of **negotiation**. The world around us has made it an essential requirement that business managers can and must negotiate. New labour legislation 'forced' managers in South Africa to face their workers more frequently and to bargain according to certain rules. The well-known Japanese business management author Imai (1986) has stated that, because of the increasing involvement and participation of workers in the world of the future, the manager's role will be mainly that of a communicator, negotiator and decision maker.

In short, a global culture has emerged which eclipses other ways of limiting conflict — negotiation instead of confrontation.

The entire world seems to agree and to subscribe to this cultural movement.

Negotiation defined

*Negotiation is a **process** of interaction between parties directed at reaching some form of agreement that will hold and which is based upon common interests, with the purpose of resolving conflict, despite widely dividing differences.* This is achieved through the establishment of **common ground** *and the creation of **alternatives**. To the present authors, common ground is not just what people **have** in common but what they **could become together**.*

Negotiation is an **exchange of information through communication.** The information is formulated as strategies and techniques. These strategies and techniques originate from the negotiation relationship between the parties and they serve to continue or discontinue the relationship. The purpose of this communication exchange is to reach agreement between parties who have certain things in common while disagreeing on others.

Therefore, negotiation, in this definition, is defined as a process. The fact that we regard it as a process is an important characteristic of the definition since a process implies that it is not an **event**.

In other words, the element of **continuity** in negotiation is very important. An event would imply that parties will only meet once and will possibly never see each other again, ever. The fact that emphasis is laid on the **process** characteristic does not mean that the strategies and tactics that are discussed in this book could not be applied in a negotiation that takes the form of a once-off negotiation.

Meeting workers regularly to appraise performance and reach agreements on future performance; dealing with suppliers about future contracts; meeting labour unions with the aim of signing annual wage agreements . . . these are all typical 'processes', while a single court case would be a typical 'event'. This implies that time and timing are crucial factors in negotiation — variables often forgotten or not mentioned in other works.

The definition implies that the processes should be directed at reaching some form of agreement. In other words, if two parties were to meet casually without the purpose of reaching some form of agreement this would not be **labelled** as negotiation. But the process could also be aimed at limiting conflict. The main implication is that **no one negotiates to avoid loss**, but to obtain 'gain'. And the emphasis is on obtaining continued co-operation.

Common ground is emphasised in the original definition and it has already been pointed out that it refers not to the past or present, but negotiation is always future orientated. A good negotiator is not someone who makes a deal, but someone who establishes a deal which will, in future, present the lowest possible implementation failure rate. Rather no deal, than a deal that continuously breaks down.

The definition refers also to the creation of **alternatives**. The creation of alternatives implies **flexibility** in negotiation since a lack of flexibility on both sides and rigidity on objectives and goals could most often lead to deadlock. The joint creation of alternatives helps also to establish a common culture through which to approach the other.

Furthermore, in this definition reference is made to **dividing** differences. This aspect of the definition should be emphasised. It implies that, although individuals may differ widely, bringing them together physically may bridge their differences, especially if both sides are flexible and are willing to create **alternatives**. Avoiding the other side just causes further problems and often leads to escalation of existing conflict. In negotiation, one should recognise differences but utilise similarities. Differences are accommodated, but similarities are used to bring unity of purpose and method.

The definition also refers to **agreements that hold**. Negotiation would not be regarded as successful if agreements do not hold. That is the real test as to whether the negotiation was successful or not. It is a process that unfolds over time, causing chain reactions with one common goal, 'peaceful' conclusions. *Finally, a good negotiator will always secure* **common ground**. *For instance, to ensure the creation of alternative solutions and in seeking areas for future co-operation, a shared goal of negotiating values before price is recommended. Finally, the skilled negotiator will obtain a commitment to always search for what may still be missing, asking not who is present but rather which party may be absent, inquiring not as to what is on the agenda but as to what should be on the agenda which is still absent. The negotiator should seek to be objective, asking not what is in it for himself but what both parties can become together. The successful negotiator will make this a visible climate, if not a culture, shared during the negotiation process.*

Many concepts are utilised in popular literature on negotiation and the concepts of *bargaining* and *negotiation* need some clarification.

There is great confusion about the difference between *bargaining* and *negotiation*. *Bargaining* is 'an agreement on terms of give and take; come to terms . . .' *Negotiation* is defined as: 'confer with another with view to compromise or agreement; arrange; bring about . . .' (*Concise Oxford Dictionary* (1982)). According to these definitions, both *negotiation* and bargaining aim to reach an agreement or compromise through the process of give and take.

Bargaining could, for example, relate to a monetary transaction between two people. It is tacitly understood by both parties that the buyer will try to obtain the lowest price that he can from the seller, so that the seller names a higher price than he would expect to get and gradually brings it down in response to the *'bargaining'* of the buyer. *Negotiation* is often said to be any other type of interaction between people that will require both parties to **compromise** in order to reach an agreement. There could be monetary issues involved, but it will be complicated by other issues that have to be part of the *negotiation*. Traditionally, in *bargaining*, each party is clear at the outset as to its real base: the buyer wants the best price he can get and the seller wants the highest price he can get. In *negotiation* both parties have to be prepared for the possibility of having to change their 'real base' (the least that they would accept in a negotiation offer) in the interests of a successful outcome to the *negotiation*. Therefore, in this book, the concepts *bargaining* and *negotiation* will be used in much the same way, implying the same purpose and having the same meaning and developing the same methods.

Collective bargaining/negotiation

Collective bargaining occurs when two or more parties consisting of groups of people act **collectively**. *The purpose is to come to an agreement on issues that concern the group as a whole.* Collective negotiation can also be undertaken on behalf of the group by agents or representatives who need not be members of the group. This form of negotiation is usually found in labour relations (Piron 1979). The present authors will address collective, multiparty and representative negotiation or bargaining.

Persuasion

Persuasion is communicative behaviour intended to **change**, *modify or shape the responses, attitudes or behaviour of the receiver. An important aspect of persuasion is* **behavioural change**. Persuasion should be distinguished from intimidation or force, where behavioural change does not occur by choice.

Persuasion is a key component of negotiation. Bostrom (1983:231) states that '. . . the really persuasive task is to get individuals to bargain at all'. Persuasion is not only found in the face-to-face phase of negotiation, but also in the important pre-negotiation phase. Persuasive communication is therefore part of negotiation and extremely useful when opinions, attitudes and behaviours have to be changed.

Mediation

Mediation is the process through which agreements are reached with the aid of a **neutral** *third party or 'helper'* (Nieumeijer 1988). The third party should have no decision-making power and have no vested interest in either of the parties. The mediator acts mainly as a communication and problem-solving **catalyst**, or as an agent to maximise the exploration and operation of alternatives, while the responsibility for the final agreement rests with the conflicting parties. Mediation should, really, bring parties back into direct negotiation again.

Arbitration

Arbitration is also based on intervention by a third party in an attempt to reach an agreement, but the final decision lies with the arbitrator. The parties no longer have the right to conclude an agreement. Each presents its case to the arbitrator, who takes the facts into consideration in forming a verdict. The arbitrator's decision is usually binding (Piron 1982:91).

Lobbying

*Lobbying is usually found in national and international negotiations, where one party tries to **pressurise** the other,* directly or indirectly, by involving other interest groups, to accept its point of view or objective. Lobbying includes influencing a person or persons influential enough to advance an issue or viewpoint (Peters 1983). Lobbying is part of negotiation, only the venue and group size vary over time.

Talks

A distinction is often made between talks and negotiation. Politicians especially prefer talks to be 'informal' meetings wherein parties will collect information and explore each other's point of view, flexibility and acceptability. Only when parties are within **reach** of each other's objectives will the talks become 'negotiations'. Talks normally involve a process of attempting to convince parties to limit the negotiation range from 'what I want', to, 'what you want', to 'what is the least you will take', to 'what is the most I can offer'. When, in other words, there is a mutual agreement within reach, the parties will negotiate.

TYPES OF NEGOTIATION

Negotiation could be classified into types, according to some critical variables such as time/timing, conflict and actors.

One could also classify objectives or outcomes, or one could classify negotiation in terms of the situations that negotiators are confronted with. The type of relationship that exists between the negotiating parties could also be a tool for classification of the negotiation processes. The use of any classification could possibly be questioned. It is our belief that classifications do help the parties to decide in what kind of situation they find themselves, so as to plan their strategies and tactics in a much more meaningful way. In this book we regard the classification in terms of Integrative and Distributive Negotiation as possibly the most important way to describe the objectives and the processes that parties confront during negotiation.

Classifying objectives

Integrative negotiation

In a simplified form, *this is a 'win more–win more' model of negotiation,* not merely the 'win–win' situation normally referred to. In this model both parties have the objective to walk away with at least a perception of having gained more than they could through an alternative approach. It is possibly the most commonly used 'model' of negotiation. In this form of negotiation disagreements are seen to be more costly than compromise; gains and losses should be equalised; and there are underlying repetitive or continuous relationships which have to be maintained as there could definitely be future dependence of the parties on each other.

Case 1.1

INTEGRATIVE NEGOTIATION

South Africa versus Angola and Cuba

The negotiation between South Africa and Angola a few years ago, with American and Russian assistance, was a good example of this approach in negotiation. Both sides, after each meeting, walked away with at least 'something' that they could take back to their constituents. An attempt was made to help each side at each stage of negotiation to gain 'face' and to make a little bit of progress. Both sides agreed that disagreement would cause the war to be extended and even to escalate, and that that would be much more costly than compromising. They tried, as far as possible, to equalise the gains and losses of each side by having detailed and specified agreements concerning trade-offs in terms of troop withdrawal and financial assistance after the independence of Namibia. The American participants at the negotiation also helped the parties to realise that a long-term relationship could be a very important outcome of the negotiations. All sides were therefore highly motivated to be flexible. The South Africans were assured of assistance internationally and of future international relationships; aspects which were very important to them at that stage. At the same time, the Cubans and the Angolans were also assured of more economic progress, something that was important to them at that stage.

There are many other examples of this form of negotiation that have taken place recently and have been reported in the press. The most important examples, however, take place every day within organisations where managers negotiate with each other about budgets and projects; where managers negotiate with workers; and where company representatives negotiate with suppliers, agents and retailers about buying and selling goods or services.

Distributive negotiation

Simplified, *this is a 'win–lose' model of negotiation.* In this model the parties go into negotiation with the objective to 'win' for themselves, regardless of what happens to the other side. It is often said that this is not really 'negotiation', for one party has to **lose**, and will seek control over the other's finances, resources or associations. The actions of the parties will be directed at the other party rather than at problem solving, and will be **offensive** rather than defensive, with **manipulation** occurring. A good example of this is a court case, some property negotiations, election issues, religious issues, divorce cases and second-hand car deals.

Case 1.2

DISTRIBUTIVE NEGOTIATION

President Paul Kruger versus Lord Milner

Chamberlain prepared for the republican government a message which, while stiffly worded, fell far short of an ultimatum, pinning his hopes on a proposal by President Johannes Brand of the OFS for a conference between Milner and Kruger at the end of May, with Bloemfontein as a venue. Milner told Chamberlain that, at the conference, he would harp on uitlander grievances in an attempt to goad Kruger into terminating proceedings, saying that although they were scarcely a good enough reason for going to war, the grievances were at least a popular and well-understood cause. At the conference, Kruger offered the franchise after seven years' residence but, in return, made a number of demands that included the incorporation of Swaziland into the SAR, arbitration over the London Convention — an on-going squabble concerning British sovereignty over the republic's foreign relations — and compensation for the Jameson Raid. Demanding that the franchise be granted after five years' residence, which Kruger refused, Milner brought the conference to an end. He did not, however, regard the talking as over for good, but wrote to a nervous Chamberlain that 'if the President is sufficiently pushed there is still a chance, though a small one, of his adopting my minimum'. He impressed on the South African League the need to keep 'cool and moderate', and not to exceed its previous demands, as this might alienate public opinion, which was 'steadily settling on our side . . .'.

On the 11th October 1899 the SAR and OFS were at war with the British Empire.

Illustrated History of South Africa. Reader's Digest 1988 (pp 242–243).

Destructive negotiation

This is a form of 'negotiation' used by some labour unions or groups of individuals that try to 'win' by losing. It is the kind of 'negotiation' where one party tries to inflict damage on the other party while at the same time not caring about the damage inflicted on itself (**'lose–lose'**). It is similar to the 'Scorched Earth' policy used in some wars where both sides suffer in the end. It is a dangerous policy. This situation can occur in an auction, in court cases and often in divorce cases. For example:

In the Gulf War of 1990–1991, Iraq was in a position where any further damage to it would hinder further USA–Arab relations. Their conjoint collapse stopped General Schwarzkopf's approach by presidential decree. To defeat Saddam Hussein would create a destabilisation process which America would find more costly than the war itself.

Destructive tactics prove nothing except that revenge and retribution can be obtained through self-destruction.

Classifying relationships
Co-operative negotiation

This is a form of negotiation in which win or lose are irrelevant; where conflict is turned into co-operation without either party entering into the competitive mode. The present authors are convinced that this form of negotiation exists which is neither 'Integrative' or 'Distributive.' Networking for the sake of involving others co-operatively would be an excellent example.

Continuous negotiation

*In this type of negotiation there is an **on-going relationship** between parties that has to be maintained throughout negotiation itself and into the future.* So, regardless of difficulties and problems, the relationship is maintained so that the parties can face one another at further negotiation sessions. To allow this, good relationships must be encouraged. Examples of continuous relationships are those between employer and employee, husband and wife, and customer and supplier.

Intermittent negotiation

This type of negotiation takes place when a problem arises that may threaten the relationship between the parties. Intermittent negotiation usually occurs when past relations between the parties have been good, but recent problems threaten the relationship. It could happen in a marriage. Another example is where failure to pay leads to an unexpected disagreement.

This kind of negotiation could also be of the **'once-off'** type. Examples of this would be buying a house or a motor car, where the buyer may never again have any contact with the supplier.

Crisis negotiation

When one party elicits a confrontation by creating a crisis before negotiation starts, the negotiation that follows can be called crisis negotiation. The crisis could be an unexpected labour **strike**, or taking of hostages or hijacking. This form of negotiation is still directed at an agreement but the bases of power from which the parties depart are very different. A crisis must be resolved. This makes it different from the previous two types of negotiation.

Classifying styles

The contact between parties who are negotiating can be Direct (Explicit) or Indirect (Tacit). Direct negotiating refers to a face-to-face situation, and Indirect negotiation refers to the use of representatives, control over the media, advertising and the like.

Direct (explicit) negotiation

Direct or explicit negotiation refers to 'face-to-face' contact. This form of negotiation is commonly used in labour negotiations, diplomatic exchanges, conflict resolution and market bargaining (Strauss 1978). In explicit negotiation the parties do not necessarily act rationally or know their own and the other's preferences or values, but they do communicate openly, making demands, stating preferences, asking for information, offering proposals and making concessions. In so doing they manoeuvre, use tactics and follow strategies that are observable by an onlooker.

Indirect (tacit) negotiation

In indirect (tacit) negotiations the use of representatives, control over the media, advertising and other third parties become the prime sources of influence. Here, messages could be passed between or among negotiators indirectly in the form of hints, signs, gossip or media reporting. As Schelling (1960) notes, this bargaining is typically used whenever communication is incomplete or impossible, whenever either party will not negotiate directly and whenever neither will trust his counterpart in a direct confrontation. Sometimes norms exist that prohibit direct negotiation, so the only way is through indirect means. Pienaar (1976) points out that in indirect negotiation parties often use phrases such as 'official sources', 'informed parties', or 'events would seem to indicate'. But, he cautions, indirect negotiation may not take the form of the written word — troop movements, the absence of a critical player or a sudden entrance into talks with another party could signal indirect negotiation.

Classifying content

Negotiation can also be classified according to content characteristics. One of the following two approaches can be used, although sometimes they could be used sequentially in one negotiation process.

The package type

When this technique is used the following steps are usually followed:

A proposed agreement could be **tendered**. When a proposal is tendered, often a party will specify aspects such as payment systems, implementation systems and dates, what sort of arbitration should be applied when a problem arises and what laws should be used if litigation takes place. Normally, in a package-type negotiation, it is assumed that the power base of the one party, normally the initiator, exceeds that of the other party. As part of the package, penalty clauses, in the case of non-performance, are specified.

Packaged negotiation is often a more rigid and a 'tougher' type of negotiation where less flexibility is possible. The package technique requires that specification and performance criteria be adhered to.

An example could be negotiation with an educational body to enrol in a certain course. The educational institution would offer a 'package' containing the courses offered, the credits and assignments required to write the examination, the dress code and transport arrangements, and many more fixed items. The prospective student would take or leave the package as a whole — it is very difficult to change variables within the 'offer'.

Progressive summarisation type

The progressive summarisation technique is based on the assumption that the power bases of the parties are equal. It is therefore a more **flexible** way of negotiating. Important subvariables exist which usually culminate in the well-known legal term, 'heads of agreement'. Inductive logic is normally used — the parties would start with reality; for example, they will discuss:

- ❏ when to **meet**,
- ❏ what they will **discuss**,
- ❏ how much **money** they have, and so on.

Then they will move, in the negotiation itself, through all these variables towards the 'heads of agreement'. In other words, **they will agree about their future relationship**. This means that the parties have started with reality and moved towards the ideal (inductive logic).

During this kind of negotiation the agenda proceeds through different stages, where agreement is reached on small sections that slowly and progressively move towards the final agreement. The implementation of each of the sections or clauses could be added or negotiated as part of the process leading up to the final heads of agreement. In the same way, security and arbitration clauses can be included in contracts negotiated by means of the progressive summarisation method.

The progressive summarisation method is made up of a series of small steps which are agreed upon; then the process is summarised to ascertain progress made; then the process is repeated. It could also comprise a series of meetings to discuss one major topic or a few minor ones.

So, in summary, the progressive summarisation technique has **multiple** and/or sequential **impact** on the other party. It makes use of slow changes in perception and attitude. Movement is gradual, and therefore the other party sometimes does not even realise that it is making big strides, because the strides are broken up into small movements toward the final stride.

> Examples can often be found in politics, as in the South African situation before the 1994 elections. The government and the ANC were involved in negotiation where they were progressively making small movements that were significant and where more parties could be slowly drawn into the process until everyone that had a stake in the outcome was involved and a final agreement could be reached.

CONCLUSION

When the team of representatives approach a negotiating situation, it is important that they consider whether they can afford distributive objectives or whether their aim should be primarily to find an outcome where both sides could gain, even if it means giving away something else in the process. When the team understands the future dependency and/or relationship that could evolve, their decisions and objectives become more rational. To some extent they will be bound by the content of the issues that they will address around the table. If they can 'break up' issues so as to have repetitive meetings, it could possibly enable them to find more alternatives and be more flexible. On the other hand, if they are far apart, it may require various indirect measures to bring them within range of each other's objectives so that fruitful agreements could be reached.

CHAPTER 2

Preparation for Negotiation

In this Chapter

❏ *Processes* involved in negotiation
❏ *Dynamic Model* for negotiation
❏ *Phases* in the negotiation process
❏ *Real Base* and *Aspiration Base*
❏ *Preparatory Phase* of the negotiation process
❏ *Legal* implications of a negotiated contract
❏ The importance of good *planning*

NEGOTIATION AS A PROCESS

Introduction

'Negotiation' was defined in chapter 1 as *a process of interaction between parties directed at reaching some form of agreement that will hold.*

A **process** would imply that:

❑ negotiation would proceed through various phases that could be repeated over time,

❑ there could be a starting point and a point where the process is completed.

Where, then, does negotiation start and where does it end?

Starting and ending negotiation

To identify the 'end' of negotiation is probably easier than identifying the start. Some negotiations will have a clear ending. For example:

> The hostage release negotiations between the United States and Iran 'ended' on 20 January 1981 at 11h45 Algiers time, when the agreement was announced between these two countries about the release of hostages and other minor aspects.

Some negotiations will be repeated over many years. For example:

> In the case of a long **relationship** between a supplier and manufacturer of motor-car parts there will be **frequent** get-togethers and negotiations about quality, deliveries, quantities, price, relationships with other manufacturers and suppliers, credit and many other issues.

We believe that most negotiations in work-life are of a **continuous** nature.

> You work with your boss today and you have to face him again tomorrow. You deal with a client today and you never know when you could meet him again. It could be five or ten years, by which time that client may have become quite a major force in the market. In this regard, it is very important to keep the **relationship** in mind at all times during negotiations.

In most cases, therefore, if we are dealing with a continuous or an integrative relationship, the relative price of conflict will be higher than in the case of a distributive or a one-off relationship.

The starting point of negotiation is sometimes more difficult to identify. It is better to refer to a **potential** for negotiation rather than to a starting point. The potential for negotiation at any given time is created by a number of factors that affect an individual, company or organisation.

THE POTENTIAL FOR NEGOTIATION

Conflict as the stimulus for negotiation

Many authors (Lewicki & Litterer 1985:4; Pedler 1977:12) agree that conflict serves as a major stimulus for negotiation. Conflict occurs when people have separate and conflicting interests and needs.

Negotiating parties may be subjected to different forms of conflict, depending on their needs and interests at that time or the needs and interests of their constituents (the people they represent). For example, they may both have a need for the same piece of real estate, the same position in the company, a similar part of the market, or equal amounts of support amongst voters.

The following three types of conflict could exist at any time during negotiations.

Approach-avoidance conflict

When your opponent in negotiation is in an approach-avoidance conflict, he will have a need to negotiate but also a fear of entering the agreement. For example:

> Management (or a trade union) could be keen to accept the counter-offer of the union but at the same time be scared of the loss of image and status if they do. In another instance someone could be very keen to obtain a franchise to sell your product but does not have the necessary financial resources to set up the infrastructure that is required as one of the terms of the franchise.

This kind of need conflict is illustrated in figure 2.1.

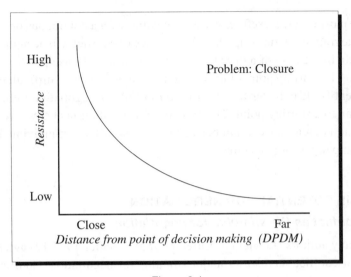

Figure 2.1
APPROACH–AVOIDANCE CONFLICT

When a party in negotiation finds himself in this kind of conflict, it would imply that when he is still far away from a final decision his resistance would be low because there is no pressure on him as yet to sign the documents. The closer he gets to the agreement, the more his resistance will increase. The problem in this kind of negotiation will be **closure**. He could possibly be trying to play for time towards the end of the negotiation.

How to end or **close** the negotiation would be the real challenge in this situation.

One method that trained negotiators use in this kind of conflict is to remove the source of avoidance first and then continue with the approach side of it last. In other words, first talk about the 'bad' news and keep the 'good' news for the last part of the negotiation. This would imply that an approach-avoidance conflict is changed to an avoidance-approach conflict.

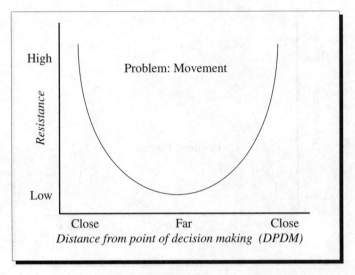

Figure 2.2
APPROACH–APPROACH CONFLICT

Approach–approach conflict

This kind of need conflict occurs when one party is confronted with two equally attractive proposals or agreements, but choosing one would imply losing the other. This kind of conflict is illustrated in figure 2.2.

Clearly, a party that experiences this kind of conflict will fluctuate between the alternatives and obtaining **movement** in the direction of one of the alternatives is the most problematic part of this kind of negotiation. For example:

> You are interviewing a prospective employee who is very highly sought after. He has had an equally attractive job offer from another company, and this could put him in this kind of conflict. The more he fluctuates between the alternatives, the closer he comes to a decision. The problem is one of forcing comparisons between the two attractive offers. Trained negotiators could, in this case, keep their best arguments until the end of the negotiation so that the applicant could be balanced in terms of his decision right till the end and when the final argument is put on the table it often sways him to the side that (in this case) the trained interviewer is on.

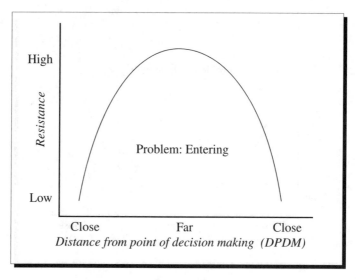

Figure 2.3
AVOIDANCE–AVOIDANCE CONFLICT

Avoidance-avoidance conflict

When your opponent is far from the point of decision making his resistance is the highest, in this kind of need conflict, but once he decides to negotiate, the conflict often disappears easily. In an avoidance-avoidance conflict your opponent would have difficulty entering into negotiation. For example:

> During the later part of the eighties the ruling National Party government in South Africa was in the conflict of either negotiating with the ANC, and then ultimately losing its power, or not negotiating and losing its power as well (due to financial isolation and international military support for its opponents).

In another example, someone who owes you a substantial amount of money, but who does not have the funds to pay you, could have the conflict of talking to you and losing his possessions, or not talking to you and being taken to court (ultimately also losing his possessions). In a case like this, the negotiating parties do not want to **enter** the negotiations in the first place, because they do not really want to choose either of the options.

In this kind of need conflict the problem is one of **entering** negotiation or of initial choice. A trained negotiator will firstly negotiate only for change in attitudes so that the other party will be willing to enter into the negotiation. This could be highly complex, involving other constituents of the opposing side, or it could be a simple case of stating your views and influencing the other party concerned. This type of conflict is illustrated in figure 2.3.

In summary, then, the **needs** of people and organisations lie at the basis of negotiating potential, especially when resources to meet those needs are scarce. It is often said that negotiation is the matching of the needs and resources of two parties, each needing the resources of the other.

Many situations could give rise to needs that in turn could lead to the desire to negotiate or to meet these needs through some means of resolving conflict. For example, after the establishment of a new government in South Africa in 1994, all international sanctions were gradually lifted. This created many opportunities and potentially beneficial negotiations with overseas organisations, especially those that stayed out of South Africa or left the country because of sanctions. Pepsi-Cola, IBM, Ford, McDonalds, Saab, Volvo and many others are examples of these companies.

Resolution of conflict

Many ways of solving or resolving conflicts will be discussed in chapter 6. Negotiation is only one of those ways. Other ways could be:

❑ **Force** (removing the object of the conflict or the competitor by strong-arm means).
❑ More 'subtle' forms of force like verbal **threats**.
❑ Communicating through **third parties**.
❑ **Ignoring** the fact that the conflict exists.

Of all the different means of resolving conflict, negotiation is without doubt the most useful. It is often said that the price of negotiation must be paid before the agreement, while the price of conflict and force must always be paid afterwards. It is often found that a party would rather go to war than be flexible and negotiate. The price of losing many lives in many wars over the years has finally dawned on society in this century. Mankind is now hopefully more mature when it comes to conflict and war. It is a pity that we often only realise the potential of negotiation after immense destruction of lives and property.

The last part of this century and the beginning of the next will hopefully be the time when the political conflicts of Israel and Palestine, of Ireland, of Angola, of Bosnia and many others can be resolved through negotiation. The potential of negotiation was dramatically illustrated by the achievements of people like Mikhail Gorbachev, F W de Klerk, Nelson Mandela and others. Unfortunately there will still be many instances throughout the world where countries will prefer war, since not all countries can find the flexibility to present alternatives that are needed to negotiate instead.

The benefits of negotiation

The more managers and other individuals learn the skills of negotiation, the less frequent will be their need to go to court or to manipulate people by forceful means. The world can only become a better one if men would rather take the course of negotiation than the course of conflict. All managers, lawyers, professional people and individuals should realise the potential for negotiation. South Africans have possibly realised that, in a 'rainbow' country of diverse peoples, the only way to solve conflicts and to realise objectives in the long term will be to become aware of the usefulness of negotiation skills and to negotiate continuously.

Fortunately, negotiation will not only help you to handle difficult conflict situations, but will enhance any individual's potential for meeting his goals in life and becoming a more effective human being. Negotiation is also enjoyable. Once this skill is mastered, it could become one of the most enjoyable parts of any manager's life. It is the one activity where he will, at one time, use most of his knowledge, experience, expertise and abilities. It is probably the activity that could be the most demanding mentally, but at the same time the most gratifying, once a relationship is established or an agreement is signed that is beneficial to both parties.

Case 2.1

THREE DAYS OF TOUGH DEBATING

(Negotiating to combat the forces of destruction and violence)

When the ANC's extended National Executive Committee met behind closed doors at a secret venue this week, there were only two items on the agenda - the country-wide violence and the negotiation process.

The extended NEC meeting was on Tuesday and Wednesday. But for Thursday's meeting the UDF, Cosatu, the ANC's internal leadership core and regional executive delegates were left out. Only the NEC was there.

For two days more than 60 delegates listened to detailed area reports on the causes of the violence that has left more than 1 700 people dead and thousands injured.

The main input on violence was from the national working group on violence, headed by Cosatu's Sidney Mufamadi, and the task force on the Natal violence, led by NEC member Jacob Zuma.

It was largely these two reports that swayed the delegates to, among other things, vote to meet with homeland leaders including Inkatha leader Mangosuthu Buthelezi. They also decided to call for a summit with the government and a conference with democratic and anti-apartheid forces to discuss 'a common strategy to combat the forces of destruction and violence'.

Although there was no objection in principle to holding a summit with the government, delegates debated at length the mechanics involved in such a summit, and the timing. There were suggestions that it be held outside South Africa to remove the territorial advantage a meeting inside the country would offer the government. A possible venue was Lusaka.

Delegates also resolved that if the summit does not yield any positive results, the option of a two-day national strike should be considered. Other strategies would include consumer boycotts, protest marches and demonstrations.

Sefako Nyaka, *Sunday Star,* 9 September 1990.

THE PREPARATION PHASE OF NEGOTIATION

Once the potential for negotiation has been established, a negotiator should be able to anticipate the major events that will occur during negotiation and prepare in advance for them.

First of all, the negotiator must know what he or she wants. In other words, determine **objectives**. After that, he will have to collect information on the kind of need conflict that he and the other side is in, the issues at stake, the legal aspects of the case, the financial implications, the form of the contract, the place of meeting, the people who will attend the meeting, the agenda and the tactics during negotiation.

Preparation - Step 1: Objectives

Objectives include stating all the goals that are to be achieved in the negotiation, determining their priority and evaluating the possible trade-offs amongst them.

Objectives may also include intangibles, such as maintaining a certain status quo or just meeting the other side again at a later stage.

In theory, each negotiator's objectives will have a 'real' base (the least he would accept) and an 'aspiration' base (the maximum he could possibly obtain). The **aspiration base** and **real base** could be different for each issue at stake, but in simple negotiations where there are one or two issues, one can assume that there will be a fairly clear range between the real base and the aspiration base. For example:

> If you are interested in buying a second-hand car from a private person who advertised it in the newspaper, and you decide to visit this individual, the price you are prepared to pay (aspiration base) may be R20 000, and you may have a real base of about R25 000 (the price you cannot exceed). On the other hand, the owner of the vehicle will also have an aspiration base (to try to get as much as possible for his motor car), and that could be in the range of R30 000. His real base (the minimum that he would accept) could be R23 000. The **negotiation** 'range' will then be between R23 000 and R25 000 (real base to real base).

The concept of aspiration base, real base and negotiation range is depicted schematically in figure 2.4.

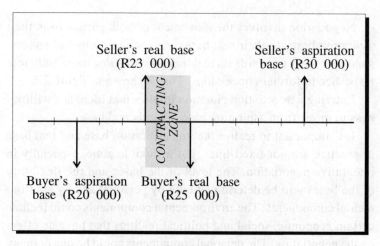

Figure 2.4
THE NEGOTIATING ZONE

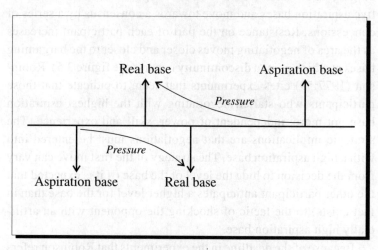

Figure 2.5
NEGOTIATION PRESSURE TOWARDS REAL BASE

Negotiation involves the movement of both parties from their aspiration bases to their real bases. As each party makes concessions and moves towards its real base, it will show more and more resistance to further concessions. This is shown in figure 2.5.

Entering a negotiation situation implies that there is a **willingness** to move from aspiration base towards real base.

It is important to realise that the aspiration base and real base in practice are not fixed lines, but a flexible zone, especially in integrative negotiation. The level of the bases and the flexibility of the bases will be determined both by personal and by environmental components. The environmental components could include certain economic, social and political realities that have an effect on the negotiation. The personal components could be one or many psychological factors such as confidence, aggression, needs at that time, or status within a certain community.

Robinson (1977) discusses the effects of aspiration and real bases in some detail. He is of the opinion that it is possible to structure a situation to alter the bargaining (real or aspiration) base of the other party. A common approach by the participants in a bargaining situation would be to start negotiations at their respective aspiration bases and move towards a consensus by a series of concessions. Resistance on the part of each participant increases as the area of negotiating moves closer and closer to the bargaining bases at which point a discontinuity occurs (see figure 2.5). Robinson (1977:59) cites experiments that seem to indicate that those participants who started negotiating with the highest aspiration base got more, independent of power, skill and experience. The strategic implications are that negotiations must be entered into with a high aspiration base. The strategy of the first move can vary from the decision to hide the level of the base (if it is expected that the other participant anticipates a higher level for the base than in fact exists) to the tactic of shocking the opponent with an artificially high aspiration base.

Because of the deadline in the experiments that Robinson refers to, and the fact that an agreement had to be reached, concessions had to be made by the participants. It was found that the least successful negotiators made the first concessions, the largest concessions and the most frequent concessions as the deadline approached. For example:

> If you are negotiating the price of canned fruit with your agent in Japan, your flight back is departing within four hours and your agent's offer is shockingly low, concessions will have to be made by one of the parties or the deal will have to be called off.

Preparation — Step 2: Analysis of the situation

In preparing for negotiation care should be taken to analyse all aspects of both your own and your opponent's position at the time of entering the negotiation. The following aspects could be of crucial importance in a pre-negotiation analysis:

❑ Are we dealing with an Integrative or Distributive situation?
❑ Is a continuous relationship of importance to both sides?
❑ Who are the constituents of each party?
❑ What alternatives exist for both sides if the negotiations fail?
❑ What are the characteristics of the content format: Progressive Summarisation or the Package format?
❑ In what need conflict are you and your opponents?
❑ What is the least that you and your opponent want to achieve after the first round of talks?

Preparation — Step 3: Identification of issues

Issues are those matters of substance that will be discussed with the opponent. Any aspect over which there could be disagreement can be defined as an **issue**:

❑ **Issues can be simple**, such as the price to be paid for a used car.
❑ **Issues can be more complex,** such as the vast array of economic data used to justify a union's wage demands.
❑ **Issues can be subtle,** such as the precise wording of a clause in an agreement (a matter on which both parties are in essential agreement, but which could easily erupt into conflict if care is not taken).

In most negotiation situations, there will be many points or issues on which agreement must be reached. These issues must be clearly identified. There is a difference between the arguments that may be used to support issues, and the various parts (issues) to be negotiated. For instance, if we were negotiating a contract for the supply of raw materials, the issues may include price, delivery times, discount for quantity, payment terms, quality and so on. For each of these issues we can present arguments in favour of our aspiration base. Arguments and issues are therefore two different aspects of negotiation. Arguments will support the issues and will be dealt with in more detail later in this book.

MacMillan (1974) suggests that one should try to identify all the issues at stake before negotiations take place. The issues could then be ranked in terms of their priority or importance to you and also in terms of the other party's priorities. Table 2.1 presents a list of typical issues that may have formed part of a negotiation for a contract to build a plant. The issues are ranked from the supplier's and from the customer's viewpoints. It can be seen that the parties in the negotiation have different preferences and this can be of great importance when it comes to planning the order in which you may want to discuss them.

Table 2.1

NEGOTIATING ISSUES: PLANT CONTRACT

ISSUE	IMPORTANCE	
	To Supplier	*To Customer*
Price	1	4
Delivery	2	2
Terms of Payment	3	5
Control of Subcontractors	4	8
Design Changes	5	6
After Sales Services	6	3
Performance Guarantees	7	1
Commissioning	8	7

MacMillan (1974) seems to be of the opinion that it is possible to develop a very detailed ranking in this way. The issues could even be numbered depending on their rankings, or classified as high, medium or low in terms of their importance to each side. That in turn could help the negotiator to plan the agenda and/or the sequence of arguments to be presented. If, for example, he knows that delivery time is a very important issue for the other side but a very unimportant issue for himself, he could start off with delivery time and it would seem as though he was making a major concession if he agreed to the delivery time issue first. Next, he could place his own highest priority on the table, especially if it is of lower priority to the other side. In that way, in theory at least, it could be possible to come to an agreement in a much more effective way with less time spent on trivial arguments. In practice, however, priorities change and even fade away. In the Gulf War of 1991, negotiation for withdrawal receded in favour of negotiation for destruction of weapons after the war.

Preparation - Step 4: Analysis of information on negotiators

It is important that you obtain information on your opponents. You will need to know their objectives, their needs and their 'personalities', if possible. A full diagnosis of the opponents might include their financial position, immediate and pressing problems, operating environment, value systems (what they regard as important in life and in the future of their company), previous negotiating behaviour, constituents (the people or organisations they represent or who are influencing them) and personal goals (such as promotion or financial gain). Also special consideration should be given to the timing of the negotiation and information should be obtained about the best time to have the first get-together. For farmers, for example, it could be just after the rainy season or just after they have received their annual cheques from the co-operatives. There could be certain times in the day, the week or the month that would be better in terms of the position of the individual or individuals with whom you are negotiating.

Where people from different backgrounds will be present, special attention should be given to cultural variables such as language, attitudes, social and religious norms, interests, connotation of translated words, forms of politeness, food, dress, possible misinterpretation of body language, stereotypes, etc. (See chapter 7 for a more detailed discussion.)

It is important to remember, however, that individuals change over time. Thus time and timing are of great importance to ascertain the relevance of information.

Preparation - Step 5: Legal implications

It could be of the utmost importance that the legal position of all parties be carefully considered, especially before some kinds of negotiations. It could be important to obtain legal advice first in the case of a complex issue or contract. It is also important to be totally aware of the definition of a contract in terms of the general law of contracts. In foreign countries it becomes even more important to consider the legal system of the country, and the role of the International Chamber of Commerce (ICC), of which most countries are members and signatories. International negotiators should realise the implications of conflict and court action in international agreements. Contracts could include an agreement on the 'country of settlement' in the event of court action.

In South Africa a contract is seen as an agreement aimed at creating a legal obligation, an obligation which will be given effect by, and will be enforced by the law (Delport 1990).

The requirements for a valid contract to come into being (in South Africa) are the following:

❑ There must be **consensus**.
❑ The parties must have acted within their **contractual** capacity.
❑ The performance must be physically **possible**.
❑ The agreement must be **lawful** (legally possible).
❑ **Formalities,** if any, must be adhered to.

If all of these requirements have not been met, there will be no contract. It is then said that the contract is void. However, even where all the requirements have been met, extraneous circumstances may have the effect that the contract may be nullified by the prejudiced party. Such contracts are said to be voidable at the instance of the injured party. Until such time as the contract is set aside, a valid contract exists. The circumstances that will render a contract voidable are cases of misrepresentation, duress, undue influence or error, or where a minor contracts to his detriment.

Delport (1990) explains the importance of three concepts in the law of contract.

❑ First is the concept **essentialia,** which are those requirements that the law prescribes for a specific contract to come into existence (e.g. a contract of sale). For such a contract these essentialia are: consensus to buy and sell, consensus concerning the item sold and consensus regarding the selling price.

❑ The **naturalia,** the second concept, are those terms implied by law in every contract of a particular kind, unless expressly excluded by the parties.

❑ Lastly, the **incidentalia** are those terms not automatically included in the contract, but which may be included by the parties by express agreement.

Parties to contracts and their capacity to act

The capacity to act (or contractual capacity) is another important consideration in the preparation for any negotiation. This refers to the capacity to carry out legal acts, such as to conclude a contract. The law recognises two types of 'persons' who may have contractual capacity.

Natural persons are divided into three categories with reference to their contractual capacity:

❑ No contractual capacity at all: infants under seven years of age.

❑ Limited contractual capacity: minors between the ages of seven and twenty-one, prodigals and unrehabilitated insolvents. These persons require the assistance of a parent, guardian or curator to enter into binding contracts.

❑ Full contractual capacity: sane, major persons.

Legal persons such as companies or close corporations can likewise have the capacity to act, but they can only contract through agents. Their powers and capacities are determined by their corporation documents.

Contracts entered into in such a manner are entered into 'on behalf of' the legal person (the company or close corporation). One person (the agent) is then authorised by another (the principal) to negotiate and conclude a specific contract on behalf of the principal, with a third party. For example, P authorises A to buy a car for P for R1 000. A makes an offer to T on behalf of P and if T accepts this offer, a contract comes into being between P and T. If A exceeds his authority, P will not be bound by the contract, unless he ratifies A's conduct. The principal will also be bound if he represents to the third party that A does indeed have the required authority.

It is therefore very important that all negotiators know their **mandate**, since the law of contract will have a very important bearing on their authority to act in negotiation.

Negotiators should also seriously consider the kind of business they are in and the kind of company or organisation they represent. Each type of business (as stated earlier) and/or type of body they represent would have implications for the legality of the eventual contract (Delport 1990:2).

Partnerships

A partnership will be bound to a contract if the other party can show that the person with whom he contracted was in fact a partner in the partnership, or that the other partners have fraudulently created such an impression, or that he has express or tacit authority to bind the partnership, or that the contract was entered into on behalf of the partnership.

Express authority can be given by agreement between the partners or can be based upon the contract of partnership.

Tacit authority can be deduced from the contract of partnership, or can be based on the fact that the contract is one which normally relates to the specific business of the partnership.

Companies

A company is a legal person and can only contract through its agents. These agents may have actual or ostensible authority to enter into agreements on behalf of the company. The third party may assume that the board of directors and the managing director will have the capacity to bind the company unless the articles of association provide to the contrary, or if the third party in fact had knowledge that that was not the case. (It is important to note that every third party dealing with the company is deemed to have knowledge of the contents of the memorandum and articles of the company.)

It is therefore necessary to ensure that an ordinary director in fact has the authority to bind the company. If a person has actual authority (that is to say, by virtue of the articles of a resolution by the board of the directors) to bind the company, provided certain internal formalities have been complied with, a third party may be assured that such internal formalities have in fact been complied with. (For example, the managing director may enter into contracts provided that, for contracts exceeding R1 million, he has the consent of the board of directors.) Persons that have actual authority to bind a company can also create the impression (or make a representation) that another person has the authority to make an agreement on behalf of the company this is a case of ostensible authority.

It could therefore be important for negotiators to examine the resolution by the board of directors before entering into a contract with the company. That copy could clarify the ability of the individual to bind the company.

Close corporations (CC)

The CC is a legal person like a company, but it does not have a board of directors, only members, who can bind the CC.

A CC will be bound to a contract entered into by a member if:

❏ this member has express or tacit authority to contract on behalf of the CC, or if

❑ the CC subsequently ratifies the act, or if the act relates to the business of the CC as stated in the founding statement or as actually carried on by the CC.

This last option will not be available to the third party if he knew, or if he reasonably ought to have known that the member had no authority to enter into the contract, or that the association agreement placed a limit on that authority, or if the specific contract could also only have been entered into with the written consent of all the members. Such consent is needed when all or the greatest part of the CC's assets or the undertaking itself is to be sold, or when immovable property is to be purchased or sold.

Case 2.2

NEGOTIATION AND THE LAW OF CONTRACT

Simpson McKie sued for R1,6 m

Stockbroking firm Simpson McKie is being sued for almost R1,6 m by a corporate finance consultancy, papers filed in the Rand Supreme Court on Monday last week show.

The consultancy, Millward Grebeck Securities (MGS), contends that under an agreement in September 1989 Simpson McKie was involved in the establishment of a new company, later to be called MGS, as a corporate finance consultancy with offices in Johannesburg and London. It allegedly represented to potential clients that MGS was an associate of Simpson McKie.

Under the agreement, Simpson McKie and MGS MD Charles Millward would hold 40 % of MGS while partner Ed Grebeck would hold 20 %.

It is alleged that Simpson McKie breached the agreement in January 1990 by denying that an agreement existed and withdrawing financial and infrastructural support.

As a result of the alleged breach MGS is claiming R1,17 m as compensation for loss of office and administration infrastructure.

MGS is claiming a further R150 000 which, it contends, is its 25 % share of a trading profit of at least R600 000 earned by the implementation of a debt restructuring scheme for Hanson Int.'s SA subsidiary Eveready.

The restructuring, originated by Millward, has increased Hanson's profits from Eveready by approximately R10 m a year, according to the papers.

Simpson McKie corporate finance director Chris Niehaus said claims
were without foundation and that the firm would be defending the
action.

An MGS spokesman said both Millward and Grebeck gave up their
existing employment to set up MGS in September 1989 on the strength
of Simpson McKie's written undertakings.

Simpson McKie has until Thursday to serve notice of intention to
defend.

Business Day, 27 February 1991.

Cession and delegation

A party to a contract is entitled to transfer or cede his rights under
the contract to a third party (the cessionary), without obtaining the
consent of the other contracting party, unless the contract prohibits
or qualifies such a cession. Whenever the right is of a personal
nature it cannot be ceded; for example an employer cannot cede
his right to services by an employee. The person who cedes can
only cede to a third party the rights that he himself has, and no
more.

Delegation, on the other hand, is the transference of the contracting party's liabilities under a contract to a third party. The
consent of the creditor is necessary for the delegation to be valid.
For example, A owes B R100. With B's consent A may transfer
his liability to C, and in effect a new contract is created.

It could be of major importance in the preparation for negotiation that companies or individuals make very sure of all the
implications of the law in each country, especially when negotiating in foreign countries. It is also of importance to consider the
legal procedure, arbitration or negotiation techniques that will be
followed should a conflict develop at a later stage.

Such procedures should, ideally, be included in the agreement.

Formalities

Formalities required by law. The general rule is that no formalities
are prescribed in respect of negotiating a contract, or the form
thereof. There are, however, a few exceptions to this rule. For
example, in order to be valid, an alienation of land or any interest
in land must be in writing, signed by, or on behalf of, the parties

(Act 68 of 1981). The object of the sale, the price and the parties must emerge clearly from the written contract, and no oral evidence will be permitted to remove uncertainties. Any amendments of the contract based on consensus must also be in writing. Antenuptial contracts must be in writing as well as contracts in terms of the Credit Agreements Act, service contracts with apprentices, suretyship contracts, and leases of mineral rights. Leases of mineral rights and antenuptial contracts must be notarially executed and registered.

Formalities required by the parties themselves. It is important that the intentions of both parties be determined beforehand. The parties may either intend that no binding contract should come into existence until such time as it is put into writing, or their intention may be that the written document will merely constitute proof of the verbal agreement. The contract will then come into existence once all the essential elements have been complied with. Amendments of the contract can then take place informally, unless the parties had agreed that it should be in writing. If the written document does not reflect the true intention of the parties because of an error or an omission, it can be rectified by means of an application to court. A, for example, sells his farm to B for R1 million, but the figure was typed as R10 million.

There are many additional legal aspects that could have a bearing on a specific kind of contract. Negotiators should also understand that legal requirements change over time due to changes in Acts as well as in the social environment. Examples of this are the 'Bill of Rights' brought into the South African legal system with the change of government in 1994, and the requirement of 'transparency' in negotiations in South Africa and all over the world. It is, however, very important that parties prepare themselves beforehand for all the elements of the law that apply to their specific case so as to avoid unnecessary psychological and financial embarrassment at a later stage.

Preparation — Step 6: Financial preparation

The financial consequences of any negotiation should be considered by the parties before they enter into any discussion of any kind. Financial consequences could be direct or indirect, or immediate or incurred over a long period of time after the negotiation. Wall (1985) illustrated the negotiation relationships by means of the paradigm depicted in figure 2.6.

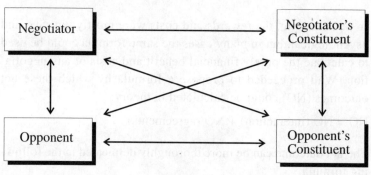

Figure 2.6
THE NEGOTIATION PARADIGM
(Wall, JA 1985)

According to Wall, negotiation relationships in a simplified form could be depicted by four parties and six relationships in this model (figure 2.6). Typically the parties in negotiation are the negotiator, the opposing negotiator, the negotiator's constituent and the opponent's constituent. Among the parties, there are six potential relationships and these can be considered as relationships of exchange in which each party receives outcomes (reward) and incurs costs as he or she interacts with the other party. The difference between the rewards and the costs yields a Net Outcome (NO) to the party for each interaction. Since each party — negotiator, opponent, negotiator's constituent, and opponent's constituent — can interact with more than one other, his or her total rewards, total costs, and thereby the difference between the two, is the summation of the rewards, costs, and NOs respectively, accruing from all relationships.

In each interaction, the rewards and costs spring from two principal sources: the ongoing interaction and the result of this interaction. For example:

> The negotiation can generate respect for the negotiator in his constituency (if he or she has sufficient verbal skills) but it can also cost a good deal of sleep. The result — perhaps an agreement — can provide a pay increase for the negotiator, but criticism from those who dislike the agreement.

In this example, the rewards and costs were mostly physical and psychological, but in many cases the same formula could be used to calculate the purely financial benefit and costs of any negotiation. Wall proceeded to propose a formula by which these net outcomes (NO) could be calculated in theory:

NO = NO (interaction) + NO (agreements)

The net outcome can be more thoroughly delineated in the following formula:

$$NO = (R_{nij} - C_{nij}) + (R_{ai} - C_{ai})$$
NO = parties' total net outcomes
R_{nij} = reward i resulting from interaction with party j
C_{nij} = cost i resulting from interaction with party j
R_{ai} = reward i resulting from an agreement
C_{ai} = cost i resulting from an agreement

For example:

> If you travel from Pretoria to Cape Town to negotiate the right to franchise karaoke bars in Pretoria, the cost of the travelling, hotel, lawyers, paperwork etc is R2 000. On the other hand, if you sign an agreement, you could stand to gain R50 000 net profit a year. If you do not sign you still learn a lot about this kind of business and meet many people in this field, enabling you to gain in alternatives. Your Net Outcome (NO), if you reach an agreement, could then be:

NO (1991)   = 50 000 - 2 000
            = R48 000
If you do not reach an agreement it will be:
            = Alternatives - R2 000
            = ?

In other words, in a simplified form, Wall's formula could theoretically be used to calculate the net financial outcome of all negotiations. The net outcome will, according to Wall, be the difference between the rewards and the costs of all the interactions, plus the difference between the rewards and the costs of the final agreement.

Negotiation can be expensive. It can be expensive to travel only to negotiate. There could be 'costs' involved in just meeting people, for example, in the context of certain sensitive political negotiations.

> An example here would be when the National Party had talks with the ANC for the first time. For many years this was something they said they would not do, and in meeting with the ANC they possibly lost some support from the conservative sector of the population.

Parties should decide whether negotiations are worthwhile financially; whether there would be benefits if an agreement is struck; how long it would take for the costs of the negotiation and other costs to be recouped; and what would be the worst scenario in terms of the costs.

Obviously, Wall neglected to consider the impact of time upon the financial equation. It is well known that product life cycle, tax benefits and capital transfers are but a few variables affected over time. A transaction may be calculated according to Wall's formula only if the influence of time is ignored and that could be a grave error.

Preparation - Step 7: Tactics

In later chapters more attention will be given to tactics during negotiation. Yet it is important that parties prepare themselves properly for the practical side of the negotiation. Here it will be important to consider:

- ❏ The **place** of the meeting.
- ❏ **Layout** of the room.
- ❏ The composition of the negotiation **team**.
- ❏ The **individuals** that will be selected for the negotiation.

- ❑ The composition and presentation of the **agenda**.
- ❑ The **alternatives** that could be proposed during the negotiation.
- ❑ The way the **problem** will be defined.
- ❑ The **time** available and the timing of the negotiation.
- ❑ The way the **climate** can be influenced.
- ❑ The aspects that you and your opponent agree upon (**common ground** variables).

It could also be important to role play a negotiation beforehand and ask 'opponents' to act as devil's advocates and to come up with extreme questions or statements so as to prepare the team for an effective response.

Preparation – Step 8: Feedback

Although feedback cannot be regarded as 'preparation' for negotiation, it is still very important that parties schedule regular feedback sessions so as to review their performance and to improve their effectiveness in future rounds of negotiations.

NEGOTIATION PLANNING: A SUMMARY

Regrettably, systematic planning is not something that most of us do willingly. Managers, for example, are much more inclined to take action than to spend time reflecting on conditions and planning. Admittedly, time constraints and work pressures make it difficult for managers to feel they have the time to do adequate planning. For many of us, planning is boring and tedious and, therefore, easily put off in favour of 'getting into the action' quickly.

In addition to devoting insufficient time to planning, negotiators frequently fail because of several weaknesses in their planning process. Authors have different views on the way that planning should be done. Marsh (1988:162) believes that there are sharp differences in the way that Japanese and Westerners prepare for negotiations.

The Japanese priorities are, first, to develop a working organisation around a discussion leader, who will usually become the spokesman, then to ensure that everyone has a thorough understanding of the issues, and, thirdly, to develop a position on which everyone can agree. This position is usually arrived at in an intuitive way, for there is rarely any discussion of position options. The essence of the Japanese approach is **organisation**, and they can be expected to come into negotiation as a cohesive team, with a single spokesman, a shared understanding of the issues and consensus on one position, even if they are ill prepared in other respects.

Planning has three dimensions: strategic, administrative and tactical. Strategic planning is concerned with long-term business goals. Administrative planning involves getting men and information where they are needed so that negotiation goes smoothly. Tactical planning simply seeks to get the best possible results at the bargaining table.

ACTUAL NEGOTIATION

There are many variables that are of crucial importance in the actual negotiation. Aspects such as the definition of the problem, the establishment of common ground, use of power, changing of attitudes and perceptions, getting a 'yes' and many other aspects will be dealt with in later chapters. There are many additional legal matters that could have a bearing on a specific kind of contract. It is, though, very important that parties prepare themselves beforehand for all the elements of the law that apply to their specific case. This will help to avoid unnecessary psychological and financial embarrassment at a later stage.

CONCLUSION

As we have stressed in this chapter, we believe planning to be one of the most important activities in negotiation. The negotiator who is well prepared will have made an effort to do the following:

❏ Understand the nature of the conflict.

❏ Understand, and clarify, what objectives he would like to achieve during the negotiations.

❏ Have information on the issues at stake and be able to evaluate the importance of these issues to both sides.

❏ Understand the needs and personalities of individuals in the other party and in his own.

❏ Have detailed information on the history of the problem, and the legal implications of actions that could be taken.

If a negotiator is able to consider and evaluate each of these factors, we believe that he could have more significant control over the dynamic process that follows. Preparation gives the negotiator a clear sense of direction and confidence. This could result in agreements of value to both parties.

CHAPTER 3

Negotiating for Climate

In this Chapter

❑ Introduction
❑ *The phases* of the dynamic agenda
❑ *Climate* in negotiation
❑ Variables that influence climate
❑ Changing perceptions
❑ The use of space
❑ Colour and its effect on individuals
❑ The effect of location and layout
❑ Communication during the climate phase
❑ Time and timing
❑ A strategic plan for the climate stage
❑ Examples of the influence of climate on negotiation outcomes

INTRODUCTION

Each 'negotiation' can be said to possess a certain uniqueness, yet there is also a commonality to the negotiation process which has been established among us. There is, for example, usually a generality in the process, though not in the content. The process of negotiation has to start somewhere, and from then on everything that happens between negotiators will influence the outcome in some or other way.

It seems that the initial stages of negotiation are crucial for the establishment of perceptions that may determine the conduct and outcome of the process. This so-called initial 'climate' or 'perception' is often the result of actions or perceived actions by contributors to the process. If participants give careful attention to this phase of the process, it can often influence the outcome significantly.

Certainly there is no doubt that it is easier to handle conflict after prolonged periods of co-operation and more difficult to establish co-operation after intense conflict. The aim should always be, in integrative negotiation, to develop **reciprocal trust** through which co-operation is encouraged. Without mutual trust the quest for co-operation becomes a very difficult process.

Theorists on negotiation have identified various phases and subphases that could be translated into fairly practical recipes that could aid negotiators in achieving success. Some of these phases are mentioned at the outset of this chapter while the initial climate phase of negotiation is also discussed in some detail.

PHASES OF NEGOTIATION

Various writers have identified certain phases that the typical discussion will go through. De Klerk (1993:1), in commenting on the process of political negotiations in South Africa between 1990 and 1993, refers to four basic phases, namely preliminary discussions, prenegotiation positioning and creating the right climate, the negotiation process itself and entering into agreements. According to De Klerk, the negotiation process itself has four sub-phases consisting of:

❑ Exploratory negotiation wherein preferences and bottom lines are discussed, information exchanged, opening gambits made, priority lists compiled, consensus reached as to areas of conflict and areas of consensus.

❑ Accommodative negotiation wherein the process of the bridging of differences and 'easy' agreements are negotiated.

❑ Confrontational negotiation wherein hard bargaining is done on the core differences between groups, where moments of crisis often arise and reciprocal blackmail is quite common.

❑ Compromise negotiation wherein solutions are found through give and take, contracts obtained and general consensus established.

According to Tuckman (1965: 98) business negotiations often take a route similar to that described above, yet he found that the process could often be simplified into four phases namely:

❑ mutual acceptance

❑ communication and decision making

❑ motivation and productivity, and

❑ control and organisation.

Depending on the formality of the interaction, the parties would therefore go through a couple of phases before they would sign agreements and end the meeting. We would like to propose that the phases of Tuckman could be modified to include the following:

Emotional phase

During this phase, the climate of the negotiation is established and the parties make contact with each other with greetings. The politeness and manner of greeting in this stage could determine the climate for the rest of the negotiations. The emotional phase of negotiations could theoretically run over a long period of time where both parties work hard at first creating the right climate before they start with the next stage of negotiation, which is a political one. It is important to realise that the climate could be influenced largely by the behaviour of the parties. It is assumed that the leader still dominates in this first stage of negotiation. He is responsible mainly for establishing the climate and the norms under which the group will operate. He is sometimes referred to as the **socio-emotional** leader because of the emotional role that he plays during this stage.

Political phase

This is the phase in which the common ground is established between the parties. The role of each individual is often defined during this stage; the rules of the meeting are agreed upon; the power and authority of the meeting are discussed and the agenda is agreed upon. A task leader usually emerges during this phase based upon the type of expertise required at this time.

Problem-definition phase

Here the group attempts to define the problem, offers trade-offs and implements the agreement. During this time, group cohesiveness is established. This is evidenced by the fact that members often stop talking in terms of 'I' and unconsciously start to use 'we'.

Constructive phase

The problem is now constructively dealt with. Experts and so-called task leaders are very active during this stage while the socio-emotional leader moves into the background.

Final socio-emotional phase

This is where closure takes place. The socio-emotional leader again dominates and during this phase, the climate for re-entry or the implementation of an agreement will be established.

THE DYNAMIC AGENDA

The above phases of group development could be transcribed into a 'dynamic agenda'.

A	C	E	G
Opening (climate) (socio-emotional phase)	Problem definition phase	Trade-offs (co-operative)	Implementation

B	D	F	H
Common ground	Trade-offs (oppositional)	Heads of agreement + security + formulation	Closure (socio-emotional phase)

During the climate phase of negotiations, the parties are dealing mainly with **perceptions** of the opposition. Most negotiations take place because the parties want to do business together. They therefore aim to create a climate that will be conducive to the agreement that they have in mind. Each party comes to the meeting place with his mind full of recent experiences. The visitor comes from his travels, with the accompanying frustrations of the airport, the railway, or the car journey, with his mind full of the work he has been doing whilst travelling. Those who have been in the office arrive frustrated, having dealt with colleagues and the everyday problems of the business world. Thus, negotiators come from different backgrounds and unless both sides have taken time to compose their minds as they arrive, they will not be in the right frame of mind.

When they enter negotiation, they enter a very critical period during which important and durable impressions are formed that will influence the whole course of the negotiation process.

The initial climate for negotiation is formed very quickly. Often stereotypes are established that are very difficult to change later. Scott (1988: 27) identified five typical types of climate:

❑ **Natural climate** in which people accept each other's natural characteristics. Negotiations are conducted in a very relaxed manner.
❑ **Cordial climate**, where a polite, sympathetic and almost friendly atmosphere exists.

❑ **Co-operative climate** where the parties work together towards an agreement for their mutual benefit.

❑ **Brisk climate** in which parties move at a measured pace towards a settlement, neither wasting time nor rushing.

❑ **Business-like climate** where the parties focus on key matters of importance to both sides, to the exclusion of everything else.

FACTORS THAT WILL AFFECT THE CLIMATE DURING NEGOTIATION

There are many small and large factors that could affect the perceptions of the other side during a negotiation. The initial stages of the negotiation set the tone for the rest of the talks. So, factors such as the first impression, politeness, personalities of the negotiators, clothing, the way the other side expresses itself, seating, the place of the first meeting, the motivation and the needs of the other party, and even the events that occurred before the first meeting, are very important.

People base their actions and reactions on their perceptions, not on objective reality. They act on their own interpretation of the stimuli they receive. Because they make decisions and take actions based on what they perceive to be reality, it is important that they understand the formation of perceptions. In this way they can more readily determine what will influence other people during everyday communications.

Perceptual selectivity

Schiffman and Kanuk (1983:142) explain that all individuals subconsciously exercise a great deal of selectivity regarding which aspects of their environment they perceive. An individual may notice some things, disregard others, and be oblivious of yet others. Overall, people actually perceive only a small fraction of the stimuli to which they are exposed. For example:

> A salesman could be talking to you. In the background you can see the gleam of the new BMW motor car; your wife is prodding you with her elbow; your little boy's eager eyes are looking expectantly at you; and

you are strongly aware of the weight of your cheque book in your pocket. Which of these stimuli will you ignore and which will demand your attention?

In general, people perceive things that promise to help satisfy their needs and which they have found rewarding in the past. They tend to ignore mildly disturbing things but will perceive very dangerous ones (for example, the house being on fire).

Perceptual selection is the process whereby people filter out most stimuli so that they can deal with the most important ones. It depends upon personal preferences and expectations and is based on previous experience.

In the light of the existence of this phenomenon, negotiations could falter or succeed on just one or two insignificant stimuli. A facial expression could cause a totally unwarranted feeling of distrust while accompanying body movements signifying 'impoliteness' or many other variables could influence this perception.

The **first impression** is one particular kind of perceptual selection since overall impressions are formed on very few stimuli that are selected in the initial period of contact.

The effect of first impressions

A wide-ranging picture of a person's personality, based on very little evidence, may be formed by a first impression. People tend to do this because they are uncomfortable with uncertainty. The mind abhors a vacuum, and tends to fill it up, if not with fact, then with inference or mere fiction.

Impressions are rounded out by certain procedures. Each person seems to have an 'inference implicit theory of personality'. This is developed from observation of people and from other influences such as reading fiction and watching movies. It leads to the belief that certain clusters of personality traits go together. A powerfully built man with steely grey eyes would be expected to snap to attention as the flag goes up, and not to cry about stepping on an ant.

The effect of the first impression (sometimes called the 'primacy effect') has been investigated by a number of researchers. It has been summarised by Haber and Fried (1975: 635) who tested the effect of the first impression as follows:

> A list of personality traits was presented to two groups of subjects. One group's list showed the good characteristics or traits (idealism and intelligence) first, and then went on to bad traits. The other group's list was the other way round. Those to whom the good traits were given, first formed a more favourable impression of the person in question and were likely to attribute good traits to him. The other group saw less favourable traits in him. What made the difference? Was it the mere fact that a trait came first or the inference of the fact that because it came first it was the dominant one in the mind of the observer who made up the list?

> In another experiment, a similar primacy effect was found when subjects were given extended descriptions of hypothetical persons. The person was depicted moving through a number of situations suggesting either loneliness, gloom and introversion or conviviality, sunshine and extroversion. When the material suggesting introversion came first, the majority of respondents envisaged an introverted personality. When the same material was presented in reverse order, so that the material suggesting extroversion came first, the majority formed an impression of an extroverted personality.

> Pursuing this study further Haber and Fried (1975:636) discovered that if subjects were warned beforehand not to make hasty judgments, they ceased to display the primacy effect. In fact, they might reverse it, forming an impression more strongly influenced by the latter and not the earlier material. When verbal material is presented, a Westerner anticipates that the important material will come first, thus showing a mental set effect. When cautioned to avoid hasty judgement, he deliberately tries to weigh all evidence equally, and he may overcompensate by weighing more heavily what he habitually under-weighs.

The halo effect

Similar to the effect of first impressions is the 'halo effect', or the tendency to perceive a person as consistently good or consistently bad on the basis of the first impression he makes. The tendency is to ascribe to that person a whole spectrum, or halo, of characteristics that bear out the initial impression. For example:

> A student who gets all 'A's on his first two report cards may continue to receive superior grades even though his work is falling off, because his teacher first saw him as an 'A' student and values everything he does in that light.

In summary

First impressions are therefore extremely important. They are often lasting and difficult to change. Negotiators should realise that first impressions are established within seconds. It is obvious that care should be taken, especially in the initial stages of negotiation, to create impressions that are conducive to the negotiations that will follow.

The influence of space

Several characteristics of people and negotiation venues, external to the other parties, will increase the likelihood of a good climate being established. External factors include such aspects as the form and size of chairs and tables, size of the meeting room and the intensity of colours in the room. The contrasting colours in the environment, clothing, seating arrangements and table arrangement.

Size of objects and spaces have special meaning in Western society. Larger spaces and sizes tend to carry with them the perception of greater importance. One kind of meaning that is assigned to space is the amount of space given to **leaders** in Western society. Status is often associated with larger spaces. For example:

Senior staff members in an organisation are given larger offices than junior members. They are also given larger desks, carpets, chairs, and motor cars. At a table the chairman is assigned more **space** than the members. In a church the minister is given huge space compared to the congregation. Unconsciously the use of space is seemingly selected by perceivers to be equivalent to status, and creates the impression of confidence and leadership. Soldiers are trained in battalions where they are given little space compared to officers. In this way they are 'conditioned' to react to orders and not to decide on any actions themselves.

It would seem that individuals can exert a more significant **role** in a bigger space. If negotiation parties are large, consisting of five or more individuals, it becomes very difficult to award each significant space and attention and therefore their roles are diminished in the process.

The strategic placing of people relative to each other could be one very influential way of procuring their co-operation, according to Knapp (1978). He refers to four basic positions relative to the other party in negotiations:

❏ The **corner** position
❏ The **co-operative** position
❏ The **competitive** or **defensive** position
❏ The **independent** position

The corner position

This position is normally occupied by people who have friendly and relaxed intentions. From this position, unlimited eye contact and close perception of the other person's movements are possible (see figure 3.1), resulting in:

❏ casual/informal talks,
❏ participants on an equal footing,
❏ ample visual and vocal communication, and
❏ sharing of material.

Figure 3.1

NEGOTIATORS FACING EACH OTHER
ACROSS THE CORNER OF A DESK

The corner of the desk still forms a limited hindrance, but it could supply security if one individual feels threatened. It does not limit the use of space on the desk itself. According to Knapp, this would be an excellent position for buying or selling negotiations. It could also relieve much of the tension of 'oppositional' negotiation and aid communication.

The co-operative position

Normally individuals use this when they are working on a similar task (see figure 3.2).

Figure 3.2

NEGOTIATORS SITTING ON THE SAME SIDE OF THE DESK

The result is often:

❑ casual/informal talks,
❑ participation on an equal footing,
❑ co-operation,
❑ inhibition of visual and vocal communication,
❑ sharing of material.

It is one of the most strategic positions by which to gain acceptance for a case. The only danger could be that the opponent could feel that 'his' territory has been encroached upon and would therefore feel threatened by the close proximity of the opposing party.

The competitive or defensive position

By sitting opposite someone, a competitive or defensive atmosphere or climate is created that can lead to (see figure 3.3):
❑ formal climates,
❑ good visual and vocal communication,
❑ adversarial or superior/subordinate relationships (especially if a desk is involved),
❑ restricted ability to share material, and
❑ psychological barriers between participants.

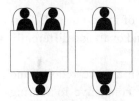

Figure 3.3

NEGOTIATORS SITTING OPPOSITE EACH OTHER AT A DESK

Argyle (1975) indicated in an experiment with medical doctors, that the presence or absence of a desk has an effect on patients' attitudes. According to his research patients are less relaxed when a doctor sits behind his desk and are more relaxed when sitting without any hindrance between them. It is sometimes referred to as a **distributive** seating arrangement or an **oppositional** seating arrangement and it often creates increased levels of tension in negotiations that could be detrimental in cases where an integrative climate is important to the parties.

The independent position

In this position there is an unwillingness of parties to interact with each other at all. It indicates a lack of interest (see figure 3.4), resulting in:

❑ casual/informal climates,
❑ independent activity/work and limited communication,
❑ participants being on an equal footing, and
❑ lack of sharing of material.

Figure 3.4

NEGOTIATORS SITTING FAR APART AT DIAGONALLY OPPOSITE CORNERS OF THE TABLE, NOT FACING EACH OTHER

When negotiators want open discussion they should avoid this kind of seating arrangement.

Table shape

The shape of tables used in negotiation is of importance. Differently shaped (square, round, rectangular, and oval) and differently sized tables could be used.

A **round table** would tend to establish a more relaxed and informal climate and it is normally very conducive to sharing information and problem solving, especially when individuals are on the same status level. To some extent it can reduce status differences. An important characteristic of the round table is the equal space allocated to each individual around the table. To allocate equal spaces around rectangular tables is much more difficult. For example:

> The Japanese refer to the 'Quality Circle' technique which is a well-known round table method for workers to solve problems and share ideas in the workplace. In the same way King Arthur designed a round table to reduce the differences in authority and perceived status of knights in his kingdom.

According to Pease (1981:120) **square tables** could create a competitive or defensive climate between people of the same status. He admits that they could be ideal for short businesslike discussions, or to establish a superior/inferior attitude. At this kind of table, Pease postulates that the individual to your right-hand side would normally give better co-operation than the individual to the left of you, whilst the individual opposite you would provide most of the opposition. Seating positions around square tables are more complicated to arrange for the right climate.

Some positions around a rectangular table are reserved for chairmen and some for followers. The 'head' of the table is usually reserved for the most important or influential person. For example:

> In the West people have grown up sitting around rectangular tables in their dining rooms. The father of the house usually occupies the position at the so-called 'head of the table'. The mother sits next to him to the left or the right. The children follow, depending on their age. The head of the table therefore has a special meaning in Western society.

Argyle (1975) indicated that the **size** of the table could be of great importance. The larger the table, the larger the distance between individuals, the easier it is to say no or to disagree. The closer or smaller the distance between two individuals, the more difficult it becomes to directly disagree with the opposition. Space should never be too big or too small.

Proximic behaviour

An important but often overlooked element of non-verbal communication is 'proximics', defined as an individual's use of space when engaged in interpersonal communication with others. According to Edward Hall (a prominent researcher of proximics), people have four zones of informal space, that is, spatial distances they maintain when interacting with others:

❑ The **intimate zone** (from physical contact to 45 cm)
❑ The **personal zone** (from 45 cm to 120 cm)
❑ The **social zone** (from 120 cm to 360 cm)
❑ The **public zone** (more than 360 cm)

For Americans, Hall (1966) is of the opinion that manager–subordinate relationships begin in the social zone and progress to the personal zone once mutual trust has developed. An individual's intimate and personal zones make up a 'private bubble' of space that is considered private territory, not to be entered by others unless invited. Proximic behaviour can create a significant communication barrier when the sender and receiver differ. For example:

> If people from different cultures get together, and the one culture is used to large personal spaces while the other is used to very small personal spaces, both would be very uncomfortable. When a South American business person is talking to an American business person at a cocktail party, the American would feel very uncomfortable with the proximity of the South American — so much so that he would not be listening to any verbal communication from the speaker.

Conflicting proximic behaviour can also affect an individual's perception of the other. There are two types of movements in and around the personal zone that have been identified and elaborated on by Pienaar (1984) as **molecular** movements and **molar** movements.

❑ **Molecular movements** are movements that are small and are made by an individual inside the personal zone.
❑ **Molar movements** are big movements that stretch out of the personal zone and into the 'unoccupied' zones around the individual. These are goal-directed movements.

These kinds of movements can be seen in the way that negotiators act around a table. A negotiator could **'use up'** minimum or maximum space around the table in his seating position, body position and in his movements. The use of a lot of space would create the **perception** of confidence, while, at the same time, influencing the individual himself, according to Pienaar, to be positive and have a creative frame of mind.

❑ **Repetitive molecular movements** are often 'destructive' in any close interpersonal situation. Movements such as small repetitive finger, hand, eye, head or foot movements are destructive towards the other party and also destroy an individual's own thinking process. They also cause defensiveness and uncertainty.

Space and seating could be used in many ways to increase the perception of power, according to Pease (1981:123). Although power will be discussed at a later stage, it should be noted that Pease is of the opinion that the type of chairs, height of chairs, placing of chairs relative to windows, and office arrangement could increase or decrease the power of the other side and could be very effective in the case of distributive negotiation.

The size of parties

The size of the parties that are brought to the negotiation table could affect the perception of power and also the climate of the negotiation. A negotiation can be conducted in one of the following ways:

❑ only one person on each side;
❑ one person meeting with a small group; or
❑ two or more small groups congregating to negotiate an agreement.

A **one-to-one negotiation** is usually very risky because each person's attributes, virtues, assets and shortcomings could have a decisive influence on the outcome of the deliberations.

One person negotiating with a small group of trained negotiators is also regarded as a high-risk situation. It is very difficult for an individual to take on a group with their multiple channels of communication and multiple interaction processes.

Small group versus small group negotiations seem to be the preferred form of integrative negotiation worldwide.

Role

The factor that influences the decision as to the size of party most markedly is that of **role**. Individual role affects climate in an important way. Role has a very important place in the understanding of group behaviour. *The role refers to the expected behaviour patterns attributed to a particular position of an individual in a group.* According to Gibson, Ivancevich and Donnolly (1991:282) a role is what an individual must do to validate his or her occupancy of a particular position. In other words, what kind of physician or patient an individual is depends upon how he or she performs the 'culturally defined' role associated with the position.

In negotiations it is of utmost importance that no one should be brought to a negotiation without a significant role to play. If the role is non-existent, the individual is open to influence or psychological 'hijacking' by anyone who would give a significant role to that person. Since having a significant role is seen as a basic need in each person, they would experience a feeling of gratification at being given a role by their own party and would therefore be no risk to their own party since they would not be inclined to give concessions to the other side.

In negotiations there are three types of roles:

❑ Socio-emotional roles
❑ Task roles
❑ Multiple roles

The **socio-emotional role** is usually filled by the leader. He is very active in the beginning of the negotiation and is involved when climate is established. He assigns **roles** to his own members. As regards the other side, he takes care of the 'pecking order', of politeness and of the maintenance of the climate. He keeps track of the progress of the negotiations and facilitates it in the correct direction.

A **task role** or **task leader** often emerges naturally in the later stages of negotiation where he becomes very active. These people are normally specialists whose input is needed in the later problem-solving stages of negotiation.

Multiple roles refer to individuals who could have more than one task or socio-emotional role. They could in fact fill two or more positions at one time.

It is important that parties who are trained as teams, should *work* as a team. Gibson et al. (1991:283) refer to the role of **followership**. They are of the opinion that followership is often ignored or even discouraged. It is, however, important in any group effort to define each role clearly so that people understand who the leaders are, and who the followers. This will prevent any concessions being made as a result of the struggle for attention and leadership within one side. Followership does not, according to Gibson et al., refer to an inferior position but rather to the redefinition of role in terms of the content of its activities. Followers could be assigned work that is delegated **and of a very high intellectual content or responsibility.**

Two other concepts that are important in the discussion of role and size of parties are the concepts of **groupthink** and **risky shift**.

Groupthink

In many situations, having a highly cohesive team of negotiators is very important for success. Yet cohesiveness could itself be detrimental to the outcome of negotiation. Janis (1973) defines groupthink as *'the deterioration of mental efficiency, reality testing, and moral judgement in the interest of group solidarity'*. In his book he described the following consequences of team behaviour that is *too* cohesive and therefore prone to the groupthink tendency:

The illusion of invulnerability

This is a typical symptom of groupthink and it occurs when members of one team believe they are invincible. For example:

> Janis cites the disastrous attempt of America to invade Cuba in April 1961 (the Bay of Pigs Invasion). Robert Kennedy stated that, with the talent of the group, they could overcome whatever challenge came their way with 'common sense and hard work and bold new ideas'.

The tendency to moralise

There seems to be a tendency, when groupthink is present, to view your own team as being right and the other team as being wrong in terms of moral criteria such as intelligence, good or bad, weak or strong.

The feeling of unanimity

Janis indicated that, when groupthink is present, members are very unanimous with regard to decision making. Later, however, some admitted that they had serious doubts at the wisdom of the decisions but did not want to stand up to the forces of cohesiveness. The individual does not want to damage the 'team spirit' in the group.

Pressure to conform

Under groupthink conditions, pressure on individual members to conform is extremely strong.

Janis gives an example:

> President J F Kennedy would bring in experts to respond to questions of his team members. The purpose was, in effect, to have the experts silence critics, instead of actively encouraging discussion of divergent views.

Opposing ideas dismissed

Any individual or outside group that criticised or opposed a decision or policy received little or no attention from the government group cited above by Janis. Even valid ideas and relevant arguments were often dismissed prematurely. Janis notes that much evidence indicated strongly that the invasion of Cuba would fail, but it was given little consideration. Thus, information conflicting with group goals can be distorted or ignored as individual members try for agreement and solidarity.

> The groupthink phenomenon could even explain such events as Watergate, the Iran–Contra affair in the United States, and possibly the decision by the National Party cabinet to accept the Separate Development policies of H F Verwoerd in the 1950s; as well as the decision by the group around Lord Milner to invade the Transvaal Republic in 1899, whatever the cost.

Certainly some level of group cohesiveness is necessary for a team to function effectively. The key here would be to define the role of each member of the team. If their roles are not properly defined, the phenomenon of groupthink could easily emerge, or worse, individuals with non-deployed roles could be 'hijacked' by the other side of the table. The role of an individual should not be subservient to the cohesiveness of the team and cohesiveness should possibly rather be waived in favour of the existence of significant role.

The risky shift phenomenon

The phenomenon of risky shift is somewhat similar to the phenomenon of groupthink. *Risky shift occurs when a group or team makes a more risky decision than any individual would ever make on his own.* Risky shift refers primarily to the tendency of individuals, when they are grouped together, to become irresponsible.

> This is often seen at soccer matches when many people who support the same team think alike and sit close together and then do things together that they would never do on their own. The terrible 'necklace' murders in the townships of South Africa were committed by groups of youths all thinking alike and acting together. On his own each would never act in a similar way.

The existence of the phenomena of groupthink and risky shift impacts on the size of negotiation teams. The ideal size of a team, considering the whole group on both sides of the table, should not be more than five to ensure effective decisions. When the group becomes bigger than about five, there will be individuals without roles, and there could be a tendency towards groupthink or risky shift decisions.

The effect of colour

Almost all physical characteristics of the meeting room could either have a beneficial or adverse effect on the negotiation outcome. The host should take great pains to arrange the physical environment to ensure an informal, comfortable and relaxed atmosphere which reduces tension, conflict intensity and the competitive instinct when dealing with integrative negotiation. If the meeting room is your own private office, your image to strangers will be reflected by the image of your office. In contrast to the highly reflective white walls of some offices and conference rooms, an intimate and friendly atmosphere can be established by a combination of sunlight from the window and the warmth of yellow-tinted light from standing and table lamps, according to Sperber (1984:31). Furthermore, lamps and other objects such as vases, abstract sculptures, plants and paintings can be selected to facilitate informality and affiliative behaviour.

With respect to the colour of walls and carpeting, according to Sperber, **blue** will not only prove relaxing for guests, but also convey the image of power and authority. **Yellow** is thought to be too frivolous and weak; **beige** and **tan** are fairly neutral; dark **brown** and **grey** are depressing; **red**, although a warm colour in small amounts, tends to excite and even frighten some people, according to Sperber.

Spoelstra (1990:73) believes that colour appreciation develops primarily from a conditioning process with the result that the effect that colour produces could vary vastly from culture to culture and from organisation to organisation. For example:

> The Japanese like pastel colours, and the Chinese prefer bright primary colours that attract attention. In Phalaborwa and Ellisras (in northern South Africa), male workers wear khaki clothes to work while in Johannesburg the khaki colour is seen as a politically radical colour that has a negative connotation for some people.

Colours are widely used for their symbolism in marketing and for the emotional effect that they create. **Yellow** is associated with sunlight and projects warmth and vitality; while **green** often conveys coolness, closeness to nature and calmness; with **red** indicating excitement, sex, love and rage.

In a discussion of literature on colour, Spoelstra (1990:74) demonstrated clearly how selectivity and preference for colour differs from culture to culture even within South Africa. Among Soweto residents, 80 % associated red with danger and 69 % associated black with death. Blue seems to be the dominant colour in advertising on television or in magazines in South Africa. Red seems to be the most controversial colour, either being totally disliked or preferred. In South Africa there even seem to be ethnic differences in colour preferences, with Xhosas preferring bright yellow compared to Zulus who prefer bright red. Black is seemingly the choice of those who speak Northern Sotho at home, compared to the preference for bright yellow by Tswana speakers in the same area. Dark violet was the colour most disliked by all ethnic groups in South Africa.

Although fashions also change radically from year to year, it would seem that darker coloured clothes worn by men are most appropriate when they go for job interviews. In offices, blue and brown colours seem to be the most appropriate in Western cities with tints of yellow or red being acceptable.

Plants in offices are becoming more acceptable as the emphasis on the **environment** is encouraged. Portraits and paintings with neutral topics by competent artists create the best climate for negotiation.

In summary then, the question is still how colour should be treated in the climate phase of negotiation. The team should be very sensitive to the choice of colour both in office surroundings and in clothes. They must realise that clothing and office surroundings will have an emotional effect on themselves and on the other side. Once they view this variable in this light they will be able to manage the climate by the appropriate choice of venue and clothing.

The effect of location

Another aspect of negotiation strategy that does not receive as much attention as it should, is the physical environment in which negotiations take place. Diplomats normally take great care in choosing locations for international talks and when unions and management decide to negotiate, they discuss the venue at great length.

The territory or 'site' of a negotiation generally has the same impact that a baseball or rugby park or soccer stadium has on the teams. Teams do better on their home ground. The home team generally has better facilities — their resources are close by, they have access to special people and equipment and luxuries that people who are away from home do not have. They know the environment better and they feel more at home. They also do not suffer from travel fatigue. The feeling of psychological support and morale is greater in the home environment.

The same is true for negotiations. Many negotiators feel more comfortable and perform more effectively when negotiating in their own offices and on home ground. According to Lewicki and Litterer (1985:144) there are some major advantages and disadvantages in the decision regarding the meeting location that could affect the outcome of the negotiation considerably. Some of the **advantages** are considered below.

Control

When the negotiators are on home ground they have control over the territory which allows them to manipulate the seating and the decoration according to the preferences for the climate they intend to have. Control could even extend to the arrangement of hotel facilities for visitors, the social activities of visitors and the way the visitors are treated in general. This includes restaurants, food and the many other customs and cultures of the host country or town. The more pronounced the cultural and territorial differences between respective negotiators, the greater the home territory advantage would be.

Assertiveness

Negotiators bargaining on their home turf are more likely to be relaxed and assertive than those on unfamiliar ground. Lewicki and Litterer (1985:145) refer to studies that clearly indicate that when individuals are on home ground they seem to talk for longer and win more settlements than those on foreign ground.

Politeness

The local rules of protocol and politeness are used in negotiation. So it would be relatively easier for those on home ground to feel at ease with the form of politeness used. Consider, for example, an individual visiting Japan and being totally uneasy about the forms of greeting and of seating and of general response to favours from the other side. Being the 'guest' not only implies socially proper norms of graciousness, but in fact may also involve a sense of **obligation** to the 'host' for his or her generous hospitality. Studies of territorial behaviour in both animals and humans confirm that aggressive displays are much more common by the owner of the location than the 'visitor'. Another aspect that Lewicki considers important is the fact that negotiators may feel that hosting the negotiation affirms a higher level of status and prestige, that is, that 'they are coming to us' rather than us going to them, which causes the home side to feel more confident to the extent that they feel they have the right to push their demands onto their guests to a greater degree. They could in fact become less flexible.

The **disadvantages** of negotiating on home ground are discussed below.

Information

When negotiating on home ground, the excuse of lack of information cannot be used against the opponents. The 'back door' outcome is not there and this limits the alternatives for the individual on home ground. Visitors could always claim that they do not have the information at hand or that the final approval must be given by the home office and therefore use time delays to get out of tight positions in negotiations. When on home turf, that claim could seldom be made with the same amount of confidence.

Guilt

When visitors have come from far afield, there could be an unconscious feeling of guilt towards them because they have gone to great lengths and incurred great costs to see you in your office. You may feel that you should at least give them something that they can take back home with them. A subtle emotional plea in this direction could be very unsettling for the party on home ground.

The aspect of gifts

Individuals that visit you from afar often bring along gifts which could cause an imbalance in the relationship between the two parties. To reciprocate would mean making a concession of some kind.

Negotiators visiting Third World countries are often extremely unsure about giving gifts and the role of 'bribes'. They think it is extremely difficult to obtain contracts and to reach agreements if the 'middlemen' in the process are not rewarded financially 'under the table'. There is obviously a fine line between 'gifts' and 'bribes', yet a negotiator should be extremely careful never to make any assumptions about bribes in a foreign country as a so-called requirement for business. Negotiators should abstain from ever becoming involved in dubious practices of this kind. In fact, the most prominent organisations in Third World countries are often those that have never allowed themselves to be drawn into doubtful practices, thereby gaining the confidence of most people. In Third World countries, governments tend to rotate at a brisker pace than elsewhere and new governments are often keen to pursue fraudulent activities which relate back to the previous regime. Actions have a way of revisiting the perpretator — ethical behaviour may be rewarded and unethical actions punished.

Neutral ground

The distinct awareness that one is more comfortable on home turf and less comfortable on the opponent's turf, pushes many negotiators to a **'neutral'** site. Yet, through international examples, we can often see the value of home ground or opponent's ground in the frequent visits paid by Reagan and Nixon to the USSR and China respectively, and in Gorbachev and De Klerk visiting the United States recently. Great advantages were gained by those visiting the opponent's ground because of the fact that they were guests, which also enabled them to return home with major concessions. On top of that they had the important impact of media coverage which caused their 'opponents' to be careful not to seem inflexible and thus to lose important political ground in the process.

> Again, this can most commonly be seen in international negotiations such as the choice of Geneva in Switzerland. In South Africa, prime ministers have negotiated on trains which were stationary on bridges over rivers demarcating the borders between countries. In this way Lord Milner negotiated with President Kruger in 1899 in a train over the Orange River and Prime Minister John Vorster negotiated in the early '60s with President Kenneth Kaunda of Zambia in a train over the Zambezi River.

In South Africa certain hotels make venues available for 'neutral' negotiations between labour and management. Sometimes, so-called 'neutral' ground could be used to great effect. For example, the President of the United States invited management and a striking union to meet in the White House to 'hammer out' an agreement. In this case the 'ownership' of location had major symbolic significance for the group that owned it. 'Neutral' turf had high symbolic significance for the parties because neither side owned it. Therefore neither side saw the other as having the potential psychological advantage afforded by territorial ownership.

The choice of ground is often indicative of the integrative or distributive attitude of the negotiators. The more distributive the negotiators are, the more the choice would tend to be for a 'neutral' location.

Case 3.1

NEGOTIATING THE CLIMATE

Scene: A conference room in Japan

The Americans are anxious. Six months after an initial meeting, Osatech, the renowned Japanese video software company, has finally agreed to meet with an American negotiating team in its headquarters in Osaka. Videomart, number one in America's video-game industry, hopes to get a licensee agreement with the Japanese company to sell its software. The Americans should be anxious. Osatech has an impeccable reputation for creating one successful game after another. Landing a contract with it would be a real coup. Now, after what seemed to the Americans an eternity, Osatech has agreed that it is in the companies' mutual interest to meet and work out an acceptable deal — or so it seems.

The meeting gets off to a good start. After brief introductions and the ritual exchange of business cards, both parties sit down at the table, the Japanese on one side, the Americans on the other. On the Japanese team are the general manager, two assistants, and an engineer who will also serve as the translator. Representing the Americans are the president of Videomart, two vice presidents (sales and marketing), and an engineer. They have no translator. Nor do any of the Americans speak or understand Japanese.

The Americans begin their opening presentation, giving a brief status report on their company, the amount of business it does, its share of the market, projected sales — a veritable 'dog and pony show'. They emphasise that Videomart has emerged as the industry leader in terms of unit and dollar volume. Repeatedly they point out that should the Japanese pass up the opportunity of doing business with them, the former would be doing their company a grievous disservice. After a lengthy public relations build-up, the Americans set the agenda, describe their product needs, suggest a time schedule and a delivery date. Item costs, they claim, can be resolved later.

During the Americans' presentation, the Japanese team has been quiet, listening attentively, occasionally nodding to one another. When the Americans finish talking, the Japanese ask many probing questions covering a wide range of issues — mostly in the category of detailed product specifications.

They wish to see the engineering blueprints for these units. What about the new game Videomart plans to introduce at the next sales convention? May they please see a working model to check for compatibility? What about delivery dates? The Americans, taken aback by the nature of the questions, decide to call a recess to think through what has just occurred. The Japanese politely agree.

Alone in their conference room, the American team is aghast.

'I don't think they understood one word!'

'How do they expect us to tell them that when we don't even have a firm commitment from them that they will join us?'

'Nervy of them! They can't really keep asking questions like that without giving a few answers themselves. They just ignored you, Bob.'

'Well, they kept nodding yes and smiling . . .'

'Can't they see what a lucrative deal this would be for them? And just think what the board will say if we don't come home with a deal!'

'I'm getting sick of the stupid request to see our blueprints before we've even drawn up the terms of a contract. Remember that article in *Fortune* about Japanese spies in the Silicone Valley?'

'Yeah well, what do you think?'

'I don't know. Two weeks and we've agreed to almost nothing.'

'Would never happen in Ohio.'

The Japanese, too, are ready to pull out. To them the futility of doing business with these Americans is obvious!

'If they are sincere, why do they keep referring to their lawyers as if only lawyers can discuss and determine minor points?'

'They are not minor points, Yoshi.'

'Yes we know that, but they don't seem to.'

'To me they are presumptuous and operate out of bad faith. They cannot be trusted.'

'But their company can help us gain the distribution and market share like no one else as they will not let us forget.'

'I hope we do not have to hear that one more time. It makes me think we should consider doing business with another company that is not so "tops".'

There was one final meeting. It too failed. The Americans went home.

From: Deutsch, M.F. 1983. *Doing Business with the Japanese.* New American Library, pp 21–25.

Politeness

The question of protocol could become complicated when different cultures are involved. Negotiators should be very sensitive about protocol and general rules of politeness. They would be expected, in integrative negotiation, to use the utmost care in this regard. Consideration should be given to pecking order and the role of each individual when greetings are made. Normally the most important persons greet each other first and then introduce their team members in sequence of importance, so that the person of least importance is introduced to the host last. Then the host introduces his members to the other side in the same way. When teams sit, hosts normally never sit first, but wait for guests to be seated before they seat themselves. Care should to taken that guests have enough space to enact their roles.

Care should also be taken that the names of the guests be remembered by each member of the host team, since accurate use of **names** eases the negotiation process. Many people find it difficult to remember names, but under normal circumstances it has been found that most people can remember five to six names when they are repeated one by one. Repetition and use of the names immediately after they are expressed could enhance retention of those names. In some cases, business cards are exchanged which will make it easier to remember names. When names are used and parties do not know each other well, they would be advised to use the most polite forms of greeting. Some individuals are very sensitive about the use of titles and surnames, especially in government and semi-government circles in South Africa and Germany. Don't try to bypass that on your own accord, but wait for the other party to suggest that you address him in a more informal manner. This suggestion should come from the most senior person in the group and should not be suggested by the junior in terms of protocol.

Clean tables

Often individuals automatically bring notes and pens to the negotiations. The best political and business negotiators of the world do not put any material on the table in front of them. They try to have as much open space in front and to the side of them as possible. Papers and notes should be kept in briefcases until they are needed.

The effect of verbal and non-verbal communication

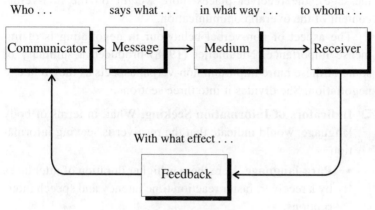

Figure 3.5
THE COMMUNICATION PROCESS
(Gibson, Ivancevich and Donnolly 1991:541)

The general process of communication is presented in figure 3.5. The process contains five elements: the communicator, the message, the medium, the receiver and feedback. It can be simply summarised as 'who says what, in what way, to whom, and with what effect'. Each of the above elements of the communication process will affect the climate of a negotiation. The communicator is responsible for communicating who he is, what he stands for, what message he brings and how he brings the message. The receivers of the message communicate who they are and what they stand for.

Messages are put across either verbally or non-verbally. However, the unintended messages that can be sent by silence, inaction or body movement can be as important as those that are verbally expressed.

Non-verbal communication

The area of non-verbal communication is an area of growing research and interest among behavioural scientists. One researcher has found that only 7 % of a message's impact comes from its verbal content; the rest of the impact is non-verbal: 38 % from vocal inflection and content and 55 % from facial content (Mehrabian 1971). When a sender's communication is contradictory (in other words, when the non-verbal message contradicts the verbal message), the receiver places more weight on the non-verbal content of the overall communication.

The aspect of non-verbal behaviour in negotiating is of immense importance. Nieumeijer (1988) produced a summary of some of these more important non-verbal aspects as they relate to negotiation. She divides it into three sections:

❏ **Indicators of Information Seeking**. What, in terms of body language, would indicate that the receiver is seeking information.

- **Para-language**. Here there is higher duration of utterances by a receiver, faster reaction time latency and speech interruptions.
- **Visual**. More frequent gazes in the direction of the other side or other person.
- **Proximic**. Shorter spatial distance in standing or seating arrangements.

❏ **Pre-articulation Processing**. Indicators of when the receiver is preparing to speak.

- **Para-language**. More frequent head nods, and chin thrusts; more expansive hand and feet movements and larger postural shifts occur in this form of reaction.
- **Visual**. Larger pupil size and increased eye blinking.

❏ **Response Selection Behaviour**. When the receiver is considering reaction to the messages received from the communicator.

- **Para-language**. Reduced verbalisations.
- **Visual**. Increased pupil size and change in eye contact.

Summarising some of the more significant research on body language, Gibson et al. (1991:545) indicated that when rapport exists, the two individuals negotiating would each mirror the other's movements — shifting body positions, dropping a hand, or making some other movement at the same time. If rapport is abruptly ended in a conversation, the 'mirror' is quickly broken. Gibson et al.

(1991:546) also classified body language into five types of expression based on an overview of the research: emblems, illustrators, regulators, adapters and affect displays.

❏ **Emblems** are gestures much like sign language: the 'OK' sign with thumb and forefinger, the 'V' sign for victory. These movements are quickly understood words or phrases.

❏ **Illustrators** are gestures that give a picture of what is being said: a raised forefinger to indicate the first point of a sender's position, extended hands to indicate the size of an object.

❏ **Regulators** are movements that regulate a conversation: an upraised palm from the receiver tells the sender to slow down, an arched eyebrow can convey a request for the sender to clarify what has been said, and a nod of the head indicates understanding.

Emblems, illustrators and regulators are consciously used by individuals. Adapters and affect displays, on the other hand, are often subconsciously communicated and can reveal much about both sender's and receiver's feelings and attitudes.

❏ **Adapters** are expressions used to adjust psychologically to the interpersonal climate of a particular situation. Usually learned early in life, adapters are frequently used to deal with stress in an interpersonal situation. Drumming fingers on a table, tugging a strand of hair or jiggling a leg or foot are all ways of releasing some degree of stress.

❏ **Affect displays**, usually subconscious, directly communicate an individual's emotions. Most affect displays are facial expressions, which are all particularly important communicators of a person's feelings. There is a long-held assumption that a person's emotions are mirrored in the face and that these emotions can be 'read' with a great deal of accuracy. Affect displays are also expressed in body positions. For example, a 'closed posture' (arms folded across the chest, legs crossed) communicates defensiveness and often dislike. Interestingly, body positions can visibly convey a high degree of rapport between the sender and the receiver.

The task of trying to 'read' an individual's body language becomes more difficult in intercultural and international environments where the meaning of non-verbal cues often differs strikingly from those back home. Consider, for example:

> A nod of the head means 'yes' in South Africa but 'no' in Bulgaria. The 'OK' sign with thumb and forefinger means 'money' in France, 'worthless' in Japan and something very obscene in Brazil. Waving, a greeting of farewell in the United States, is a grave insult in Greece and Nigeria.

Verbal communication

Henderson (1989:27) is of the opinion that some facial expressions account for more than half of a total impression, yet believes that vocal tone can represent as much as 38 %. Psychotherapists use voice characteristics such as pauses, vocal tone, pitch and enunciation to determine some personality or behavioural traits, such as introversion, extroversion, anxiety, intelligence and leadership potential. Pienaar (1991) divided voice characteristics and meanings in the following manner:

❑ **Plosives.** These are the way sounds such as 'd', 'k', 't', 'p' and 'b' are pronounced by the communicator. Overemphasis on the plosives could indicate varying levels of aggression.

❑ **Vowels.** Where the vowel sounds 'a', 'e', 'i', 'o', 'u' and 'y' are emphasised, it could indicate flexibility, complacency and accommodating behaviour.

❑ **'S' sound.** An emphasis of this sound in speech could be an indication of social sensitivity.

❑ **Pitch and volume** of the voice. Normally, high pitches and high volumes would be used for words that require 'low intellectual' functioning, such as swear words, shouting and screaming and emotional tones. The lower the pitch and volume of the voice the greater the ability of the individual to concentrate on intellectual processes. An example would be the mathematics class in which it is very difficult to do complicated calculations if there is no silence. On the other hand, in a disco, physical and emotional reactions are due partly to the high volume and pitch of the music.

❏ **Silence**. In many ways silence could have more meaning than voice. It could often be an indication of strength and emotional control.

Language is made up of vowels, 's' sounds and plosives in most cases. An overemphasis of any of these in speech could, according to Pienaar, be an indication of underlying conflict or intense feelings around the negotiating table. It could also be used by negotiators to create a climate conducive to the objectives they plan to achieve.

Noise

Noise in the environment can often affect the climate in negotiation as well. Pienaar makes a distinction between three types of noise: pink noise, white noise and pure tones.

❏ **Pink noise** refers to a group of infrequent sounds, of varying pitch, that come across infrequently during negotiation. The noise of building contractors next door, shouting, hammering, honking of motor-car hooters, screeching sounds, slamming of doors and so on are pink noises. These noises tend to **stagnate** people and cause an inability to think creatively and constructively during a negotiation.

❏ **White noise** is a noise that is continuous. It is usually of the same frequency and volume and is so unending that it is hardly noticed consciously by individuals negotiating. Sounds such as a train passing in the distance, air conditioners humming in the background, neon lights humming and the continuous sound of motor cars in the street are white noise. White noise tends to repel and cause either a negative climate or a tendency to postpone whatever is being discussed.

❏ **Pure tones** tend to attract people and therefore the tone of voice and soft music could be important in setting climate. The impact of pure tones on an individual's frame of mind is well known since we know that music is often used to encourage people to relax and to create certain 'moods'. Certain kinds of music have proved successful in stimulating creativity and the voice itself can have a soothing effect or can be conducive to the negotiation process.

The effect of time

Time is probably one of the most underrated variables in negotiation. The control of time and timing strongly influences the climate for negotiation. Researchers have found that the frequency of negotiation contacts is often positively related to the success of these contacts. Thus, in the first place, it seems better to negotiate more frequently for shorter periods, than to try to solve the problem at one session. Timing has also received attention in literature on negotiation (Lewicki & Litterer 1985). Consideration should be given to the best time for a negotiation appointment.

❑ The best time of the **day** for the particular company could be in the morning or the afternoon. Morning appointments seem to be better on the whole since people are fresh and intellectually more active than in the afternoon. It also provides the opportunity for parties to have lunch after the negotiation so as to conclude agreements in a more 'visible' fashion.

❑ The time of the **month** could be important. Some companies are very busy at the end of the month and have little time for meeting guests.

❑ The time of the **year** could even be considered. For some companies there are financial year ends, others are prone to seasonal change (especially those that deal with the farming industry) and there are times when the cash flow is low in some companies.

❑ The best time in terms of the **needs of companies** or individuals should be considered. These could be times when business is slow during periods of unrest and strikes, times of organisational change and new appointments and many other factors that could affect the climate.

❑ The **previous history** of timing during past negotiations should be considered, since what happened in the past could affect the feeling around the table when the parties meet again.

Time and timing are also important since control over time could affect the power of each party. Although power will be dealt with later in this book, the effect that time has on power is that the closer parties get to deadlines, the more power can be wielded to encourage them to come down to their real bases during negotiation.

Case 3.2

NEGOTIATING CLIMATE

The man with space

It is nine o'clock in the morning at work. Peter and seven other individuals, all working on a marketing strategy for 'Calps' cooldrink, are still waiting for John to arrive. Finally he enters the room. John is immaculately dressed. The white shirt is in sharp contrast to the dark, expensive suit and the floral tie of the latest design. He moves to the head of the table with confidence. He sits down and, while spreading his arms wide in front of him on the table, he looks at each team member, in silence, with empathy. He is the only one without a single note in front of him.

'Well, gentlemen,' he begins in his normal, deep voice, 'this is certainly an important day . . .' He hesitates a long time, making eye contact with each member around the table once more, then continues:

'No South African will ever again come out of a Pick 'n Pay store without a bottle of Calps as part of his weekly shopping after we have concluded our strategy . . .' While he is talking, both Jim and Mac, who sit on either side of him, nod in agreement.

John suddenly turns his head to the left. 'Not so, Carl?' Carl nods. 'Yes, you do have a point,' he says.

Peter is sitting at the end of the table. His hands are covering his chin. He is deep in thought. 'How does he do it? John is on the same level as me, why can't I be like him? If I make statements like that, no one will even listen to me!'

CONCLUSION

What is important is that the negotiator remembers that it is within **his** ability to influence the climate of any meeting considerably through good planning and concentration on some of the variables discussed in this chapter. It is within reach of virtually anyone to create a climate conducive to the reaching of mutual agreement.

The claim is sometimes made that some of the strategies discussed could be construed as an overuse of influence and therefore manipulation. The ethical aspect of negotiation will have to be considered by all readers of this book. However, individuals should realise that relatively small variables related to 'personal' behaviour could have a large effect on the perception by the group of that individual. This perception could significantly enhance the negotiation process.

CHAPTER 4

Negotiating for Common Ground

In this Chapter

❑ *Common Ground*, Framing and Prospect Theory

The basis of Common Ground:

- The relationships between the parties
- Needs and fears of parties
- Objectives and information
- Personalities around the table
- The role of time and timing in negotiation

❑ *Power*

- The sources of power
- The use of power
- Examples of power in action
- 'Laws' for the deployment of power in practice

INTRODUCTION

Although the establishment of climate is of crucial importance in the first phase of negotiation, it is important to realise that climate should be maintained throughout the negotiation and even beyond. Any of the variables discussed in the previous chapter could affect the climate in the later stages of a dynamic agenda.

'Small talk' about matters such as the weather, rugby, health and other trivial matters of common interest usually follows the introductions and is quite normal. Small talk could have an important effect on the climate of the talks and could even be more influential if it is directed towards the issues that are to follow later. So, related small talk will make the transition into the problem stages of negotiation somewhat easier. For example:

> The subject of rugby could lead on to a reference to the rugby stadium's new grandstand, for which the steel beams are to be manufactured by one of the parties — an issue to be discussed later in the negotiation.

Very much in line with the dynamic agenda discussed in a previous chapter, the first phase of negotiation is of a socio-emotional nature. After the small talk comes the question, whether expressed or not: **'Why are we here?'** or 'Why have you called this meeting?' This is regarded as an extremely important stage of negotiation. The way that the initial objectives are framed has an important effect on the outcome of the negotiation. If there is no commonality in the framing of the objectives it could cause the negotiations to start off with parties opposed to one another instead of being bound by common ground.

It should be noted that one of the first recognised conventions of negotiation is, that as part of the problem definition, **time** parameters should be established before or early during the negotiation process. This implies the negotiation of the time to start and end the negotiation process, as well as the general management of time-related events during the process. Not only does this provide an easy early common ground issue, but it also determines critical elements for timing, as will be illustrated later in this chapter.

FRAMING AND COMMON GROUND

Common ground could be defined as those issues which are relevant to the problem on hand and are reciprocally agreed upon. It specifically refers to what the parties aim to achieve together (Becoming) rather than what they could achieve independently or in opposition to one another. Such a focus on common ground renders the entire negotiation process future directed (Becoming) rather than stagnating in the futile exercise of trying to resolve, as opposed to overcome, past and present differences or conflicts (Being).

Framing refers to a process of defining the problem in such a way that it reflects issues of possible consensus rather than issues of dispute. Since so much of problem solving depends upon how the problem is defined and understood, framing is an essential process of summarising the common ground issues of problem definition. One could therefore frame a 'threat' as 'no, a warning', or disguise 'threats and opportunities' as 'strategic issues'. According to Neale, Huber and Northcraft (1987:229) the framing of objectives or decisions has considerable impact on the outcome of bargaining and negotiation.

Framing under conditions of uncertainty

Under conditions of uncertainty or fear, people tend to reduce alternatives to dichotomous and oppositional dimensions, i.e. 'yes or no', 'north or south', or 'fight or flight'. For example, play a simple word association game where you say a word and then wait for the first word that comes from a group of people. Words like: good, man, yes, north, etc. You will observe a preponderance of oppositional and dichotomous respones.

People tend to polarise their thinking when making choices. This tendency is accompanied by sequential thinking, like 'and then'. Negotiation is by definition an agreement which takes place in circumstances which vary in their degree of uncertainty. Naturally the players will begin to entertain prospects of gains and losses, amplified by the tendency to continue with 'and then' arguments, to the ultimate level of reductionism. Tversky and Kahneman (1990) also explore this in their famous Prospect Theory, which has since been researched by many, both quantitatively and qualitatively, and has many implications for negotiators.

Prospect Theory

In an elaboration on the influence of framing, Neale et al (1987) refer to the so-called *'Prospect Theory'* which states that decision makers seem to treat the prospect of gains differently from the prospect of losses. Individuals are risk-averse (they prefer a certain outcome) when evaluating potential gains, and risk-seeking (they prefer a gamble) when evaluating potential losses. Often, whether the decision maker is evaluating the prospect of gains or losses, it is simply how a question is framed which counts. For example:

'Is the glass half full?' or 'Is the glass half empty?'

Prospect Theory states that significant losses always loom much larger than significant gains. People tend to avoid risks when seeking gains but choose risks to avoid sure losses.

Here is another example:

Compare the choice between
(*a*)a sure gain of R3 000, and
(*b*)an 80 % chance of winning R4 000 and a 20 % chance of winning nothing.

Prospect theory would predict that an individual given this choice would choose (*a*).

Compare this to the next choice:
(*a*)a sure loss of R3 000, and
(*b*)an 80 % chance of losing R4 000 and a 20 % chance of losing nothing.

According to prospect theory, the individual would, in most cases, choose (*b*).

Therefore, in the face of losses, individuals tend to take higher risks than in the face of potential gains. For example:

If negotiation with a labour union is framed in terms of the potential losses for the company, this could increase the likelihood of negotiators engaging in the risky behaviour of conflict escalation, impasse, strike or third party intervention. Alternatively, when the objectives are framed as a potential gain in common ground (what can be gained by both parties settling and reaching agreement), the likelihood of negotiators choosing the certainty of a negotiated settlement would increase.

Framing and Prospect Theory

In a recent study of the impact of framing on collective outcomes, Neale and Bazerman (1985) found support for their contention that negatively framed negotiators are less concessionary, resolve fewer conflicts and have less successful contracts than positively framed negotiators (where the objectives were framed as potential gains instead of potential losses).

Neale et al. (1987:230), in an examination of the literature on framing in negotiations, found that framing of negotiations in a multi-opponent, multitrial market has a significant impact on performance. Positively framed negotiators completed significantly more transactions than negatively framed negotiators in one extended study. While there were no differences in average profit per transaction which could be attributed to the manipulated frame, a total profit per participant over the course of the transactions was greater for those negotiators who had been positively framed by task characteristics relative to negatively framed negotiators. However, the data revealed an interesting and unexpected finding. When the simulation was role symmetrical (potential profits were the same for buyers and sellers), there was a significant effect of **role**. So, the role of the participant (whether that of buyer or seller) has a marked effect on profitability, independent of the framing manipulation. Thus, it is very difficult to separate the effect of **role** and that of **framing**, on any negotiation outcome.

When, for example, the roles of buyers and sellers were given to participants, Neale et al. (1987:231) found that buyers in a symmetrical, competitive market simulation consistently outperformed sellers. They also found that, apart from framing objectives in terms of gains and losses, and apart from the effect of role, **goal setting** and **perception of power** also seemed to be extremely important variables in the determination of the outcome of simplified simulated negotiation situations.

They continued to try to determine why it is that when the role of one participant is framed as that of a seller and the role of another participant is framed as that of a buyer, the buyer would outperform the seller in most cases. One explanation would be that sellers initiate actions that have the objective of gaining a transaction, while on the other hand the buyer responds to the seller's initiatives and focuses on what must be given up in the exchange. He has the objective of averting losses (the loss of money in the transaction). Buyers would therefore be negatively framed and sellers positively framed. According to the previous explanation, the buyers would then be the more risk-seeking negotiators because of the negative frame and they will therefore be willing to demand a higher premium for a negotiated settlement. Thus, negatively framed negotiators will benefit from the additional premiums demanded, while positively framed negotiators will benefit from their willingness to complete transactions and reach agreements.

Case 4.1

PROSPECT THEORY

A car manufacturer

A large car manufacturer has recently been hit by a number of economic difficulties and it seems possible that three plants will need to be closed and 6 000 employees laid off. The vice president of production has been exploring alternative ways to avoid the crisis. She has developed two plans.

Plan A: This plan will save one of three plants and 2 000 jobs.

Plan B: This plan has a one-third probability of saving all three plants and all 6 000 jobs, but has a two-thirds probability of saving no plants and no jobs.

Which plan would you select?

Prospect theory predicts that most people would choose Plan B.

Aside from Prospect Theory, Tversky and Kahneman have also identified the influence of two other phenomena, which they refer to as Availability Theory and Representative Theory.

Representative theory

This theory proposes that people believe lots of detail because it seems more lifelike. This, despite the fact that it is known that Probability Theory statistically demonstrates that the likelihood of any event decreases as a related and integrated whole, as new facts are added. Take any seven assumptions, each of which one may be 90 % certain of, and the probability of them happening together statistically is reduced to less than 50 %. Clearly, $0,9 \times 0,9 \times 0,9 \times 0,9 \times 0,9 \times 0,9 \times 0,9$ = less than 0,5! The implications for negotiators are clear: the more the words, the weaker the argument.

Availability theory

This theory states that, despite man's empirical and scientific knowledge that statistics is the most accurate and certainly the most reliable forecasting method, he stubbornly refuses to apply this knowledge in practice. Instead man usually believes an $N = 1$, i.e. one other person, particularly when that person uses a lot of words (Representative Theory). For example, at any gambling event one could walk up to a perfect stranger and 'give him a hot tip' — the chances are very likely that he will take that tip despite what statistics state or may predict.

Framing with representative and availability theories

It must be clear to the reader that the above-mentioned theories of Tversky and Kahneman (1991) imply that gossip can be a scientifically proven phenomenon, i.e. lots of trivial detail from one source.

How should we respond to our knowledge of the concept of framing and prospect theory?

The information seems to indicate that negotiators should:

❏ Try to frame their objectives during negotiations in terms of **gains** and not in terms of losses, especially in integrative negotiation.

❏ Ask their opponents to **put themselves in their shoes**. This would mean that they would be able to identify with your frame, which would influence their attitude considerably.

❏ Use **questions** to negotiate for agreement on objectives. In other words, common ground should not be regarded as a statement by one side but should be negotiated for. This would involve a question to the other side, waiting for a response and an answer, followed by an agreement on the objectives of the negotiation.

❏ When negotiations are framed negatively, it would be of the utmost importance to try to get out of the high risk response that this elicits, by creating as many **alternatives** as possible for the other side to consider. This would mean that the opponents would be moved from decision making to **choosing** alternatives which is a much more positive and integrative approach. Another response to negatively framed negotiation, according to Nierenberg (1973:110), is to create a positive reaction by redefining the negotiation role (to the other side) and by eliciting acceptance for that redefinition. For example:

> Frame the other side as a seller instead of a buyer. Instead of trying to sell products to an organisation like a big supermarket, it could be effective to ask them, at the beginning of the negotiations, whether they are selling shelf space, since you are in the market to buy up shelf space.

❏ When objectives are framed, the more **details** that are supplied and the more lifelike it seems, the more trustworthy it will seem and the more the other side will identify with the frame. This would cause commonality between parties regarding the frame and objectives of the negotiation.

❏ Be careful, in the beginning of negotiations, not to react too quickly to indications of negative framing on either side. Use your power only to **reward** those behaviours that are positive during the initial stages of integrative negotiation and never use your power to punish behaviour, especially in these stages of negotiation.

Entrapment (or the negotiator's dilemma)

To reach a common ground agreement in the initial stages of talks could be extremely problematic. The reason is that many variables, especially at this stage of negotiation, could affect the parties on both sides of the table. These 'unavoidable' actions and situations cause the parties to react in ways that can only have a distributive outcome. The result of not reaching an agreement on a positive and constructive common ground is the so-called 'negotiator's dilemma' or 'entrapment'. The conflict between the objective of the talks and the parties' own emotional reactions to the situation around the table leads to this 'entrapment'.

Negative emotional reactions towards individuals because of a negative frame or because of the way they behave during the first phase of negotiations, could lead the negotiator to forget the objectives of the negotiation itself. Emotions could easily over-power objectivity, resulting in missed opportunities. Emotions often tend to overpower cognitive logic, and can cause negotiators to try to avoid losses. The type of loss incurred at this stage would be the termination of the negotiations as quickly as possible without causing too much animosity. If this reaction occurs on both sides of the table one can imagine that the results of such talks will be mediocre or worse.

How can negotiators avoid this dilemma and the resulting entrapped position? Although it is difficult to distance oneself from emotional responses, it is of the utmost importance that parties prepare themselves extremely well for this occurrence during discussions. The negotiator should prepare himself with appropriate reactions to emotional outbursts on either side. Al-though the handling of emotional, irrational and aggressive behaviour will be dealt with in detail in chapter 6, here are some techniques that could, meanwhile, be helpful:

❏ **Declare** the feelings caused by the opponents around the table.
❏ **Caucus** or ask for another meeting later so that any form of illogical reaction (that might be occurring) can be cleared up to gain a more balanced approach in the negotiations.
❏ Keep the negotiation **objectives** in mind at all costs.
❏ Consider whether their reaction is a typical first impression reaction or whether there is real ground for being negative in the discussion.

COMMON GROUND QUESTIONS

Apart from the fact that parties should be aware of common ground during negotiations, it is also of importance to reach an **agreement on common ground** in the initial stages of negotiation.

To enable a group to reach an agreement on common ground, it is important that questions be asked of the other side on what they agree on. Once they agree on certain principles, objectives or fears, it can be minuted and used as the basis for the rest of the talks.

Asking questions

Questions are very useful in this phase of negotiation. To make only common ground statements without a response from other members in the group is of little use. Common ground agreement is only reached once everyone around the table has had the opportunity to consider the question and to respond to it.

One of the strongest common ground questions that could be asked is:

'Why are we here?'

Then agreement can be reached on critical aspects that are shared and should serve as a 'guiding light' during the talks, such as:

'Let us agree that we are here to . . . :'

❏ Consider **alternative** ways of working together in the future.

❏ Agree that it is not **us versus you** but rather all of us choosing amongst ourselves different systems that are going to be followed in the future to help all of us to work together.

❏ Agree on **what we are to become** and not what we have been. Therefore what happened in the past is not important for this meeting since we are only here for the future.

❏ Agree that to **compromise** would be better than to go to war (court), since if the parties go to war, both sides are going to lose much more than they will gain in the long run.

❏ Agree that both sides are going to be **flexible** on the issue to be debated. Flexibility will be the guiding principle of the negotiation since inflexibility leads to loss on both sides.

❏ Agree that the parties would prefer not to go to court to settle the matter. To achieve this both sides will need to be flexible on this issue, meet each other halfway and explore **alternatives** so that there are no losers in the process.

❏ Agree that, at all costs, there will be **no losers**.

❏ Agree that during these meetings the parties will be **sensitive** to each other's feelings on the matters to be discussed.

❏ Agree that the parties are in the negotiation together and will **support** each other.

❏ Agree to find ways of becoming **wealthy**.

There are many agreements of this nature that could be added to this list so as to create the necessary common ground climate in the negotiation. Common ground is therefore characterised by words such as 'we' instead of 'I'; 'future' instead of 'past'; 'all of us' instead of 'we'; choosing alternatives instead of 'you should decide'; and 'help us' instead of 'make a concession'.

There is a danger that negotiations could easily become a distributive affair once each side has made statements regarding its point of view, if they never reach the stage of **listening** to the other side and of responding to **questions** about what they all agree on. Without the use of questions it is difficult to imagine parties reaching an amicable agreement of any kind. It is therefore important also to consider the way in which questions could be used in negotiations. Nieumeijer (1973) has analysed various forms of questions and the resultant effect on negotiations in some detail. She developed the following classifications of questions:

Five functions of questions

❏ To get attention. These questions are used to prepare the other side for what is to follow. Example:
   'How are you?'
❏ To get information. Example:
   'How much is it?'
❏ To give information. Example:
   'Did you know you could handle this by using the left lever instead of the right?'
❏ To stimulate the thinking process. Example:
   'What would you suggest we do about this?'
❏ To bring to conclusion. Example:
   'Isn't it time to act on this?'

The present authors think the questions below are important and should be added to the above 'functions'.
❏ To obtain control. Example:
   'What is your name?'
❏ To make a statement. Example:
   'Have you ever lied to someone?'

Clearly, the authors can only concur with the statement that a negotiator must never ask a question to which the negotiator does not already know the answer.

Types of questions

Questions that are often useful in negotiation:

❏ Open-ended questions: These questions cannot be answered by a simple 'yes' or 'no'. They usually begin with WHO, WHAT, WHEN, WHY, HOW, WHERE, and EXPLAIN PLEASE. Example:
   'Please explain why you follow this approach.'

❑ Open questions: This type of question invites the other person to express his **opinion** freely. It gives him latitude in answering. Example:
'Will you tell me, Tom, what this looks like to you?'

❑ Leading questions: These are questions that give direction to the reply. Example:
'Then couldn't you send a letter to Tom?'

❑ Cool questions: These involve little emotion. Example:
'Now, what would you say that the next step in this arithmetic problem is?'

❑ Planned questions: These are part of an overall logical sequence thought out in advance. Example:
'And after you take care of the first part, what would your suggestion be on this?'

❑ Treat questions: These questions have subtle, hidden compliments. Example:
'Could you help me, Joe, with one of your excellent suggestions?'

❑ Window questions: These questions help the questioner to look into the other person's state of mind. Example:
'Why do you feel that way about her?'

❑ Directive questions: These focus on a particular, understood point. Example:
'How excessive do you think the cost might be?'

❑ Gauging questions: These give feedback about the state of the other person. Example:
'How do you feel about this; how does that strike you?'

Questions that can cause difficulty during talks:

❑ Close-out questions: These force the other person into your preconceived point of view. Example:
'If you were convinced that the action was destructive for you, you wouldn't take it, would you?'

❑ Loaded questions: These questions put the other person on the spot, whatever his answer may be. Example:

> *'Do you mean to tell me that your solution is the only solution to this problem, and the right one?'*

❏ Heated questions: These questions reflect a good deal of feeling toward the respondent. Example:

> *'Having already spent a great deal of time discussing the problem, don't you think we should move on?'*

❏ Impulse questions: These questions just occur to the questioner. Example:

> *'By the way, how do you think your boss would handle this situation?'*

❏ Trick questions: These would appear to require a frank answer, but are actually going to put the respondent on the spot. Example:

> *'What are you going to do about your marital problem — get a divorce, separation or annulment?'*

❏ Reflective or mirror questions: These simply reflect another point of view or your own. Example:

> *'Here's how I see it, don't you agree with me?'*

Nierenberg (1973:110) believes that the ability to ask constructive questions will enhance the outcome of negotiation considerably. He says that the judicious use of questions can easily secure immediate attention, maintain interest in the item under discussion and direct the course of the conversation. The opposition can very often be led toward the conclusion that is desired by clever questioning. The use of questions in a negotiation as a means of recognising **needs** (and common interests) generally involves four decisions:

❏ What questions to ask
❏ How to phrase the questions
❏ When to ask questions
❏ What effect the questions will have on the opposition

The importance of phrasing a question properly is well illustrated by the following story:

> A clergyman asked his superior, 'May I smoke while praying?' Permission to smoke was emphatically denied.

Another clergyman, approaching the same superior, asked, 'May I pray while smoking?' To the question thus phrased, permission to smoke was granted.

When to ask a question is equally important. Many a jury has been hung when the foreman started off their deliberations with, 'Let's find out where we stand before we begin the discussion' or 'What do you think of this plan?' The timing of this question tends to freeze people into an immovable position.

Answering questions

Although it is important for a negotiator to improve his ability to ask various kinds of questions to control the directions of the negotiation, it is also important to be able to answer questions in such a way that there will be a constructive outcome to the talks. Answering questions can be classified into two groups: a constructive response to questions and a destructive response to questions.

The **constructive response** to questions will entail a response that will lead the discussion back to common ground issues and to positive outcomes in a negotiation. These responses could be:

❏ To **declare**. This is to state clearly what is happening to the negotiation by the current line of questioning. In this case the negotiator will air the feelings that are aroused by this line of questioning. By declaring the true feelings that are aroused by the discussion or questioning, misunderstanding and a breakdown in communication can be avoided. For example:

> 'If you phrase it that way it makes me feel that you are not as positive as I thought you were about this venture. Am I correct? Or would you like to rephrase the question?'

❏ Asking for **suggestions** on possible ways to help the group to reach constructive conclusions, is another response to questioning.

❏ To **remind** the group that both parties are present to choose alternatives rather than to set one party against the other.

❏ In some cases **silence** could be the most suitable response to difficult questions.

There are also **destructive responses** to questions. Nierenberg (1973:133) believes that the following responses could help the negotiator to stall, play for time or be on the winning side (in other words, follow distributive tactics) in negotiation:

❏ Answering questions in such a way that the person is left with the assumption that he has been answered. For example, just the question *'Why?'* or the response *'You should definitely know the answer to that question.'*

❏ To answer incompletely: The answer will only address part of the question or even a section that is not related to the initial question. For example, *'How did you like my wife's dinner?'* The response could be: *'She certainly sets a beautiful table and the silver was especially fine.'*

❏ To answer inaccurately: Here the answer could start off by saying, *'As I understand your question . . .'* and then redefine the question in the way in which the party wants to answer it.

❏ Leaving the other person without the desire to pursue the questioning process further. Such an answer could be, for example, *'That's one of those unanswerable questions; the future holds the key to that problem; it would serve no purpose in this instance to speculate on the future.'*

Nierenberg also believes that excellent ways to get out of difficult questions would be to use **humour** in the answer, to counterattack immediately using the questioner's background in the counter-attack, or refer to someone else such as 'Why don't you ask Mr Murray those questions instead of me?' Another response to a line of questioning could be:

❏ 'What are you leading up to?'
❏ 'Get straight to the point.'

The present authors, however, are convinced that the best way to answer a question, is to ask a counterquestion, e.g. 'Why do you ask?' or to merely put the negotiation process back on its future-directed course: 'Tell us what you are leading up to, and we can get straight to the point.'

TIME AND TIMING — THE HIDDEN DIMENSIONS OF NEGOTIATION

Few theorists and professionals in the field of negotiation stress the importance of power, information, accommodation, planning, and other such dimensions. However, they all agree implicitly that the new frontiers of negotiation will mean dealing with time and timing. In practice, even if only in the strategic aspects of planning for negotiations, the crucial influence of time demands scrutiny (Pienaar 1995).

However, in this section, the influence of this pervasive factor will be scrutinised and practical implications for practitioners will be explored.

Common ground, time and timing

Time and timing of questions are variables which have permeated the entire text so far. Pienaar (1992) in a paper on project management made the statement that time and timing are forgotten intervening variables in marketing, sales, production and finance. He stated that 'during the 1990s speed will be the currency of choice. Since many negotiation processes are not infinite but finite, the timing of opening, closing and struggles for movement should be considered within definite parameters. But more importantly, if they can use time and timing as an issue of common ground then they capture a unique vehicle for the control of the entire process, e.g. 'Can we continue to the next topic on the agenda?', 'I think that we should demonstrate **movement** to our constituents', etc. If parties cannot even agree on time dimensions, how can they agree on anything else?

Human experience, time and timing

Man is aware of time both psychologically and physiologically, placing great importance on it. Man's experience of the duration of time or of time limits is subjectively judged and defies objective analysis.

Time impacts on one's cognitive experience of reality; and emotionally it impacts upon our experience of the past, present, and future. Migration through time is therefore far more complex than migration through space, because it is so subjectively experienced. The reciprocal interaction between subjectively experienced time frames and emotional states, like fear or anticipation, makes social passage through time seem empirically undefineable. However, the latest available research begins to demonstrate that at least some phenomena are open to scientific scrutiny and highlight their heuristic value.

Strategic planning and time

In an earlier chapter, the importance of preparation and planning was emphasised. Planning has to do with the future. However, very few writers have ever examined the time dimension of strategy. Consider the following as a typical scenario in business: Two executives of a company are involved in strategic planning for a corporate takeover, each heading a division and its workers. Executive 'A' believes the most realistic revenue expansion over the next five years to be in the order of R500 m. His colleague and rival believes that R220 m may be the most likely figure over the same period, and would therefore aim at a far more conservative expansion.

It would only be realistic to characterise the difference and subsequent recommendations in terms of the relative assertive or risk-taking propensities of the two executives. Consider, however, the probability that one of them has the innate and learned ability to project further into the future and grasp better the flow of events over time to come.

Psychological research has shown that individuals differ in their extent of **future orientation**, just as people differ in risk propensity, confidence and even intelligence. Elliot Jacques (1982) has described these phenomena and denoted the temporal horizon of an individual to be 'the longest forward planned task in the individual's active present'. Thus, the future orientation of decision makers is crucial in planning for negotiation. Furthermore, the normal assumption was that the executive with the longest time perspective also has a superior long-range view or the **competitive edge**. This, however, can only be true when the overall environment is tranquil — but the reverse should be true under conditions marked by turmoil. Thus, we need to be able to use negotiators with different abilities for different scenarios.

However, it is normally assumed that all executives have the same undifferentiated ability to grasp the future. It should be understood that time horizons of leaders have decisive impacts upon their planning: executives with a long-term perspective are obviously superior when the future is predictable. However, when turmoil and 'critical events' are the order of the day, the person with the short future orientation may be more adaptive.

Thus, the future orientation of a negotiator may be a crucial variable in his ability as a strategic negotiator. The most superficial search into existing theory and research demonstrates that this field is lamentably neglected. However, some exciting work has recently been done on this previously hidden dimension. Madriakis (1990) claims that time is more fundamental to strategy and negotiation than space. He explains that other variables of time awareness have a critical influence upon the planning aspects of strategy and negotiation.

Different ideas of time
Clock time

Madriakis (1990) points out that the planning horizon ability of individuals is not the only variable that affects negotiating ability. Physical time is the most widely prevalent view of time and is also known as **clock time** or calendar time. Since time, in this context, was considered to be flowing in a linear fashion and in one direction, the assumption is accepted that to become efficient means utilising whatever time is available. The goal then becomes one of limited time utilisation — speed up all processes to get the objective satisfied. This 'Fast Cycle Capability' of individuals has become desirable, as this quotation illustrates:

'Cutting-edge Japanese companies today are capitalising on time as a critical source of competitive advantage, managing time the way most companies manage cost, quality or inventory.'

Clearly, the negotiator's emphasis upon his 'fast cycle capability' becomes another very decisive variable, other than the 'time horizon' factor.

Calendar time

However, as Pienaar (1988) remarked: 'God created time so that everything should not be happening at the same time and thus become Murphy's Law, that is, if anything will go wrong, it will do so at the same time as everything else.' This clearly implies that if one acts by fast cycle capability alone, one would lose the critical advantage of timing. The **absence of time horizons** precludes the opportunity for timing. An appreciation that time is not necessarily limited provides the opportunity to use time during planning and implementation. The appreciation of time as a process rather than an event instructs the planning and timing process, potentially leading to an advantageously timed agenda. Most practitioners and theorists agree that any agreement without implementation difficulties is preferable to any contract or agreement with implementation difficulties. Only the planning of timing can provide this.

Time frames

Timing is probably one of the most critical variables in the negotiation process. One of the basic conventions of negotiation is that time frames, relating to the negotiation, should be negotiated early or before the negotiation proper. To agree that the parties will meet

for a set period of time with regular intervals of rest and delibera-
tion between sessions, sets definite time frames and realistic time-
bound objectives. An agreement that, 'We will meet from 10 a.m.
to 11 a.m. to match agendas', not only freezes the objectives and
anticipation but also is an agreement that forestalls poorly discussed issues, which may cause implementation difficulties later
on during the process. It also prevents the inhibitive influence of
fatigue and irritation. It does not have to mean the retardation of
the overall time perspective of the negotiation but in fact allows
for the introduction of a method which not only facilitates but also
accelerates the process of negotiation. This method is known as
the Progressive Summarisation Method. This method implies the
summarisation of agreements up to a specific point in time and
focuses upon progression to whatever is left on the conjoint
agenda.

Being versus becoming
Mission focus

Not only do people differ in their time horizons and their abilities
to turn from an expected 'fast cycle' demand to a controlled
process approach, but they also differ in their awareness of being.
They are not always aware of being in a state of becoming. In a
sense, one could say that people differ in their ability to pull their
attention away from the immediate and focus upon **'that which is
still missing'**. For example, most companies now have mission
statements — but how many of those statements reflect what the
company is currently doing and neglect to explain and describe
where the corporation is heading? The present authors are quite
convinced by current literature that individuals differ profoundly
in their ability for creative thinking and the recognition of this
ability in a negotiator will have a profound impact upon the
outcome of the negotiation process.

   In a recent debate on AIDS, two clearly identifiable groups
emerged: those who focused upon the epidemiological aspects of
its incidence, the geographical distribution, etc.; and another,

which focused upon the future of helping behaviour between individuals and nations, economically, socially and otherwise. Both made useful contributions and made the audience aware of the impact of loss. However, one individual focused upon the problem in a totally new way: he sketched a life after AIDS and made all aware of the gains made on scientific, economic and social fronts. And suddenly the 'problem' was changed into the 'challenge'. People were made to understand that mankind had faced similar challenges in the past and will assuredly face them again in the future, but it was emphasised that society must become a 'learning' one. Miles and Snow (1978) state that 'truly prospecting (learning) organisations search for new ways of doing business to feed forward into present behaviour and actions'.

Time and shared values

However, merely to be creative is not enough: Leonardo da Vinci discovered nothing that was used during his own time: only centuries later would, for example, the aircraft be developed. It is imperative that individuals within negotiating teams share the values of the **'Being'** and **'Becoming'** time perspectives. Otherwise one man's fantasy will never become a shared goal. This is, in fact, what common ground is all about, i.e. what different parties can become together.

Time and speed

Clearly, the ideas of time and the perspectives of time for man cannot be overemphasised. The criteria for determining planning horizons are many but here are a few examples: the expected growth rate, interest rate forecasts, validity, the product's life cycle, payback periods, lead time between planning and actualisation, and accounting periods. The mechanistic character of these approaches, coupled with non-recognition of the subjective future orientation of negotiators, renders them risky. Negotiations empirically proven to be the best are those where long and short-term horizons are considered, where the speed of the entire process is recognised to be important, and where a creative and often **'miss-ing'** vision is sought (Tregoe & Zimmerman 1989).

If time and timing are not understood as cause–effect contingencies, a negotiator is clearly on far too risky ground. Let's compare two recent events. Negotiators were acting with 'fast cycle' orientation during the Gulf War, deadlines were issued and a military confrontation was inevitable because of Iraq's too hasty invasion and the lack of a visionary insight by USA diplomats. Iraq is as strong today as before the Gulf War. Clearly the message is that sometimes it is as important to watch the calendar as it is to watch the clock. The second example is that of the former Yugoslavia, where diplomats only became involved after the disintegration of the country into different states — when the fighting in one state, Bosnia, rendered this imperative. Clearly, here the process of negotiation was entered into too late. Hence the axiom that because the price of conflict can only be paid afterwards, the price of freedom must be paid beforehand, that is, paid timeously.

Examples can also be seen in the business world. The cyclical impact of timing can clearly be seen during the high season which is normally the low season for most of the building industry. If a buyer from a large retail store gets to know the target dates of representatives of some manufacturers, he can delay the negotiation until the representative is willing to make the most concessions, i.e. days before the deadline. The slogan 'offer stands as long as stocks last', normally means that the firm is overstocked with that particular item. Any businessman knows that by negotiating time periods and timing, he can affect **cash flow** markedly. Similarly, time and timing are critical for entering into negotiation, maintaining the **movement**, and finally, obtaining an agreement.

Time as a resource
The price of time

The interdependency of goals and means in the sphere of decision making is critical. In this section we shall explore how time dimensions can be visualised as the 'means' component. Lakoff and Johnson (1980) have discussed the metaphorical concept of 'time is money'. Some of the metaphorical concepts of time are: 'I don't have the time to give you', 'How do you spend your time these days?', 'You need to budget your time', etc. They suggest that the practice of conceptualising time in terms of money — a limited resource and a valuable commodity — results in the fact that we understand and experience time as the kind of thing that can be spent, wasted, budgeted, invested wisely or poorly, saved, or squandered.

It may be useful to draw an analogy between time and money as different forms of organisational resources. In other words, like money, time can be considered an exchangeable resource in the securing of objectives. This kind of approach is routinely found, for instance, in project resource allocation problems. The trade-off is between project duration and project cost, so that short completion times are bought by proportionately high resource commitments. Stated differently, negotiation or planning objectives are easily carried out through the bargaining of such resource units, where the metrication is universally understood. These resources are the exchange currency or medium of negotiation for deciding upon the planning objectives. Effective negotiators consider timing as a critical variable. Examples of where time is a resource are easily identifiable in all fields of negotiation. In retail, it could be the terms of paying for produce sold. In politics, it could be the timing of an election. In production, it could be the prime determinant of the number of shifts or even jobs. Hence, competent negotiators are not only aware of time as a **restraint** but also as a **resource**.

Multiple impact negotiation

The most basic mistake that any negotiator can make, is to believe that he is negotiating with only one party at one time. The fact is that at any one point in time, most often more than one party's interest is at stake. For example, if a retailer is negotiating with a chain store outlet for shelf space, he has some other party (often even another brand from the same organisation!) negotiating for the same space. Each party in the entire negotiation has a different time horizon, purely because of different objectives: the chain store for special prices on its 'special' occasion, the second party to meet monthly targets, and the third party to introduce a new product — clearly, they negotiate for time frames, fast cycle horizons, and far-sighted horizons respectively. They may think that they are at odds with one another but, in effect, if they consider time, they may discover that by co-ordinating they could establish greater common ground and all benefit. The fact is that Multiple Impact Negotiation implies that multiple parties impact upon one another on multiple occasions through a multitude of people. What compounds the equation is that time in Multiple Impact Negotiation is affected by conflict and co-operation.

One of the peculiar features of history is that **time always erodes advantage**. Every invention sooner or later leads to a counter-invention; elsewhere in the book, it is referred to as 'the law of countervailing power'. Every success contains the seeds of its own overthrow.

The red queen phenomenon

The phenomenon known as the Red Queen in biology explains why all progress is relative. The concept of the Red Queen comes from the chess piece that Alice meets in *Through the Looking Glass*. She perpetually runs without getting very far because the landscape moves with her at equal speed. The faster one runs, the more the world runs with one and the less one makes real progress. Every creature, animate or organisational, is in a Red Queen chess tournament with its clients, with its competitors and, above all, with its peers in and between organisations. (See *The Red Queen* written by Mark Ridley, 1994.)

Just as parasites depend on their host and yet make it suffer, and animals exploit their mates and yet need them, so the Red Queen never appears without another theme being sounded: the theme of **intermingled conflict and co-operation over time**. Every businessman knows that he needs his clients and yet exploits them. Every producer of a product needs an outlet for those products i.e. clients—yet he exploits them and vice versa. This is one of the great recurring themes of human nature, the balance between co-operation and conflict. It is the key to economics and is the quest of every negotiator.

Tit for tat: co-operation and conflict

Co-operation and conflict appear to be contradictory but, in fact, they are the source of new ideas. The effective negotiator perceives their interrelationship as the relationship between answers and questions, or questions and statements: the one begets the other and only sequential logic links them. In practice, the effective negotiator bases his entire control on these two variables, time and timing. However, when more than two parties are engaged simultaneously, the problem of time and timing is incredibly complex and no definite prescription can be offered, except to state that it will always remain advisable to use the Progressive Summarisation technique to keep the time units of negotiation within manageable proportion.

But more importantly, it impacts on the **deployment of power**. During the late 1970s, Robert Axelrod, a political scientist, developed a programme for simple strategies which man could use for dealing with his fellow man (Wilkinson 1995). Should he be invariably **generous**, always a selfish **aggressor**, or a clever **cheat**? What should he be? The simulations showed that the generous would soon be wiped out by aggressors. But aggressors would also soon wipe out one another. Cheats are eventually found out. After the development of several strategies, it was found that one simple rule worked best: tit for tat.

'Tit for tat' implies that people should 'do unto others as they will do unto you': meet aggression with aggression (noting that parity must be maintained), and generosity with equal co-operation. This strategy enables negotiators to reap the benefits of co-operation but avoid being exploited. Robert Wright (1995) in his recent book *The Moral Animal* refers to this as psycho-evolution. The present authors refer to it (later in this chapter) as one of the 'Laws of Power'. This law refers to 'parity in power' in the same way as Wright did, but it also adds that the amount of power deployed should be equitable. Furthermore, our view on the critical value of time and timing, parity in power in the above sense, should be retained for calendar time. However, consideration of clock time may require alternative power deployment alternatives. The authors will return to this issue in a later section of this chapter.

Time and power deployment

Since power is always relative and changing, the good negotiator should enter and close all negotiations within an **inferior status position** — but he must also be reminded to maintain a symmetrical relationship when referring to his own competency, his organisation and its products. However, in the light of the previous section, he must move from entering to closure within predetermined time schedules. An example of this is the current openness of the Russian scientific community to expose the technology that they have kept under utmost secrecy for the last few years. Anyone interested in any of this technology has, at the most, two years to move from entering into negotiation, to completion of an internationally secure contract. That is merely because by then all those 'new' technologies will be known and duplicated worldwide. Clearly, the Russians' power position will erode during that period of time unless they can maintain the competitive edge and an internationally competitive edge in their technological niche. Often it is imperative to leave the time and timing of a product launch visible, so as to keep competitors out of already established consumer markets.

POWER
Power defined

The study of power and its effect is important in the understanding of negotiation and relationships (or common ground) flowing from any negotiation. Every interaction and every social relationship, inside and outside organisations, involves an exercise of power.

Gibson et al. (1991:329) see *power as simply the ability to get things done the way you want them done.* The power of the manager who wants increased financial resources is his ability to get the desired resources.

Power involves a relationship between two or more people. Robert Dahl (1957:202), a political scientist, captures this important relational focus when he defines power: 'A has power over B to the extent that he can get B to do something B would not otherwise do.'

A person or group cannot have power in isolation; power has to be **exercised** or **deployed** or have the potential of being deployed in relation to some other person or group. Power for the present authors is similar to a currency exchange: it is meaningless unless linked or compared as an exchange commodity. Power is never linked to price, but always to value.

Parity in power

The concept of **parity** in power is important in any relationship, since in negotiation *parity of power is the perception, by one party, that the other side possesses the ability to counter any form of power with a similar or different form of power that would render the further escalation of power useless.* As stated, parity in power refers to balance in power deployment. Parity in power is a key factor in the behaviour of a successful negotiator and will be returned to later in this chapter.

In the literature, a distinction is made between power and authority. *Authority is regarded as the formal power that a person has because of the position that he or she holds in an organisation* (Gibson et al. 1989:330). Directives are orders from a manager in an authoritative position and are followed because they must be followed. So, persons in higher positions have **legal** authority over subordinates in lower positions. Power is vested in a person's position, it is accepted by subordinates and it is used vertically in organisations.

Influence is merely the potential of power deployment and is therefore the least amount of power that a person can deploy. To execute a karate punch on someone would demonstrate relative power; however, to warn the other side that the person has a black belt in karate would merely display the resource, i.e. the potential of it being deployed. However, when power is used as a threat, the negotiator should remember that a threat retains its power provided that it is never executed. Upon delivery a threat loses all its value.

Interpersonal power

French and Raven (1959:150–167) suggested five interpersonal bases of power: legitimate, reward, coercive, expert and referent power.

Legitimate power

Legitimate power is derived from the ability to influence because of position. Legitimate power is similar to Max Weber's (1946:324) concept of authority. A person at a higher level has power over the people below. However, each person with legitimate power uses it with a personal flair.

Subordinates play a major role in the exercise of legitimate power. If subordinates view the use of power as legitimate, they comply. However, the culture, customs and value systems of an organisation determine the limits of legitimate power. In other words, there are times when people respond to directions from another, even directions they do not like, because they feel it is proper (legitimate) for the other to tell them and proper (obligatory) for them to obey. This is legitimate power.

According to Lewicki and Litterer (1985:247) it can be shown quite convincingly that legitimate power is at the foundation of most of our social structures. When individuals and groups seek to organise themselves into any form of a **social system** — a family, a combat unit, labour union, a work group, a sports team — they will almost immediately form a social system. A 'leader' will be elected or appointed; informal rules will evolve on how decisions will be made, work divided, responsibilities allocated and conflicts managed. Without this social ordering, chaos would prevail. Group co-ordination would take a long time. Even in informal groups that have no formal roles defined, members may press for this type of definition in order to facilitate group functioning.

The need for social ordering and social structure, then, creates the basis for legitimate power. People are willing to vest rights, responsibilities and power in an office, title or role. By their acceptance of the same social system that gives the power or the power base, they are **obligated** to obey its directions and follow its influence.

There are several ways to acquire legitimate power:

- ❑ It may be acquired by **birth**.
- ❑ It may be acquired by **election**.
- ❑ It can be **awarded**, in the manner of positions in an organisation or in a military establishment.
- ❑ It can be acquired through the use of a **title**.
- ❑ It can be acquired through the ability to **control** rewards, punishments and resources and by converting these into obligations.
- ❑ It could be **'taken'** by one individual in a disorganised or loosely structured group, provided that this is accepted by the majority of the members of the group: the 'chairman' will have legitimate power in a meeting; the most senior manager in a meeting of managers; and the president in a meeting of the South African cabinet.

Legitimate power is used in many ways during negotiation. People with a lot of legitimate power could use their positions of authority to 'instruct' other parties to follow certain procedures. Depending on the authority of the individual, the other players in the negotiation could follow whatever is decided, relying totally on the abilities of the individual in authority.

This could be the reason why, in conflict situations such as those experienced in South Africa during 1990 in Welkom between the AWB and the ANC, the Minister of Defence was called in to try to settle the dispute. Primarily because of his position he was better able to diffuse the conflict than anyone else in the same circumstances. In the same way, Mr Nelson Mandela was called in several times to settle disputes between two factions within the black community of South Africa, since his position enables him, more than anyone else, to be of influence in those circumstances.

Sometimes one party will use legitimate power as a **tactic** against another party by:

❑ bringing in someone who has the influence to make important decisions, and who has **credibility** with the other party; or by

❑ assigning a lot of legitimate power to an individual or individuals within opposing parties so as to use the need for power and status that exists in all individuals to get major concessions from them. This is sometimes referred to as 'ingratiation' or as 'stroking'.

It is important to note that legitimate power can only have influence if it is **recognised** by other individuals because it occurs only in a social structure. Some negotiators may attempt to deny the other party some of their legitimate power by:

❑ denying them an opportunity to talk;

❑ preferring to make reciprocal offers while insisting the other party continue to make concessions;

❑ ignoring prior agreements on how to proceed; or

❑ denying that any one of the other party can have any legitimate position of significance.

In such situations a negotiator could find it necessary to establish some minimal legitimate authority before proceeding, and in some cases may in fact be advised to refuse to proceed until the other party shows by his or her behaviour, that the authority is in place. Once a small, secure base of legitimate authority is established, a negotiator can, according to Lewicki and Litterer (1985:249), extend it (like a drill sergeant).

Reward power

Power can be derived from the ability to reward compliance. Reward power is used to back up legitimate power. If rewards or potential rewards such as recognition, a good job assignment, a pay rise, or additional resources to complete a job are promised, the employee may reciprocate by responding to orders, requests and directions, according to Gibson et al. (1991:331).

Rewards are often monetary but can also be intangible. Research has shown that verbal approval, encouragement and praise are frequently good substitutes for tangible rewards. Experiments on the use of positive reinforcement and behaviour modification in the classroom and work setting have shown that **verbal rewards** could take the form of:

❑ extreme politeness,
❑ compliments, and
❑ praise for past behaviour.

Non-verbal rewards could take the form of:

❑ giving individuals in the other party more space at the table;
❑ nodding of the head to indicate approval and acceptance;
❑ eye contact to indicate attention; and
❑ open and non-aggressive gestures to indicate acceptance and respect.

Rewards could also take the form of verbal promises of financial benefits to be gained by establishing a relationship.

Research reviewed by Lewicki and Litterer (1985:243) supports the view that rewards tend to be used in the following circumstances:

❑ The power holder expects resistance from the target.
❑ The target is perceived as dissimilar to the power holders and when rewards (primarily money) are most likely to be used to prevent the recurrence of resistance in the future rather than to eliminate the present resistance.
❑ Persuasion efforts fail or are likely to fail.

The **potency** of reward power is traceable to simple principles of reinforcement as a mechanism for shaping and changing behaviour. Impressive results have been obtained by psychologists who have advocated the use of reinforcement and behaviour modification programmes in industrial settings, creating rewards and positive incentives for the desired changes in behaviour.

Ingratiation

Ingratiation is sometimes called the art of flattery, and is an example of the use of reward power in social settings. Friedman, Carlsmith and Sears (1974) provide interesting overviews on the impact of ingratiation in interpersonal situations. Most of us know that if other people like us, they will be more willing to do us favours or carry out actions we request than if they dislike us. This fact forms the foundation for one very common technique of influence: **ingratiation**. Briefly, *ingratiation involves one person's efforts to increase his or her appeal to others*. Once this preliminary goal has been attained, attempts to influence these individuals — to get them to change their behaviour in desired ways — are initiated.

Liking

Several different procedures seem to be effective in this regard:
❑ Individuals seeking to increase others' **liking** of them can convince these persons that they **share** basic values or are similar in other ways.
❑ The most common tactic of ingratiation involves the communication of high personal regard to the intended targets of influence. This tactic, usually known as 'other enhancement', often takes the form of **flattery** — exaggerated praise of others. And often, it succeeds: praising others does increase their liking of the flatterer.

Flattery

It is, according to Friedman et al. (1974), possible to go too far. If the recipients of flattery realise that it is being used to influence them, they may react in anger rather than with enhanced liking of the flatterer. For this reason, less direct techniques for communicating positive feelings to others, such as hanging on their every word, encouraging them to talk about themselves, or the emission of positive non-verbal cues are often more successful. Such tactics are very common in many negotiation settings. It is important for negotiators to recognise these techniques for what they are: preliminary steps in the process of gaining compliance.

In general, however, the use of **reward power** seems to be very effective, especially in the longer term. Reward power is sometimes used together with coercive power and these two can be subject to semantic confusion. It is important to describe coercive power before comparing it with and evaluating it against reward power.

Coercive power

Coercive power is the opposite of reward power. *It is the ability of the power holder to take something away from the target person or to punish the target for non-compliance with a request.* For example:

> Coercive power could be the threat to strike from a labour union; the threat of blocking promotion or transfer of a subordinate for poor performance; it could be the threat to go to court; it could be a threat of non-payment; it could be the threat to go public; and it could even be a threat of bodily harm.

All of these practices have an important element of **fear**. The fear that these threats will be used is called coercive power.

Lewicki et al. (1985:244) are of the opinion that the conditions for the use of coercive power are similar to those described in the use of reward power: the target is dependent on the power holder in some way and the punishment can be administered in a manner that will ensure the target person's compliance. Actions to harm the other side in some way, or the imposition of sanctions, are most likely when the other side in negotiations is attempting to use this form of power. This usually occurs when expectations of successful influence by one party are the lowest.

In South Africa coercive power has been used a great deal in business and politics in the last decade.

> South African business and work communities are constantly under threat of stayaways, sanctions, bankruptcy, strikes, terrorism and dismissal. In the townships of South Africa there is a very real threat,

sometimes even of death, to people if they do not comply with the wishes of the power holders. Sanctions were used against South Africa by the international community to force the government of the day to comply with standards laid down by the rest of the international community. Even sports bodies found that they had to change their constitutions and their mode of operations drastically under the threat of non-participation in the international sports arena.

Positive and negative sanctions

Kipnis (1976) stated that *'sanctions, whether positive or negative, are most likely to be involved when **expectations of successful influence are lowest.** Positive sanctions appear to be preferred when the power holder wishes to retain the goodwill of the target person, or when the power holder anticipates that their compliance is likely to drop off in the future. Negative sanctions appear to be preferred when the goodwill of the target is less involved and the influence attempts are directed at changing some behaviour rather than maintaining it.'* An example of negative sanctions is if one side of the negotiations states:

'If you have not released all the political prisoners by the end of the month, our party will start with mass action and a countrywide stay-away.'

An example of a positive sanction is:

'If you do release the targeted number of political prisoners by the end of the month, our party will be willing to negotiate the first principles of a new constitution.'

Victims

It is often pointed out that **victims** can be left in the wake of the use of coercive power. This is probably why the use of coercive power could be effective but is often shortlived in its effect, with a long process of rebuttal later on. The price of integrative nego-tiation seems to be paid before the actual agreement is reached, while the price of war is often paid afterwards (and in many cases, for centuries after the war has taken place). There are many examples of feuds still existing, resulting from wars that took place before the birth of Christ. The core of the feelings created by those feuds still exists today.

Fear

Coercive power can be exerted in many ways. In virtually all of these forms of coercive power, **fear** is present. It is important to elaborate a little on some forms of coercive power in practice and the effect that fear has on an individual.

Threats induce fear, and fear, since time immemorial, has been used by people to induce others to comply. Priests and gurus of all denominations have promoted the concept of the god-fearing person. The impact of such practices has even filtered down to present-day child-rearing practices. For example:

> Parents tell their children that God will punish them if they do not do what their parents expect them to do.

According to Friedman et al. (1974) results of many experiments indicate the following:

❑ Some fear arousal appears to increase compliant behaviour.
❑ Specific fears help to encourage compliance but have little effect on attitudes. For example:

> If a group of young 'comrades' threaten an individual with a 'necklace' death in a South African township, this will cause the resident to stay away from work or do whatever the threat requires of him, but this threat will not necessarily change the resident's attitude towards the cause or the 'comrades'.

Attitude change and fear

Arousal often changes **attitudes**, but it is not too effective in increasing **compliance** unless it is paired with a specific plan of action. For example, the fear of lung cancer could change the attitudes of a smoker, but it will still be difficult for him to change his behaviour and to stop smoking without a plan of action on how to go about it. In these days of fear arousing doomsday campaigns in many vital areas such as crime, ecology, equality, smoking and birth control, this two-step process between attitude change and actual compliance should be kept in mind. Therefore, if the ANC wants to use a threat effectively in negotiations, it should not only threaten mass stayaway action, but add a suggestion as to what the government may do to avoid these actions. This will make the threat more effective.

Case 4.2

THE FEAR OF THREATS

Death threats cause school closure

The PAC and its student wing, the Pan African Student Organisation, have condemned moves to close the Mamello High School in Virginia in the Free State, PASO national organiser Mr Eugene Motati said yesterday.

He said thousands of African students faced a bleak future following the decision by supporters of the MDM, Cosas, Sayco and the ANC to 'forcefully close down' Mamello High School in Virginia's Meloding township.

'The action by these people who do not have the interests of the oppressed at heart comes shortly after the joint efforts by PASO and PAC branches to normalise schooling in the area.'

'With the support of students, parents and teachers, PASO and the PAC had succeeded in normalising education in Meloding but these ANC supporters resorted to threatening teachers with death unless they completely stayed away from school premises,' Motati said.

He added MDM supporters had also launched 'a witch-hunt' for PAC supporters with the view to discouraging them from supporting the normalisation campaign.

'PASO condemns in the strongest possible terms this destructive move as it is to the disadvantage of the students,' he said, adding that PASO called on the MDM, Cosas and Sayco to rescind the decision to abolish schooling in the area.

The Sowetan, 4 September 1990.

Obedience

During the years 1933 to 1945, millions of innocent people were killed in Nazi Germany's gas chambers. The deaths of these people were engineered by a single person who, through a series of commands (combining authority with fear), gave orders to have the grim deeds carried out. The fabric that binds command to action is **obedience**. According to psychologist Stanley Milgram (1963) obedience is the psychological mechanism that links individual actions to political purpose. It is the dispositional cement that binds men to systems of **authority**. Because people tend to obey orders, history has witnessed many atrocities. Some historians suggest that during the course of history more hideous crimes have resulted from obedience to authority than from any type of rebellion.

The problem of obedience to authority is age old and has been recognised for thousands of years. This is one of the reasons why people with authority can be extremely effective in negotiations with subordinates. Obedience to authority is treated in the biblical story of Abraham and discussed in psychological terms by Plato.

Plato, for example, argued that responsibility for crimes committed on command rests with the authority rather than with the person who carries out the order.

To illustrate this relationship Milgram (1963) conducted a highly controversial experiment on obedience to authority.

The Milgram experiments on obedience

The subjects in the experiments were adult men drawn from a variety of occupations and social positions in the Connecticut–Newhaven area. Upon arriving in the laboratory each subject was introduced to his supposed co-subject, a man of about fifty who was actually working with Milgram. The two were asked to draw lots to determine who would be the 'teacher' and who the 'learner'. The drawing was rigged. The real subject always became the teacher. The experiment was ostensibly designed to find out about the effects of punishment on learning in spelling new words.

Whenever the learner made a mistake, he was to be punished by an electric shock. A shock-generating machine was used. It had thirty switches on it, the first delivering fifteen volts, the second thirty volts and so on up to four hundred and fifty volts where the switch was labelled, 'Danger — severe shock — XXX.' The teacher (the real subject) then took his place at the shock-generating machine where he could not see the learner (Milgram's confederate). The plan was for the learner to make many mistakes in repeating words given to him by the teacher. With each mistake, the teacher was told to increase the shocks. At seventy-five volts, the teacher could hear grunts coming from the learner, who was actually faking, as instructed by Milgram. At one hundred and fifty volts, the learner shouted, 'Let me out!', and said that his heart could not stand the pain. He began to yell. He let out an agonising scream at two hundred and eighty-five volts and refused to go on, but seemingly kept trying and made even more mistakes.

Most of the teachers became very upset. Some asked the experimenter whether it was proper to continue. No matter what the teacher asked or how he protested, the experimenter only said, 'The experiment requires that we go on.' The subjects were also told, 'You have no other choice; you must go on.' Milgram wanted to know how many subjects would defy the orders to go on and how many would continue.

Before these experiments were conducted, forty psychiatrists were asked their opinion about whether the subjects would quit. Only 4 % of the subjects, the psychiatrists predicted, would continue to shock learners who failed to respond. But, out of a total of forty subjects, twenty-six (65 %) obeyed the experimenter all the way to the very highest level of the shock generator (XXX).

These men were not abnormal. In fact, most showed extreme signs of emotional strain and psychological conflict during the experiment. They trembled, bit their lips and dug their fingernails into the palms of their hands. They repeatedly asked for the experimenter's permission to stop. Yet they continued increasing the voltage. Milgram stated:

'I observed a mature, initially poised businessman entering the laboratory, smiling and confident; within twenty minutes he was reduced to a twitching, stuttering wreck, who was rapidly approaching a point of nervous collapse . . . Yet he continued to respond to every word of the experimenter and obeyed to the end.'

After the experiment, the subjects were all told the truth. The shock-generating machine delivered 'nothing at all'; it was a sham. During the experiment, every subject was convinced that the learner was another subject like himself.

Milgram's experiments have produced much controversy over the ethics of the procedure. Some opponents of this type of research maintain that many of the subjects suffered long-term psychological harm. Milgram flatly rejects this idea and points out that the sessions all ended with a complete debriefing.

Why did the subject obey the experimenter? Although he possessed no specific power over the subjects, he appeared to be a powerful person of authority. The experimenter created an **illusion of power**: he dressed in a white lab coat, was addressed by others as 'Doctor', and was very stern. The subjects perceived him as possessing **legitimacy** to conduct the study. The experimenter apparently did an excellent job of projecting the illusion of having power.

The Milgram experiments indicate that exercising power in an authoritative way is not the only way that power can be exerted. Coercive power is often exerted by individuals who have only minimum or no actual power. An individual may be able to influence others significantly simply because he or she is perceived to have power. By being obedient to any individual around a negotiating table one is actually identifying with that individual. His power is shared. Once his authority is accepted it is almost as if a common ground is accepted in the negotiation.

Comparing reward power and coercive power
Although coercive power sometimes results in amazing short-term effects, it would seem fairly clear that reward power is, according to Lewicki et al. (1985:247), far more likely to produce desired consequences, with less close observation and control than coercive power. Yet, efforts at coercion are a common occurrence in negotiation. When simple persuasion fails, when tempers flare, when self-esteem is threatened, or when the vision of material gain overshadows the understanding of the potential cost of its use, the efforts at coercion through threats and hostile language are likely to increase. It is at these times that the emotional expression of anger, or feelings of frustration and impotence may overwhelm the rational understanding of the effectiveness of reward strategies.

Expert power

A person who possesses expertise that is highly valued has expert power. Experts have power even when their rank is low. An individual may possess expertise on technical, administrative, or personal matters. The more difficult it is to replace the expert, the greater is the degree of expert power that he or she possesses. Expert power is sometimes referred to as **information power** and is often a personal characteristic. For example:

> A secretary who has a relatively low-level organisational position may have high expert power because he or she knows the details of operating the business — where everything is or how to handle difficult situations.

The influence of information

According to Lewicki et al. (1985:249), men and nations will act rationally when all other possibilities have been exhausted. Within the context of negotiation, expert power is the most common form of power in use. Expert power refers to the persuasive, influential nature of the information itself. It refers to the accumulation and presentation of information that will change the other's point of view on an issue.

Lewicki et al. (1985:251) are of the opinion that expert power is a special form of information power. Information power can be used by anyone who has studied and prepared his position for negotiation. Expert power, according to this author, is accorded to those who are seen as having mastered and organised a great wealth of information.

Case 4.3

THE USE OF INFORMATION POWER IN NEGOTIATION

South African coal versus Nippon steel

We arrived at the venue well prepared (we thought) and soon got down to business, quoting our price, which we knew was cheaper than any other. Then the dreaded words from Mr Shibuya that I'll remember until my retirement . . . 'Please Mr Smith, explain to us how you worked out your price, because we also worked out your price for you and get a different figure. We do not mind paying you a premium.'

Shibuya then commenced to put an impressive document on the table: on that they had detailed figures of SATS tariffs, on tonnage, on insurance, on the cost of **our** administration. What audacity! Yet they were right: on closer inspection we could not fault them on a single point. Their figures were even more recent than ours. They had better information on our own product than we ourselves! How on earth do you counter this across a table?

Smith, G.H. *The Study of Business Negotiation in Japan.* Unpublished AEP Script. School of Business Leadership, UNISA.

Lewicki et al. are of the opinion that there are methods by which a negotiator can establish him or herself as an **expert** in the eyes of the other party:

❑ By making credentials like university degrees or licences known. Some physicians hang degrees and certificates on their walls.
❑ By citing facts and figures.
❑ By 'name dropping'.
❑ By citing examples of detailed experiences gained in well-known institutions overseas.
❑ By being known through the press or through other people, or through writing articles in well-known journals (by being visible).

Presentation of information

Within the context of negotiation, information power is at the heart of expert power. Even in the simplest negotiation, the way that information is presented could make a large impact on the outcome. In the light of this it can be seen that visual aids like charts, graphs and good statistics have a great impact on the negotiation. Market research on other prices in the area, on consumers' opinions and on financial position and the interest of suppliers is important information to gather when preparing oneself. Care should be taken that information is trustworthy, since if it is proved to be untrue this could damage the trust built through negotiation in a very serious way.

Information power is often used in a distributive way so that information is manipulated to control the options open to the other party. For example, the others' choice of behaviour is influenced by sending him positive information about the option we want him to choose, or by concealing information about an option we don't want him to choose. In some cases **experts** are brought into negotiations since people are less likely to argue with a perceived expert in the area of his expertise. To really take on the challenge, the non-expert would probably have to consult with another expert, which is costly, time consuming and somewhat risky. The lack of confidence of the non-expert is often quite visible in his body language, posture and manner of speaking.

Countering good information

Countering information power can be a real problem. When information or an expert is brought in to counter the other side's information, it can lead to an escalation in conflict with either a negative result of no resolution of the conflict and hence no agreement; or a positive result which leads to a search for other alternatives which could be beneficial to the negotiation process. So the best approach would be to:

❑ Explore all the information at hand.
❑ See an expert for what he is. All experts have abilities in a certain field, but seldom over the whole field covered by the negotiation.
❑ Either specify or generalise depending on the posturing of the opposition. For example, if the opponent comes with very specific information, an effective counter would be to return with very general information. For example:

> When selling a training package to a big organisation that has specific details on the prices of similar packages in the rest of the market, it could be a useful counter to give them general information on the perception of managers regarding the value of the training package. On the other hand, if the opposition provides general information like the perception of managers that this kind of training is not very valuable, an effective counter would be the use of very specific information such as how the profits of the different companies who used the package have changed after they have done the course.

There are other ways to counter different forms of power which can also be used in the countering of information power, especially in integrative negotiation. These will be discussed towards the end of this chapter.

Referent power

It is common to identify with and be influenced by a person because of his personality or behavioural style. The charisma of that person forms the basis of referent power. A person with charisma is admired because of his or her personality. The strength of a person's charisma is an indication of his or her **referent power**. **Charisma** is a term used to describe the magnetic personalities of some politicians, entertainers and sports figures. Some managers are also regarded by their subordinates as extremely charismatic. Referent power is sometimes referred to as personal power. Referent (or personal) power is based on the target's attraction to the power holder — liking, perceived similarity, admiration, desire to be close to or friendly with the power holder. This attraction may be based on physical attractiveness, dress, mannerisms, lifestyle or position, but can also include friendliness, congeniality, honesty, integrity and so on.

Truly charismatic people — those who have a unique blend of physical characteristics, speech, mannerisms and self-confidence — are able to influence very large groups of people by their actions. Referent power is based on the need of an individual to identify with people of influence or attractiveness. The more the target admires or identifies with an individual, the more referent influence the power holder has and the more control he can exert because of this identification. This form of power is often regarded as one of the strongest in negotiation.

Lewicki et al. (1985:253) are of the opinion that referent power is at the basis of a relationship between two parties. Since there is a strong psychological relationship between the perceived similarity, liking and attraction of the other person, a power holder may work to establish referent power by building a relationship. That is one of the reasons why relationships between a supplier and a consumer are built upon the relationship of the individuals within the participating organisations. Those individuals do not have to be the most senior people in the organisation, but could be people who have an abundance of personal power, which creates very strong relationships. Such relationships are based on expectations of trust, openness, honesty and co-operation. The target is often attracted to the power holder because of the referent power, and trusts that the power holder will not abuse his power and endanger the relationship.

In international negotiations governments recognise the importance of sending professional negotiators or individuals with special qualities of referent power to negotiate on their behalf. If personal power is abused by any side it can lead to tremendous distrust between the parties involved. Personal power is seldom associated with destructive tactics of any form, because individuals with an abundance of personal power will often try to find those agreements that could benefit both sides so as not to leave any victims in their wake and thus lose their source of attractiveness.

The personal integrity of an individual in the opponent's team could be a very strong form of common ground in negotiations. Many negotiators fall back on the integrity of the parties and the relationships built up between individuals as the strongest bond that exists between negotiating parties. The very existence of this bond will encourage them to find solutions for any conflict that may occur.

Other forms of power
Indirect power
The previous discussion focused on the direct way of using power in negotiation. All forms of power can, however, also be used indirectly. In the use of indirect power, the power holder can use a third party to channel the power through to the target.

So, in the case of **reward power**, instead of complimenting the opponent on his integrity at the table, it could be an even greater reward if that statement were made in the press. For example:

> Mr De Klerk has often said, in the press, that Mr Mandela is a man of integrity. This is an even greater compliment than saying it to him directly, especially if it is well reported in the press. In the same way one party could state of the opponents that they are very tough negotiators, which could be construed as a compliment and could enhance their position within their own constituencies.

In much the same way **coercive power** could be used in an even stronger way by making announcements visible to the outside world. For example:

> Statements can be made in the press regarding the inflexibility of the other side (a union or another political party, for instance), which could result in pressure on the difficult party by the community. A third party, who could be a very credible source, could inform the other side that the opponent will definitely go to court if some concession is not made during the negotiation.

Information power could also be used or misused in an indirect way. For example:

> Recently a case was reported in the South African press about a property sales organisation that used 'illegal' ways to bring down the prices of property in certain areas on the Rand. They used third parties or intermediaries to approach the seller of the property and make ridiculously low offers continuously. After receiving five or six offers of about 50 % lower than his asking price, the property organisation would approach the seller with a price slightly higher than the price offered by the five intermediaries. By that time the seller was convinced that his original price was much too high and that he had better accept the highest offer which, in virtually all the cases, caused the seller to sell the property.

This is an extremely negative or even unethical way of using information power in the property market.

Information could also be used positively by reporting it in the press, on TV or in journals where it will be seen by opponents. Information could also be passed on to experts by a third party in the form of an inspection of the facilities the opponent is considering accruing.

Legitimate power is used indirectly when the one side in the talks calls individuals to the meeting with an abundance of position or legitimate power (or authority) on their side of the negotiation to independently persuade the other side that they should seriously consider the offer of their opponents. They could be senior members of the company who thus have authority over individuals on the other side. The representative could be an important business associate, a person in government, a legal expert or even a judge.

Finally, **referent power** is used indirectly when the power holder uses a third party who is well liked, respected or trusted by the target in a negotiation. This is well known in the field of advertising. Celebrities are brought in to endorse products like Edblo mattresses (Bruce Fordyce) and insurance (Gary Player). Regardless of whether the individual is an expert on the product he is advertising or not, it is felt that his popularity (or personal power) will encourage consumers to associate themselves with him and thus with the products he is advocating.

Associative power or coalition power

This form of power is used indirectly when, for example, a book is being advertised through third parties who are well known or respected and who feature on the back cover of the book. For example:

> Henry Kissinger states, of a recently published book, that 'it should be made compulsory for every soldier in the world to know this book from cover to cover. If this were done, mankind would no longer feel the need to wage wars'.

The power of weakness

Friedman et al. (1974) discussed at some length the important forms of influence called **guilt and sympathy**. Many studies suggest that one way to manipulate people is to make them feel guilty. Advertisers are only too aware of this principle. For example:

> The telephone company tries to get you to spend money on long distance calls by asking you when last you telephoned your mother. Beggars exploit the sympathy of people in the streets.

One of the most interesting examples of the use of generalised guilt to manipulate people is an analysis of the brainwashing techniques used by the Chinese during the Korean war. These are cited by Friedman et al.:

> Western soldiers in prison camps were encouraged to confess all their misdeeds. At first the soldiers only confessed small things, but with encouragement they began to confess greater transgressions. After a while they began to confess very personal thoughts about themselves, their fellow soldiers, their captors, and their country. Because of these confessions, the soldiers developed tremendous feelings of guilt. Once the soldier had been made to feel guilty, the captors were more able to gain their prisoners' compliance to their requests than before.

In the same way virtually all individuals will have guilt feelings after using too much force, especially coercive power, on someone else. For example:

> A father who has given his child a hiding will often feel very guilty soon after the occurrence. As a result of this he will become highly susceptible if the child were, shortly after the incident, to ask a favour of him.

The power of 'weakness' can also be applied to the handling of strenuous relationships. Most people will have **guilt feelings** if they have lost their tempers with other people in their offices or during a negotiation. They will often avoid those they have clashed with. However, it could be better to confront the individual who caused feelings of guilt, remembering that he will possibly be more susceptible to manipulation in this case.

During negotiation it is very difficult if one team is entering the talks with an inferior status position (or weakness). For example, if one team says: 'You are Eskom. You are a very big and powerful organisation. We are very small. We are totally dependent on you.' If it does that, there will be nothing left of them and they will all lose their livelihood.

This could be a very complicated situation, especially for the negotiators on the Eskom side.

Countering power

The question of countering the above forms of power often arises. If a combination of the different forms of power is being used to a point where it becomes destructive to the negotiation, how could it be countered by the other side? There are a number of rules whereby **parity** can be established, thus enhancing the feeling of common ground in negotiation as a possible first step.

One of the most effective ways to counter the excessive use of power is therefore to **collapse** your own power base. For example:

❏ If one team attempts to counter power with the same amount of power as the other team, this can lead to an escalation of power. In this situation, if one team assumes an **inferior** position in the negotiation relationship (thus collapsing their power base), the other side is unable to escalate their power further. For example:

> If several warriors charge towards a closed door with a battering ram, and someone opens the door at that moment, this would cause 'parity of power' because they would fall flat on their faces.

❏ Another method of collapsing power is to **apologise**. The words 'we are sorry' are some of the most powerful words that can be used in negotiation situations. This could render it impossible for the other side to escalate power any further.

❏ Another method could be to say 'please just walk over us, you can do it — so please just go ahead and do it!', thereby **challenging** them to the extreme to execute their hidden threat.

❏ **Hunger striking** of political prisoners has become common in South Africa. A **'hunger strike'** or **personal suffering** is yet another way to collapse power. It is a very powerful way to induce the government to release the prisoners, especially if this form of power is accompanied by extensive press coverage. Mahatma Ghandi realised this and became one of the most powerful people in India through his policy of non-violence and martyrdom. He used to gather people, sit down in a street and block it, even while military tanks rolled towards them. The events on the Tien-an-men Square in China, when thousands of people sat down (with no violence), thus assuming a position of weakness, are still clearly remembered. Their only strength lay in their large numbers.

❏ Another means to counter excessive use of power is the **declare response**. This method has been referred to previously, where the actual feelings aroused by excessive use of power by the other side are made visible and are announced. In this way the use of power will become a point of discussion in the negotiation, thus preventing the further escalation of power. One side could say:

> 'Your bringing in experts has made us feel inferior. This could cause us to be influenced emotionally by their extensive knowledge and authority and to make premature decisions. We believe that this is an unfair advantage. Could we please have the opportunity to consult sources of similar expertise and then continue with this discussion?'

❏ Another form of countering power could be **silence**. Absolute silence, with no response at all, could be very powerful. Some teams prefer to ask for a caucus or play for time, which are other forms of the use of silence.

When teams have ample time on their hands it is sometimes easier to regroup and to work out countering strategies than to use the above techniques.

The laws of power deployment

We have selected and drawn a number of conclusions and implications from the above. The present authors realise that many of the postulates have not yet been tested empirically and yet are bold enough to postulate these as 'laws of power deployment'. Some of them are postulates that have a certain degree of validity at this stage, in the light of worldwide negotiation tendencies, although they have not yet been substantiated by research.

❏ Power is relative and **dynamic** and **ever changing**; it is a source of interpersonal energy (MacMillan 1974).

❏ Power is a **basic human need** and a basic requirement for the successful adaptation to life (Künkel, under the influence of Freud and quoted by Palland and Jonges 1966).

❏ The law of countervailing power: Power deployment seems to be matched, over time, by a **counter-deployment** of power by another actor.

❏ The law of **parity** in power: Parity in power development assures non-escalation of conflict — the balance of power also allows interpersonal control.

❏ Whenever power is based upon **common ground** and not on issues of difference, the authority of the actor is enhanced faster and further.

❏ If an actor relies on **one form of power** for too long, all other sources of power will diminish.

❏ Any attempt to utilise power outside the range of power will tend to reduce the power. So, when all sources of power have been deployed without success, a person **loses his self-control** and is at the mercy of his environment. Following on this, the excessive deployment of power always leads to **social rejection**.

❏ 'If you can lick everybody in the world you will never have peace again' (Muhammed Ali).

❏ To **collapse** one's power when the other actor has been deploying all his power, leads him to want to escalate when it is impossible. He will then **succumb to fear**.

❏ Power of authority should be linked to **responsibility** and **accountability**. If not, it has extremely negative consequences.

❏ To expand power — **share it**.

❏ Recognition of **security**, the social **role** of an actor and the **power** of the individual will lead to a decrease of power deployment.

❏ The deployment of power for the purpose of accumulating power for the sake of power has negative consequences.

❏ Only the strong can afford to be weak; the weak can seldom afford to be weak. In fact, the strong, by being weak, become even stronger.

❏ **Victims become aggressors**; the worse the victimisation, the worse the aggression.

❏ Power should be deployed in all group decision making. Whoever does not deploy his or her power becomes a **risk** in decision making.

❏ The deployment of power leads to **creative conflict**, which in time creates alternatives for decision making.

❏ Of all the types of power — referent power, expert, legitimate, reward and coercive power, indirect and coalition power — the form of power that is the strongest and the broadest seems to be **referent power** (French & Raven 1959).

❏ If the power of an actor is not recognised, the actor is forced to increase the amount of power deployed.

❏ If your opponent is stronger than you, **don't fight him**. If equally matched, you can offer battle (Sun Tzu 1988).

Case 4.4

COMMON OBJECTIVES

The man with power

. . . I am still pondering on John's obvious 'charisma' when he automatically continues . . . 'Guys, why are we here . . . The way I see it is we are to come up with a clear-cut strategy on **how** to introduce Calps into the South African market, not so?' Everyone seems to agree. I feel the tension creeping up to my throat. What is going wrong? (Or **who** is wrong, maybe I am wrong?) I hesitate. Everyone seems to agree with him. Why am I the one that has to be unpopular again? I start to talk, but find myself stuttering . . .

'John, guys, this is not the way I understand it. We are not supposed to be talking about the "hows" — only the "ifs" at this stage. In other words, should we go for Calps or shouldn't we?'

Just one glance in the direction of John and the others makes me realise that, again, I'm in the old 'not-you-again-stupid' corner.

'Look here, Kevin,' John begins with sympathy in his voice, 'I spoke to David (our managing director) last night. No question we're on the right track!'

I wonder why he has to refer to the MD. I decide to pursue this just one risky step further.

'I am sorry fellows but, really, the feeling that I have now is that you are all unanimous and I am the spanner in the works . . . While at the same time you make me feel that if I question you I am questioning the MD. I don't think it's fair.'

'No, please, Kevin, it is your right. Please continue . . .'

'OK guys,' I stumble on, 'Can we please just look at last week's minutes of the management committee's meeting so as to understand exactly what we're supposed to do today.'

There is an uneasy silence. I look up into John's face. The look he gives me is either one of 'fear' or hate. He knows that he is wrong. He also knows that he is trying to manipulate us all.

He hesitates and his sudden small hand movements are enough to tell us all that his is different from ours. We have arrived at parity.

'OK guys,' John says, 'I suppose it will not do any harm to first do what Kevin proposes . . . .'

CONCLUSION

The common ground phase of negotiation can possibly be called the most crucial phase of the talks.

❑ 'Why are we here?'
❑ 'What do we agree on?'
❑ 'What is still keeping us apart?'
❑ 'When shall we deal with it?'

These are possibly some of the most important questions to be asked at the beginning of the talks. The perception of power can cause many 'imbalances' and individuals or teams can be led to 'expect' the other side to act in preconceived ways.

No negotiator can bypass this important phase of the process, although this will be the toughest part. Negotiating the correct framing of the problem (the reason for him being there) and the perception that 'they are equals' (parity) could lay the foundation for reaching agreement that will impart value to all parties concerned.

Pienaar remarks (1995:7) that under conditions of uncertainty people experience fear or anxiety. This seems to compel most to seek clarity by 'staring into shadows or the darkened corners of their environment more intently' whereas 'under conditions of security and certainty people focus upon more real issues, readily visible variables'. He warns that under conditions of uncertainty people could miss the obvious by wasting time and energy on searching for evidence to support their own fantasy, often in vain. But, he also warns, people with a misguided sense of security are blind to what is being presented to them. He stresses the need to 'always look for what is missing' and to remember that common ground is founded on trust. Fear should never be allowed to dispel trust. Risk taking is part of openness to amazement, discovery and gain. Common ground is the conjoint effort of parties to pursue gain, to minimise loss and commit themselves to continued reciprocity.

CHAPTER 5

Persuasive Communication

In this Chapter

❏ *Information* and information sequencing for presenting and negotiating issues

❏ *Attitudes and Opinion sway* through the use of Bales's and other techniques

❏ *The role of needs* and personality in negotiation

❏ *Strategies* aimed at compliance

❏ *Concepts* such as:

- Labelling
- The 'good man–bad man' principle
- Cognitive dissonance
- The gain–loss phenomenon

INTRODUCTION

In the previous chapters attention was given to the establishment of climate and ways and means by which to influence the important climatic phase in negotiation. Following on climate, the importance of common ground was stressed, as was the necessity to negotiate for common ground by means of questioning, framing and power.

Assuming a conducive climate in terms of the objectives of the talks has been created, and assuming the existence of an awareness of common ground in terms of goals and relationships, negotiators still have to reach amicable agreements before they can conclude their interactions. Issues will now be laid on the table; offers and suggestions will be made; the opposition will be convinced by means of information, opinions and suggestions to accept the proposals and the negotiators will need to be able to manage whatever deadlocks, conflicts or emotional outbursts occur as a result of bargaining.

Good negotiators should also be able to facilitate movement towards decisions in such a way that everyone around the table will accept ownership of those decisions and agreements. What is the impact, then, of the way that information is presented on the negotiating process?

OPENING PROPOSALS

When negotiations begin, the negotiator is faced with an important problem: What should the opening offer be? Will the offer be seen to be too high by the other party and contemptuously rejected? Should the opening offer be somewhat closer to the resistance point, and thus suggest a more co-operative stance? Could a modest offer have been lower, either to leave more room for manoeuvring or to achieve a lower eventual settlement?

The fundamental problem is whether the opening offer should tend towards the upper extreme or more towards the low end. Lewicki et al. (1985:90) indicate that negotiators who make extreme original offers (sometimes referred to as 'banana offers'), believe that they achieve a more satisfactory settlement than those who make modest opening offers. There are at least two reasons for the advantage that accrues from an extreme opening position:

❑ It gives more **room for movement** in negotiation and therefore allows more time during which one can learn about the other's priorities and therefore influence the other.

❑ It can create, in the other party's mind, the impression that there is a long way to go before a reasonable settlement is achieved, and that more **concessions** than originally intended may have to be made to bridge the difference between the two opening positions. In distributive negotiation this seems to be a common practice.

The disadvantages of extreme initial offers are:

❑ They may be **summarily rejected** by the other side and cause opponents to lose interest in the possibility of an agreement.

❑ They communicate an attitude of **'toughness'** that may be destructive to the long-term relationship.

There are a number of approaches that seem to be effective in persuading individuals to accept a more extreme request than they (would) normally have accepted. These techniques are sometimes named **'violation of expectation techniques'**. By making use of the **contrast** in what is expected and what is offered, bigger than normal concessions are often gained. Friedman et al. (1981:341) cite three techniques that could all be classified as techniques where perceptual contrast is used in gaining advantage.

The foot-in-the-door technique

This technique is employed explicitly or implicitly by many propaganda and advertising campaigns. Negotiators also use it to encourage the other side to agree to something they usually hesitate about. *In this technique members of the opposition are encouraged to agree to a small, insignificant request and once this agreement is reached, they are asked to agree to larger and more important requests.*

A study by Friedman and Fraser (1966) demonstrated this effect:

> Experimenters went from door to door telling housewives that they were working for the Committee for Safe Driving. They said that they wished to enlist the women's support for the campaign and asked them to sign a petition which was to be sent to that state's senators.
>
> The petition requested the senators to work for legislation to encourage safe driving. Almost all the women contacted agreed to sign. Several weeks later, different experimenters contacted the same women and others who had not been approached before. At this time, all the women were asked to put a large, unattractive sign which said: 'Drive Carefully' in their front yards.
>
> The results were striking. Over 55 % of the women who had previously agreed to sign the petition (a small request) agreed to post the sign, whereas less than 17 % of the other women agreed. Getting the women to agree to the initial request more than tripled the amount of compliance to the later request.

This effect was replicated by many other studies cited by Friedman et al. (1981:342).

There is an old saying 'give them an inch and they will take a mile'. It refers to the fact that individuals seeking compliance from others often begin with a small and trivial request. Then, once this has been granted, they escalate to larger and more important ones. An example of this is:

> The salesperson asks the potential customer to receive a sample or brochure describing his company's products.
>
> Only later, after his request has been granted, does he try to close an order. This technique is also referred to as the 'office romance syndrome', where individuals within the company ask potential partners out for coffee. Their requests then increase slowly until there is a more serious and permanent 'relationship'.
>
> In South Africa, the public has become used to the practice, particularly amongst politicians, of using the foot-in-the-door technique to get laws passed or scrapped. In the eighties the P W Botha government started to dismantle the apartheid laws that were instituted in the early sixties. In the dismantling process they started with very small concessions, increasing them slowly, with the result that the public, after a while, became so used to these concessions that larger concessions seemed to be trivial.

If the 'Group Areas Act' had been scrapped at the beginning of the process, it would have caused a major upheaval, but later seemed like a small concession.

When an initial small request is agreed to, people seem to undergo a shift in their self-perception. They now see themselves as more helpful and co-operative than before. Since this shift is often flattering, they then experience internally generated pressure to agree to later and larger requests: only by doing this can they maintain their improved self-image.

Negotiators could make use of the foot-in-the-door technique by starting the talks with the words: 'Let's agree in principle', which is a very small request, so that later on, the size of the requests can be increased. Another tactic could be to say: 'Let's just test the market for our product; there will be no charge for initially listing our products on your shelves; once we've determined consumer reaction, we can start talking about cementing a more permanent relationship, payment and other details.'

Door-in-the-face technique

Whereas the foot-in-the-door principle consists of first making a small request and later following it up with a larger request, *the door-in-the-face principle consists of first making a large request and then following it up with a smaller request, but the smaller request is still larger than what was anticipated by the opponent.*

Cialdini et al. (1975) demonstrated how the making of a large request first, and then a small request, can have an important effect on compliance. It can even have a stronger effect than the foot-in-the-door technique.

In Cialdini's study some subjects were asked to contribute time to a good cause. Some were asked first to give a lot of time and when they refused, as almost all did, the experimenter immediately said that perhaps they might agree to a much smaller commitment of time.

Other subjects were asked to commit only the smaller amount of time, and a third group were given a choice of the two. Although 16,7 % in the small-request-only condition and 25 % in the choice condition agreed, 50 % who heard the large request first agreed to the smaller one.

The door-in-the-face method will be familiar to anyone who is engaged in a bargaining situation with a used car salesman or a labour union. The tactic is to ask for the moon and settle for less. The more that is asked for at first, the more can be expected in the end. The reduction of the demands appears to the other person to be a 'compromise', and the amount of the compromise seems small in relation to the first request. In a compliance situation such as asking for charity, the same might apply — 25c does not seem much money when the organisation initially asked for R100.

This technique is sometimes referred to in companies as 'a banana offer'. When confronted with ridiculous first offers, negotiators should realise the effect that it could have on the reaction to subsequent offers. The banana offer refers to the fact that only 'monkeys' would accept these offers. Compared to the first request the second one seems mediocre, although, in fact, the second request is also a very big one.

Techniques such as these are common in everyday life and in politics as well.

> Your wife could come home from a shopping trip and comment about the ridiculous prices of R400–R450 charged for ladies' shoes. When you express shock at the possibility of having to pay that much, since it would come out of your cheque account, she replies that she was very fortunate since she was able to procure shoes for R200, which seems to be much less than the initial prices she mentioned, but is, in fact, still a lot of money for a pair of shoes!

> In politics, an announcement could be made by the Minister of Finance that the prices of certain items must be raised by substantial amounts. As a consequence, the expectations of the public are raised to that effect. When the eventual announcement is made, the price increase is much lower than the public anticipated, and they feel a sense of **relief**, although the price increase may still be substantial.

The 'low-balling' technique

This technique also seems to increase compliance, but for different reasons. Cialdini et al. and Cacioppo, Bassett and Miller (1978) demonstrated this procedure and the effectiveness of this in various studies on compliance. *The technique of 'low-balling' is to*

gain compliance to a small request (or any request for that matter)
and then immediately increase the size of the request slightly.

Many of us have experienced the feeling of buying a new car for
R113 000 and then having to pay for extras such as another R3 450
for air conditioning, R2 959 for a radio, R2 890 for a sun roof, in
addition to the original price. Similarly, 17 % does not appear to differ
much from 18 % on a hire purchase contract, but when paid off over
48 months, it could add up to quite a substantial amount.

A supplier may encourage the store owner to replace his old machinery
by stressing all the benefits and profits to be obtained by doing so. The
supplier may suggest, or even clearly state, a 'low-ball' price which is
unreasonably favourable to the store owner, to entice him or her to
evaluate the new machinery and to continue with further negotiations
towards purchase. Once the store owner is convinced that it makes
sense to replace the old machinery because the supplier is offering a
good buy, the supplier puts the next stage of the gambit into operation.
This involves the ploy of the 'external factor' or the 'bland withdrawal' (see below). The store owner fills out a purchase order for new
machinery, only to be told that the price has just been raised and there
is nothing that the supplier can do about this increase as it came from
top management.

The ploy of *'bland withdrawal' or 'the external factor'* involves
a tactic that makes use of a fictitious or actual change away from
a previously stated position of commitment. It may really be due
to circumstances that are beyond the control of the negotiator and
may be used in place of the 'external factor' in a situation which
changes the previous position, commitment or concession.

In this case, the supplier initially implies or indicates a 'low-
ball' price proposal in a vague or ambiguous manner. After the
store owner accepts the machinery at the price mentioned, the
supplier informs the store owner that there must have been some
misunderstanding. The supplier explains that such a low price
could not have been mentioned and simultaneously whips out the
price sheet showing the higher price of the machinery. This adds
credibility to the fact that there really was a misunderstanding and
the supplier never offered the price the purchasing agent heard. In
South Africa there seems to exist a practice among building
contractors and computer firms to tender an extremely low price,
just to get in. Once they proceed with the contract, the contractor

starts to identify additional work and then increases its prices slowly but continuously and after a period of time, you may realise that you are totally dependent on the contractor. Being at the someone's mercy does not provide an ideal scenario for negotiating one's freedom.

The theory behind 'low-balling' is that, if the increased price for the new machinery is still reasonable, the store owner will go through with the purchase because a lot of time and money has been spent in evaluation and negotiation, and there is still a chance of a fair deal.

Sometimes in negotiations this is referred to as the **'Caesar's Declaration'**. In labour union negotiations in South Africa, well trained negotiators have tried this method, seemingly with some success. After reaching an agreement, one side would state: 'We are happy — we think we have an agreement, just add something that we can take back — put the "cherry" on the top — and we will sign the papers.' Usually the other side will respond with some small concession just to ensure good relations. That extra small percentage wage increase or few days' leave would not have been there without the 'Caesar's Declaration' or 'low-balling '.

The explanation for the effect of 'low-balling' is not clear, but it seems to involve the difficulty people have in **rejecting a request** once they have complied with it. Even though the request has actually changed somewhat, the person has agreed and has more difficulty backing out of it than if he were presented with a large request in the first place. For example:

> You might ask someone to help you carry a suitcase up the stairs, and when the other agrees, you might say: 'Oh, I didn't mean that small case, I meant this trunk. You don't mind, do you?' The other person never actually complied with the request to carry the small case. Instead, the larger request is substituted for the smaller one, and often the person agrees. In this example, if asked to carry the big trunk first, he could say that he was very busy or that he did not like moving or he could offer any number of excuses for why he could not help. Once he has agreed to carry the small suitcase, however, most of these explanations no longer work. He could still say that he had a bad back, but obviously he does have the time and does not hate moving (since

he has already agreed to give the time and energy to move the small
case). In a sense he is trapped. He has been tricked into doing something he might not have done if asked directly.

Many people could, quite rightly, have **ethical** objections to the
use of some of the above methods since they tend to manipulate
others into positions that they would not, under normal circumstances, have taken. It has been stated that the foot-in-the-door
technique is ethically the most 'natural' and possibly the one
technique that is the most defendable of the three. There are people
who have ethical problems with the other two techniques as well
but there are those who defend them. For example:

> The government could argue that adding 13 % sales tax to all pur-
> chases is quite an 'ethical' procedure since it is used by everyone else
> in the world, although it may consist of a 'low-balling' procedure
> whereby individuals are not hurt that much by the sales tax, provided
> that it is within certain limits.

As far as door-in-the-face is concerned, the same argument may
be used.

> Government agents could argue that it is their duty to make unpopular
> laws more **palatable** to individuals. Laws such as those against
> drunken driving and the use of alcohol while driving are justified
> through television advertisements with horrendous pictures of acci-
> dents, shown to demonstrate the effect of drunken driving so as to gain
> the compliance of the public for the fairly 'reasonable' legislation on
> drinking and driving.

In discussing the above techniques it becomes obvious that there
are many **ethical** questions regarding the use of contrasting offers,
such as the above. It is not the purpose of this book to provide
ethical rules or regulations about the use of some of these techniques, but it would seem reasonable to accept that the continu-
ation of positive relationships, even after the agreement has been
signed, could be a very important criterion in determining the types
of procedures to be used in the negotiation.

Case 5.1

FOOT-IN-THE-DOOR

South Africa regains sugar quota

South Africa has regained its quota to export sugar to the United States, Mr David Hardy, export manager of the South African Sugar Association, confirmed yesterday. It will come into effect on September 1.

But the measure is largely symbolic — it would probably be equivalent to **one shipload** of sugar and in financial terms an extra R12 000.

Mr Hardy said that the quota was determined each year and published in mid-September. South Africa would have 2,3 % of the total which for last year would be 48 000 tons.

But Mr Hardy thinks that the quota figure for the coming year is likely to be drawn on the present overall 2 100 000 tons as a result of world over-production.

It will mean that South Africa can diversify its markets further. It has not sold any sugar to the US since sanctions came into effect in September 1986, but has no problem in disposing of all its export sugar in spite of the loss of several markets following the imposition of sanctions.

The Natal Mercury, 31 July 1991.

PRESENTATION OF INFORMATION ON ISSUES

There are three key elements in the process of persuasion:

❑ **the sender** — the person or persons who is/are attempting to persuade the target;

❑ **the target** — the person or persons to be persuaded; and

❑ **the message** — the content that the sender wants the target to believe, accept or understand.

Dimensions of each of these elements may be used separately, or in combination, to bring about a successful persuasion outcome. Obviously, facts and ideas are important to the process of changing another's opinions and perceptions on issues that are on the agenda. Yet there are many ways in which facts can be selected, organised and presented. Let's first consider how messages can be organised so that a target can be moved from his original position

regarding the issues under discussion, to a new position, which is
the position preferred by the sender.

Presenting information

There are many approaches that can be used to change the target's
opinion. Some of these will receive attention later in this chapter.
One approach recently hypothesised by Pienaar (1984) for the
changing of an opinion, is the 'Bales Method' of information
presentation that seems to be extremely effective.

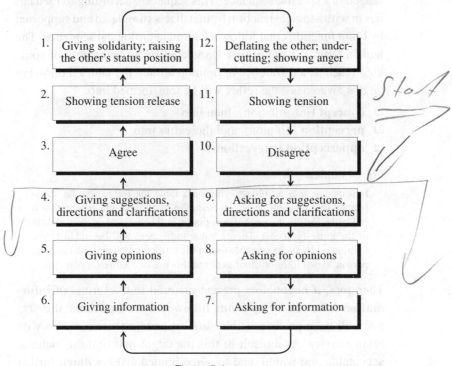

Figure 5.1
BALES'S INTERACTION PROCESS ANALYSIS

Changing opinion: the Bales method

Pienaar (1984) based his method of opinion sway on the interac-
tional matrix that was used for small group analysis and developed
by R F Bales (1950). Bales claimed that while individuals interact

in small groups they are able to respond in twelve possible ways. He numbered these twelve reactions and used them as a checklist to analyse the behaviour of individuals in small groups. His checklist is still used today and is referred to as the Bales Interaction Process Analysis. The interaction analysis is depicted in figure 5.1 in a simplified form.

Pienaar believes that opinion change will be facilitated when a negotiator arranges some of the Bales reactions in a certain manner. In this way **information, opinions and suggestions** will be arranged in a specific sequence. This sequence, according to Pienaar, ties in with a logical reaction format that is stimulated and supported by brain functions that follow a natural neurological sequence. The human brain is usually first stimulated by an awareness of some kind (such as a difference of opinion around the table). Following on this awareness, the reflex will be transformed into:

❏ **concept** (information), then into
❏ **perception** (opinion), and thereafter into
❏ **apperception** (suggestions).

For example:

> If someone sees an object lying on a table the reflex will be transformed into concept, at which point the individual will realise that it is a knife. Following on that, an opinion will be formed on the function of the knife (percept). Then a value judgement will be added to the opinion, such as the possible use of the knife for killing a man and the person's own likes or dislikes about this use of a knife (appercept).

Therefore, if negotiators present material in the format of **information** followed by **opinions** followed by **suggestions**, this format will have an 'irresistible' logical pattern that coincides with brain activity. As a result of this the target will find the material acceptable and would tend to agree immediately, without further consideration. At a later stage he could realise that he did not think the proposal through properly and could reverse his decision. (This could be the danger in the use of the Bales method of opinion sway as hypothesised by Pienaar.)

In practice, Pienaar believes that the need for opinion sway could be stimulated initially by a difference of opinion at any point during negotiation. If the target requires a price of R100 for an item, and it is unacceptable to the sender, the latter could follow a step-by-step procedure that could result finally in the target agreeing with the sender and thus changing his original position on the price. The stimulus for employing the Bales method would be a so-called 10 reaction on the Bales Interaction Matrix. The method should be used in the following manner, according to Pienaar:

❑ **Step 1** (9 on the Bales matrix):
   'Would you clarify that please?'
   The sender should wait for a response from the target.
❑ **Step 2** (8 on the Bales matrix):
   'Therefore in your opinion . . .' (Here the sender would frame the opinion of the target.)
   The negotiator should wait for a response.
❑ **Step 3** (7 on the Bales matrix):
   'On what information do you base your statements?'
   The sender should wait for a response.
❑ **Step 4** (6, 5, 4 and 3 on the Bales matrix in sequence).
   From here onwards the sender should provide **information**, **opinion** and **suggestion** in a continuous manner without allowing any response. The whole sequence should be completed as quickly as possible. You will give **information**, and then add:
   *'And therefore in my **opinion** . . .'*
   and then add:
   *'And therefore I would like to **suggest** . . .'*
   ending with:
   'Don't you agree . . . ?'

According to Pienaar this method can be extremely influential if used with confidence. However, Pienaar stresses that care should be taken that relationships are not destroyed in the process since this method could be perceived as highly manipulative by the other side. For example:

John: 'We would like R100 per batch for the coming year.' (10)

Bill: 'Would you clarify that please?' (9)

John: 'Well, according to us, with an inflation rate of 15 %, R100 is a fair price, since last year we charged R90 for it and this increase actually constitutes less than the 15 % inflation rate.'

Bill: 'So, in your opinion, if the increase is below the inflation rate, it is a fair price?' (8)

John: 'Yes, we think it is fair because a lot of other costs, such as labour expenses, have gone up in the meantime, and compared to other competitors in the market, this is still very reasonable.'

Bill: 'Do you have any other information that will justify this price of R100?' (7)

John: 'Yes, we think that it is a very fair price, since Company B will charge you anything from R110 upwards, and is not able to give you the service that we do.'

Bill: 'Well, according to our information at this stage, because of the favourable exchange rate of the rand, we can import this product from both Japan and Germany for less than R90 per unit, delivered at our premises, with an international guarantee attached to it. In the light of the high inflation rate and high production costs, in our opinion this is the time to fight high prices. Our customers are not inclined to pay any more than R90 for this product. I would like to suggest that you really reconsider the price that you are offering, since to us it seems to be a little bit high, don't you agree?' (6, 5, 4 and 3)

John: 'Yes, but . . .'

Changing behaviour: the Bales method

According to Pienaar (1984) the above response of Bales could also be used to secure behavioural commitment in a negotiating situation. When the questions and answers are rearranged with this objective in mind, the technique becomes less manipulative and more conducive towards integrative negotiation. When the matrix is employed for behaviour change or commitment, the target is involved in each phase of the Bales process.

❏ The sender would start by asking for **information** from the target, responding with his own information and then immediately attempting to move the discussion into the opinion level by asking a question or opinion of the target.

❏ He would then wait for a response and then respond with his **own opinion** but, after giving his opinion (regardless of what it is), he would then immediately try to move the discussion on

to the suggestion level by asking the target for his suggestions
(and wait for his response).

❑ He will then respond with his own **suggestion** (that could be
an adaptation of the target's suggestion). According to Pienaar
the suggestion level of the matrix (point 4 and 9) would involve
a highly positive phase of negotiation where negotiators can
remain as long as is feasible. On this level there are seldom
highly emotive differences between the parties as can occur on
the opinion level (5 and 8) or the information level (6 and 7).

If negotiators are also **flexible** while they are exchanging suggestions, the chances of a settlement become highly probable in
virtually any negotiating situation. Agreement can often be
reached and many alternative types of agreement are possible.
These could include an agreement to meet again, or to continue the
negotiation and/or the relationship after that session has been
completed.

These two methods can be depicted graphically, as shown in
figure 5.2.

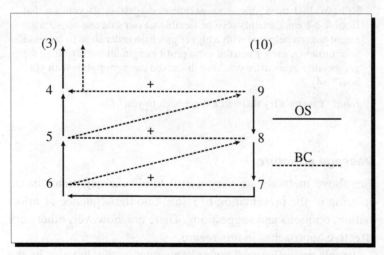

Figure 5.2
THE BALES METHOD OF OPINION SWAY (OS)
AND BEHAVIOURAL COMMITMENT (BC)

For example:

> Bill: 'On what information do you base your price of R100 per item?' (7)
>
> John: 'Well, the inflation rate is 15 %, our labour costs have gone up by 15 % in the last year and so have the prices of most of our competitors. We believe this is a fair price to charge.'
>
> Bill: 'Well, our information is that we can import this product from both Japan and Germany for R90 per item delivered to our premises. These are high quality products with an international guarantee. (6) John, in your opinion, could you match this offer?' (8)
>
> John: 'Well, as I said before, it is very difficult for us to go down on the quoted price and still be in business. We believe that this is a very fair price to charge you in the light of what I have said before. It is going to be very difficult for me to convince my management otherwise in the light of profits going down in this business.'
>
> Bill: 'Well, in our opinion, we would like to support South African products, but not at a price that is higher than what our customers are prepared to pay. (5) However, because we would like to do business with you again, how would you suggest we proceed from here?' (9)
>
> John: 'Well, I suggest that I go back to management so that we can consider your arguments in this case and see what we can do in the light of our previous long-standing relationship.'
>
> Bill: 'Well, I think that is an excellent suggestion. If you are that flexible we can certainly also be flexible on our side and see to what extent we can help you with a bigger purchase order so as to increase your turnover, giving you the same profit margin ultimately. Shall we get together again after you have discussed these proposals with your boss?' (4)
>
> John: 'Yes, let's try that and I'll get back to you.' (3)

Message structure

The above methods are very useful to aid the negotiator in the ordering of the presentation of issues into the sequence of information, opinions and suggestions. There are, however, other very effective approaches in this regard.

People are influenced not only by what is said, but also by the way the words and the sentences are **arranged**. The question therefore is: should the most important information or strongest arguments be placed at the **beginning**, the **middle** or the **end** of a presentation? Should counterarguments or opposing ideas be mentioned at all?

Lewicki et al. (1985:187) are of the opinion, in the light of research, that the structure of logic in the message, as in the Bales method discussed above, does not have as significant an impact on moving opponents in negotiation as does the structuring of material. It has also been found that people remember the beginning and the end of a message better than they do the middle. So, according to Lewicki et al., opinion change mostly occurs over a longer period of time in a negotiation rather than via a 'quick-fix method' of a few questions and answers based on a single recipe.

Some principles in the ordering of information are :

❏ In negotiation, given that there is **new material** in the presentation, on a topic **important** to the listener, it is usually best to put the most important and persuasive material towards the **end** of the message.

❏ For those messages that the sender feels the target will **like**, the important points should come **first**.

❏ When the sender is not sure about the target's interest or familiarity with the arguments, he can take the safe route and make his strong point at **both** the **beginning** and **end** of his presentation (Lewicki et al. 1985:188).

Bettinghaus (1966) concludes that one aspect of message construction seems to be very clear: important information should never be in the middle of a message. He recommends that:

❏ When the topics are familiar, interesting and/or controversial to the target, the important points should be made early, exposing the target to the **primacy effect**. This effect occurs because the first item in a long list of items to be presented is the one most likely to be remembered. Thus messages that are desirable to the target should be stated early, before presenting something the other will not want to hear.

❏ In contrast, when the topic is uninteresting, unfamiliar or not very important to the target, the most critical points should be placed at the end of the message to take the advantage of the **recency effect**. The recency effect is the tendency for the last item presented to be the best remembered, and this should be considered when the message given is likely to be contrary to a current point of view.

One- and two-sided messages

In negotiation there is a dilemma: should the message be constructed in such a way that one side or both sides of the issue are presented? Should only the positive points of the product be mentioned or should some of the problems the client may have with the product also be pointed out?

This problem is often dealt with by completely ignoring arguments and opinions that might support an opponent's position. Some politicians not only do not mention their opponent's point of view, but make a policy of not even mentioning their opponent's name.

An alternative approach to ignoring the competition is to mention and describe the opposing point of view and to show how and why it is less appropriate or desirable than the presenter's point of view.

Which of these approaches is more effective?

Bettinghaus (1966) has concluded the following about one-sided versus two-sided messages:

❏ Two-sided messages (those that mention and then criticise the competition) are more effective with better **educated** opponents.

❏ Two-sided messages are more effective when the other party **disagrees** with the position of the sender.

❏ Two-sided messages are preferable when the other party will be exposed to arguments and points of view **different** from the one advocated (that is, other people who try to persuade the target toward **their** points of view).

❏ One-sided arguments are more effective when the other party is already in **agreement** with the sender's point of view.
❏ When presenting two-sided arguments it is more effective to present **the preferred arguments** last.

So, in summary, when dealing with reasonable, intelligent opponents, it is a mistake to ignore the impact of counterarguments. The target will be formulating them as the sender speaks, and it is to the advantage of the sender to address and refute them by using two-sided messages, stating his own point of view last.

Repetitive summaries

In a previous chapter, reference was made to the Progressive Summarisation Method in negotiation and the effectiveness of frequent summaries. Pienaar (1983) is of the opinion that the second Bales method, designed for the use of ensuring commitment, could also be effectively used in a slightly modified way by frequently summarising after each position on the Bales matrix has been reached. So, after 'information', the negotiator could summarise the information presented; and then move on to 'opinions', after which the summarisation could follow again. The same could be done for suggestions.

In this way **effective chairmanship** could often be facilitated through the method of repetitive summaries.

It seems certain that **repeating** a point could be an effective way to communicate messages around a table. McGuire (1973) found that restating a point is very effective in changing opinions the first few times, but **loses** its effectiveness if repeated too often. The effect of drawing regular conclusions is also discussed at length by McGuire.

Sometimes writers or speakers lay out a line of argument, and then state their own conclusion. At other times they encourage the receivers to **draw their own conclusion**. Letting the other side draw its own conclusion (but still the conclusion **you** want drawn) can lead to a very effective presentation.

McGuire also found that the drawing of **explicit conclusions** for the audience seems to be, in general, an extremely effective technique of securing agreements. A conclusion or a summary of what preceded in the negotiation can often constitute an agreement or be an important benchmark. It can then be referred to and even guide or facilitate movement during subsequent talks.

Length and content of sentences

The **'sixteen-second rule'** in negotiation has been mentioned by Spoelstra (1991). He postulated that not even a genius can concentrate while listening to the spoken word for more than a very short period of time without a pause of some kind. He therefore believes that all utterances of negotiators should preferably be short and to the point. Negotiators should aim to stop after the point has been made and not continue with words that do not add to the content of the issue.

Some communicators are extremely good at changing their tone of voice frequently or bringing in pauses of sufficient length to continually hold the concentration of the listener.

The **choice of words** that make up sentences is important. Some words are loaded with emotion and controversy and could create a negative climate or atmosphere merely by their use. There are 'good' words to describe something and 'bad' words to describe the same concept. For example:

Regime/Government

The difference in meaning is not that great, yet, depending on which word was selected, a negative or positive feeling could be created in the minds of the opposition about the attitude of the speaker.

So it is clear that most concepts can be described with negative or positive connotations. Newspaper editors are extremely proficient at handling words and sentences that describe events or concepts to indicate the newspaper's stance on a matter.

Lewicki et al. (1985:203) refer, in the light of the above, to the effect of **paraphrasing** in negotiation. Paraphrasing confirms that both parties in the negotiation know that they have understood each other accurately. It is important to repeat in your own words what someone else has said, thus indicating that you understand him clearly. Literal repetition is not necessary, but repetition in the negotiator's own words could have an important effect of clarifying the discussion. It is best, according to Lewicki et al., not to wait until the end of a long message, because the message may be forgotten. Instead, it is best to paraphrase what has been said after each major point. For example: 'Let me see if I understand the point you have just made . . .' This kind of sentence could be repeated and corrected many times until both sides are satisfied that the point has been understood correctly. This forms a **summary** that could constitute an **agreement** in the negotiation process.

Changing attitudes on issues

While debating issues, negotiators have to deal not only with opinions, but also with deeper and more emotional attitudes. An **opinion** is defined as *a belief or conclusion held with confidence, but not substantiated by positive knowledge or proof;* or *an evaluation or judgement based on special knowledge given by an expert* (Reader's Digest 1984:1197). An **attitude** is defined by Steers (1991:76) as *a predisposition of an individual to respond in a favourable or unfavourable way to objects or persons in one environment.* It is, according to Steers, a like or a dislike with a strong cognitive (intellectual), affective (feelings) and intentional component. An element of feeling or emotion is present to a much larger degree than is present in an opinion.

Negotiators often encounter people who have strong attitudes about certain issues. They may have strong feelings and are often emotionally affected by certain statements about the issues discussed. For example:

> A reference to an individual in government could evoke strong attitudes from opponents to government. A derogatory statement about a product could offend someone who has strong positive attitudes about that product.

> Another example could be a reference to previous mistakes that were
> made, not realising that someone around the table was involved in the
> mistakes at that stage.

Steers (1991:77) postulates that individuals have feelings or attitudes about virtually everything they encounter in life. It is therefore justified to state that members of negotiating teams will have
strong attitudes about virtually every issue that is on the table.

The question is how to change those attitudes. Previously we
suggested that sometimes an opinion (which by definition is much
shallower than an attitude), could be changed by a simple process
of logic that induces a 'Yes' answer. In the case of changing
attitudes the process is more complicated and more time consuming. Let's consider some of the methods that could be used to
change attitudes, specifically during negotiations.

The cognitive dissonance approach

The cognitive dissonance theory of Leon Festinger (1957) assumes that there is a tendency toward cognitive consistency.
According to the theory, ***dissonance*** *exists between two cognitions*
which are inconsistent with each other. A cognition may be a fact,
a belief or an opinion about anything, including one's own behaviour. Any two cognitions can be **consonant** — that is, consistent
with one another, or **dissonant** — inconsistent, or irrelevant,
where the existence of one implies nothing about the other. According to Festinger, any person whose behaviour is inconsistent
with his values will experience cognitive dissonance. Someone
who is very religious could be having an extramarital affair, for
example.

Dissonance creates psychological tension, which people feel
pressurised to remove or reduce. Dissonance is much like any other
drive: if we are hungry we do something to satisfy our hunger; if
we are afraid we do something to reduce our fear; and if we feel
dissonance we do something to reduce it. The two main ways of
reducing dissonance are to:

❑ add **consonant** cognition; and

❏ change **dissonant** cognitions so that they are no longer inconsistent.

Dissonance is similar to the feeling of having doubts, or second
thoughts about something. People will have more dissonance if:

❏ the decision is psychologically or financially important; or
❏ there are few or no alternatives to the decision on the table. For
   example:

> If an ultraleftwing labour union representative negotiates with an
> ultrarightwing manager about racism and the equal treatment of staff,
> it could create dissonance in the mind of the conservative. According
> to Festinger's theory the conservative manager will, in this case, do
> something to reduce the dissonance. There are only a few choices open
> to him:
>
> • He can change his attitude about the inferiority of other races.
> • He could add new information to justify his old stance on other
>   races.
> • He could disregard the request from the labour union as a ridiculous
>   ploy to antagonise management.
> • He could remove himself from the negotiation (flight reaction).
>
> If the labour union's arguments are supported by the fact that manage-
> ment is legally incorrect, and that non-compliance with the request
> would bring about strike action or even closure of the organisation, it
> is obvious that the manager is in a very difficult situation.
>
> Festinger suggests that if the labour union negotiator continues to
> argue with the manager until he agrees to change the system to the
> extent that unequal practices will be changed, the only way for the
> manager to reduce his dissonance would be to **justify** his agreement,
> and that can only take place if he changes his attitude regarding
> segregated facilities. This is based on the assumption that the labour
> union does not put too much pressure on the manager to conform to
> its wishes.

Dissonance theory predicts that once a decision is made, or once
an action is taken, such as the purchase of a new product, attitude
change will most certainly follow.

   One behaviour that almost always arouses dissonance is **decision making**. Festinger refers to this as 'post-decisional dissonance'. After a decision has been made, all the good aspects of the

unchosen alternative and all the bad aspects of the chosen alternative are dissonant with the decision taken. For example:

> If we decide to buy a Mercedes Benz instead of a Honda, the Mercedes's speed and stylishness and the Honda's crampedness and homeliness are consonant with the decision. But the price of the Mercedes and its reputation of being expensive to repair, and the reputed inexpensiveness and ease of upkeep of the Honda, are dissonant with the decision.

Dissonance can be reduced by changing the **evaluation** of the chosen and unchosen alternatives. Increasing the attractiveness and value of the chosen alternative reduces dissonance, because everything positive about it is consonant with the decision.

Dissonance can also be reduced by **lowering** the evaluation of the unchosen alternative. The less attractive it is, the less dissonance should be aroused by choosing the other.

Therefore, after someone has made a decision, there is a tendency for him to increase his liking for what he has chosen and to decrease his liking for what he did not choose. After choosing the Mercedes over the Honda, he tends to rate the Mercedes even higher and the Honda even lower than he did previously. This is supported by many studies referred to by Friedman et al. (1981:407).

This theory implies something very important for negotiation: it predicts that once people make a decision to take a certain course of action, their attitudes will change accordingly. Therefore, attitudes do not cause behaviour; rather, behaviour is at the root of all attitude change. Many authors on management have realised that productivity causes job satisfaction and not the reverse.

If your opponents can be encouraged to say 'Yes, we'll do it', the agreement will most certainly cause attitudes to change. If they can be encouraged to act, they will have to **justify** their actions (and become more positive about their agreements).

Cognitive dissonance theory is sometimes referred to as the 'theory of justification of actions'. Often, the only justification open to individuals is to change their attitudes and to defend whatever decisions they have taken. This is why it is important to encourage opponents to indulge in some action that is contrary to their normal behaviour as a first step towards attitude change. For example, this action could be:

❑ To **encourage** the other side to agree to another meeting.
❑ To **lunch** with the other side.
❑ To spend money on something small as an **appetiser** for the main product that is to come later if an agreement is signed.
❑ To invite the opposition to agree to come to **visit your plant**.
❑ To invite the political party to agree to make a **public announcement** about something.
❑ To encourage both sides to agree to make a **statement** to the press.
❑ To encourage the other side to join you in watching **cricket or rugby** the coming Saturday.
❑ To encourage them to agree to **try out** the product.

These types of actions (getting individuals to indulge in goal directed behaviour) cause attitude changes provided not too much or too little pressure is imposed.

It is important for negotiators to take cognisance of the role of the intensity of pressure on individuals to change their attitudes. It would seem that, if **too much** pressure to change is used, the recipient will experience very little dissonance because he could justify his actions by saying 'He gave me no choice'. If, on the other hand, **too little** pressure is administered, very little dissonance will be created and in some cases old attitudes will persist and could be strengthened in the process. The best approach is to use 'just enough' pressure. For example:

> If a racially prejudiced white worker refuses to share toilet facilities with black workers, it will be of very little use just asking him to think it over, as this will be pressurising him too little. It could in fact reinforce his attitude about segregated toilet facilities. The answer would be to argue with him until he agrees to try it out for a period of time. Once he responds by sharing his facilities, he will have to justify his action to his peers and support groups to the extent that he will have to change his attitude.

Communication strategies in attitude change

In general, characteristics of the communicator that imply that he is well versed in his subject (is an expert), is being honest (has no ulterior motive), or is likeable, increase the effectiveness of the communication, according to Friedman et al. (1981:377). Since derogation of the source of communication is one of the ways of avoiding attitude change, these variables relating to the communicator are extremely important. Any dislike of the communicator, or lack of trust in his competence or credibility makes it relatively easy to reject the message by attacking him. In this way the target frees himself from the pressure of worrying about the complex details of the message itself.

Negotiators tend to concentrate on general rules that increase the effectiveness of the message rather than on the content of the message itself. This is because they are looking for general laws that can determine the effectiveness of all messages. Given a particular product or opinion to sell, a number of variables in the communication itself have important effects on the amount of attitude change that is produced.

Discrepancy

As mentioned earlier, one source of stress (dissonance) in any influence situation comes from the discrepancy between the target's initial position and the position advocated by the communication. The greater the discrepancy, the greater the stress.

> If someone who thinks that Hendrik Verwoerd was a great prime minister hears a communication arguing that he was mediocre, the individual's attitude is under pressure. If the communicator argues that Verwoerd was a terrible prime minister, there is much more pressure.

If on a scale there are two points of discrepancy, two points of attitude change are necessary to eliminate them. If there are five points of discrepancy, five points of change are necessary. An individual who changes his attitude under pressure from a discrepant message, must accordingly change it more with greater discrepancy. However, the relationship between discrepancy and amount of change is not always that simple. There is more stress with greater discrepancy, but it does not always produce more change.

For negotiators, this is an important issue. If the negotiator is aware of a huge **discrepancy** between his communication and the position of the target, how radical should the message that is communicated to the other side be?

It is known that, as discrepancy increases, the individual will find it increasingly difficult to change his attitude enough to eliminate the discrepancy. Moreover, an extremely discrepant statement tends to make individuals doubt the credibility of its source. So at high levels of discrepancy, the stress tends to be reduced more by source derogation than by attitude change, according to Friedman.

Therefore negotiators need to keep in mind that if they advocate messages that differ greatly from the present position of the other side, the chances are that the other side will doubt the credibility of the message. So, radical statements are high-risk statements, even if they are based on fact. Many studies have shown that as discrepancy increases, attitude change becomes more difficult, and rejection of the communication becomes easier.

The only moderating factor seems to be the **credibility** of the communicator himself. To some extent, the higher the credibility of the communicator, the more successfully will he be able to avoid a highly discrepant position. If someone deeply respects the teacher who makes a statement about Hendrik Verwoerd, it is harder to decide that he is incorrect. Similarly, a source with lower credibility makes rejection relatively easy.

In conclusion, the safest and most effective approach would be to advocate messages that are fairly low in discrepancy relative to the position of the other side. If someone makes a statement that Hendrik Verwoerd was not a great prime minister, but nevertheless a good one, the opponent is likely to be somewhat influenced. There will be some pressure on him to change his attitude in the direction of the communicator's and, if the communicator presented a fairly persuasive argument, the target would be moved somewhat from his previous position. In this situation, it is difficult to reject the moderately credible communicator, but relatively easy to change one's attitude the little bit required to reduce the discrepancy.

Fear arousal

Arousing fear is one of the most natural ways of trying to change attitudes. Advocates of population control warn of mass starvation; environmentalists warn of mass lung disease, skin cancer and polluted oceans, dams and streams; economists warn of rising unemployment; religious leaders frighten their followers with threats of eternal damnation and suffering; anti-smokers warn of cancer and early death. Given a particular argument in favour of a position, how does the amount of fear aroused affect the success of the argument and thus attitude change?

This relationship has interested researchers for a long time. Janis and Mann (1965) have suggested that the relationship between fear and attitude change depends on the **level of fear** involved. They argue that at low levels of fear, more attitude change is produced, but at the point where fear becomes too intense, a defence mechanism is aroused that produces less change. For example:

> If you have a fairly neutral attitude towards the effect of cholesterol on health, high fear arousal could be very effective in making you aware of the danger of high cholesterol, and changing your attitude to eating habits. If you are a lifelong smoker and a high fear arousal message is directed at you about the risk of lung cancer it could provoke too much fear and, since it is very difficult for you to prevent lung cancer after many years of smoking, the message could have less effect.

To sum up, the evidence indicates that under most circumstances **arousing fear** increases the effectiveness of persuasive communication. But arousing **too much** fear may be disruptive. Causing a person to be too frightened can make him either so paralysed that he is unable to act or so threatened that he tends to deny the danger and reject the communication. Aside from such cases it appears that fear-arousing arguments are more effective in producing attitude change than are arguments that arouse little or no fear.

Similar conclusions can be drawn about the effect of threat (a form of fear arousal) on attitude change during negotiation. Studies cited by Friedman et al. '(1981:417) suggest that severe threats should be avoided wherever possible. The smaller the threat used, the more attitude change is to be expected. For example:

> If a parent wants to teach his child to be honest, he should try to do so without using strong threats. If he succeeds by using only mild threats, the child is more likely to accept the value that honesty is good and stealing bad. If, instead, the parent uses strong threats, even if they seem to be successful in making the child behave honestly, it is less likely that the child will accept the value that honesty is inherently good. He may decide that honesty is the best policy if there is a chance of getting caught, and therefore act honestly when his parents are present. When the threat (parent) is removed, he will have experienced little internal attitude change to make him sustain honest behaviour.

Labelling

The concept of labelling has received some attention by authors on attitude change. *Labelling implies that, if people's image of themselves is reinforced by providing a name or label for them, it tends to make them behave consistently with the label provided.*

> In a study by Kraut (1973), people were asked to contribute to charity and were labelled either 'charitable' or 'uncharitable', depending on whether they had contributed. Other subjects were not actually given any label. Later, they were asked again to contribute. The labels had the effect of making them behave the way they did the first time — those who had given the first time and were labelled charitable gave more than those who were not labelled; and those who had not given and were labelled uncharitable gave less than if they had not been labelled.

The concept of labelling can also be referred to as **'as if'** behaviour. Steele (1975) provided evidence that if the label is a negative one, for example, 'as if' you are a racist, it will sometimes have an even more drastic effect on attitudes, since individuals who have been given a negative label will sometimes try to prove the opposite in the presence of someone else.

> Steele phoned people and said that it was common knowledge that they were (were not) involved in the community or said something negative that was irrelevant to the community. He then asked them to help to

form a food co-operative for the community. He found that when he labelled someone in a positive way this would increase attitude change and compliance. But, frighteningly, the negative 'name calling' (labels) produced even more compliance than the positive one. This was presumably caused by the fact that the subjects felt that the label was unfair and they wanted to show that they were, in fact, community minded.

The consequence of attitude change in a negotiation situation could be quite dramatic. The effect of labelling would imply that if the technique of 'positive lying' (as if it were the truth) were used, it could in fact change people's attitudes. For example:

If a manager says to a subordinate, 'You are well known for your excellent human relations' (as if it were true), even though the manager has had many problems with this individual because of a lack of proper human relations, this could lead him to be more sensitive to other individuals than he was before.

The label seems to affect the person's self-image. Sometimes a **label** can solidify that image and make the person behave consistently with it; at other times, the label can make the person worry about his image and try to do something to improve it. When combining this research with that of the previously discussed 'foot-in-the-door' technique, and also the theories of cognitive dissonance, it appears that cognitive elements, and especially what the person thinks of himself, play an important role in changing attitudes and gaining agreements.

The labelling principle reminds one of the so-called 'self-fulfilling prophecy', which advocates that we tend to give labels to ourselves, and, over time, become like them. Parents can cause a great deal of harm to their children if they constantly refer to them as 'lazy' or 'slow'. Over time, these children could start to believe that they are not as able as their peers and could suffer from lack of confidence and a negative self-image.

The gain–loss phenomenon

The principle of **reciprocity** is very important in all publications on negotiation. In the negotiation of issues, individuals are often very sensitive about the perception of **trade-offs** that are taking place. It is normally assumed that there should be a feeling of **parity** in this phase. The feeling should at least exist that reciprocity will take place at some stage during the negotiations.

Reciprocity possibly controls one of the rewards most central to a human being: a person's feeling of affection and goodwill towards the other side. But Arenson and Linder (1965) suggest a complication in the simplest version of the reciprocity principle. It is not always the number of rewards another person gives you; sometimes it is whether these rewards are **increasing** or **decreasing**. They argue that we like best those people who show increasing liking for us, and dislike most those who show decreasing liking for us. According to this **gain–loss** principle, we do not react as extremely to those who are more steadily positive or negative towards us.

> In Arenson and Linder's study, subjects heard a confederate making either positive or negative statements about them, and the subjects generally reciprocated the confederate's evaluations. But the experiment included one other variation — a condition in which the confederate began by making negative statements about the subject and became more and more positive in his descriptions throughout the course of the experiment. By the last few interviews he was making as many positive statements about the subjects in this condition as he did when he was positive throughout. In other words, some subjects heard a confederate who liked them at the beginning and continued to like them, whereas other subjects heard a confederate who did not like them at the beginning but ended up liking them. Although in both these conditions the subjects liked the confederate, they liked him even more when he began critically and ended positively than when he was positive throughout.

Arenson and Linder suggested that the initial negative statements caused the subjects more anxiety and self-doubt, all of which were painful feelings. When the statements gradually became more positive, they were not only rewarding in themselves but they also reduced the previous negative feelings.

For negotiators this seems to indicate that there is much more attitude change to be gained in **slowly increasing rewards** to the other side (such as smiling, agreeing, complimenting) compared to being agreeable throughout the negotiations. Moreover, being continuously negative, in the light of these findings, will also produce little attitude change from the other side.

The 'good man'–'bad man' technique

In international spy novels this technique is claimed to be used by interrogators to gain compliance or to change attitudes dramatically in the matter of a short space of time.

In this technique the team is made up of a 'good man' and a 'bad man'. The bad man will commit atrocious, aggressive and sometimes violent acts against the target. The good man will then appear after the beginning of these acts, and in the presence of the target, complain about the treatment of the target and then ask the aggressor to stop his acts of aggression. He will then ask the target for concessions so as to enable him to put a stop to the aggressive acts of his counterpart. In many instances the target will comply by giving information or acceding to the requests of the 'good man'.

This technique is sometimes used in an adapted form in negotiations where a very strict, meticulous, 'nit-picking' individual is chosen for the team of negotiators. In the same team there is also an extremely compassionate person. The latter will ask for a concession in an extremely modest and polite way. When the concessions are not given, the 'nit-picker' will start objecting to the style of negotiating that the 'good man' in his own team is using. He will object to his extremely soft stance and to the fact that he is not getting concessions with that approach. It is important to remember that the complaint is directed at his own team member and not towards the other side, thus avoiding leaving any victims on the other side of the table. The 'good man' will then turn to the opponents and request a small concession in the light of the problems that he is experiencing. In many cases the opponents will, because of the tension in this situation, try to form an almost 'joint team' with the 'good man' and try to isolate the 'bad man' in the process. At the same time huge concessions are often made to help the 'good man' to 'pacify' the 'bad man'.

Techniques such as the above are often labelled as unethical and should be used very carefully. Remember that these techniques can also surface during negotiation in very subtle forms. It is important that negotiators recognise 'good man–bad man' techniques and the possible effect that they could have on them and therefore to recognise it for what it is.

To counter techniques such as these negotiators could inter alia:

❑ Ask for a **caucus**.
❑ Ask for a **recess**.
❑ Answer them with **silence**.

Helping behaviour

There are many ways that one party can ask for and expect help from the other side during a negotiation:

❑ by doing them a **favour**;
❑ giving them **time**;
❑ giving **information**;
❑ **lending** them a hand; or
❑ responding to a **request** for help.

In his book *Sociobiology*, E O Wilson (1975) proposed that altruistic behaviour in humans is genetically determined! Altruism is defined as any act that benefits another with no expectation of return. In negotiation the concept of **prosocial behaviour** is used and defined as an act where someone will help another *but often for concrete reasons*.

Wilson gave many examples of altruism in the animal kingdom, for example:

> In termite hives, the soldier termites will defend a nest against an intruder by putting themselves in front of the other termites and thus exposing themselves to danger. Many soldiers die so that others may live and so that the nest itself survives.

> Parents will often sacrifice themselves when their young are threatened. This is most evident amongst birds — they have a variety of techniques designed to draw off or distract threats.

> In the same sense, a fireman will rush into a burning building to save people although his own life may be in danger.

Altruism and prosocial behavioural tendencies of individuals seem to make them feel especially responsible and thereby increase the amount of help they are prepared to give. If someone in negotiation, in the presence of others, requests help from the other side to solve the problem, they could obtain large concessions and even attitudinal changes because of the natural tendency of people to **help** others and to experience satisfaction from doing this.

Violation of target's expectations

Violation of expectations occurs when the listener expects one style of delivery from a speaker and then experiences a totally different style. For example:

> The expectation before the so-called 'Rubicon' speech delivered by President P W Botha in Natal in 1985 was that wide-ranging changes were to be announced in the South African government's policy, but he announced virtually no changes, thus violating everyone's expectations. Large attitudinal changes occurred as a result of this, as was evident from the reaction of the rest of the world and from the fact that the value of the rand dropped considerably soon after the speech was delivered.

When a negotiator expects to face a very aggressive opposition, but is actually confronted by a very soft-spoken and flexible person, this can cause a significant attitudinal shift.

> After Nelson Mandela's release from jail in 1990, he addressed an audience consisting mostly of businessmen expecting a radical individual, having built up a perception of him as a 'violent terrorist'. When he arrived, he was conservatively dressed and greeted his audience in a quiet, relaxed manner and then proceeded to put forward some modest proposals for social change along with some sensible ways of financing those changes. The audience was surprised, then impressed and in many cases won over.

According to Lewicki and Litterer (1985:191) this process may also work in reverse. Audiences who expect a quiet, controlled, highly rational discourse may equally be persuaded by an emotionally intense speaker because they are unprepared to defend themselves against such passionate persuasion.

CHARACTERISTICS OF THE COMMUNICATOR

Sun Tzu (1988:8) stated the following, many years before the birth of Christ: 'Know your enemy, know yourself, and you can fight a hundred battles without disaster . . . ' In negotiation this prophetic statement should be taken to heart. Negotiators should evaluate their own strengths and weaknesses and also those of their opposition. The credibility and characteristics of the source in any communication can often account for a major part of movement attained during negotiations. Let us consider a few personal characteristics that are important in a negotiator.

Successful negotiation behaviour

Carlisle (1978:7) has indicated in his study on the behaviour of negotiators that skilled negotiators show marked differences in their interactions when compared with average negotiators. They use certain types of behaviour significantly more frequently while they tend to avoid others. He found that skilled negotiators use 'irritators' five times less often than average negotiators.

'**Irritators**' are certain words and phrases which are commonly used in negotiation and have negligible value in persuading the other party but do cause irritation. According to Carlisle an example of this is the term 'generous offer' used by negotiators to describe their own proposal. Similarly words such as 'fair', 'reasonable', and other terms with a high positive value loading have no persuasive power when used as self-praise, while serving to irritate the other party because of the implication that they are unfair, unreasonable and so on.

Carlisle also found that skilled negotiators make only half as many **counterproposals** as average negotiators (a counterproposal being either a whole new issue that clouds the negotiation, or not listening, or blocking or disagreeing during the discussions).

Skilled negotiators seldom allow themselves to be drawn into **defend/attack spirals** (counterattacking or defending with the result of conflict escalation)—in fact, only one third as often as average negotiators.

Skilled negotiators also seem to use fewer reasons to back up arguments (about 50 % less reasons). Skilled negotiators tend to advance **single reasons** insistently, only moving to subsidiary reasons for their arguments if the main reason is clearly losing ground, according to the above research.

According to Carlisle, skilled negotiators tend to give an advance indication of the class of behaviour they are about to use. So, instead of just asking 'How many units are there', they will say 'Can I ask you a question — how many units are there?', giving warning that a question is coming. Instead of just making a proposal they will begin, 'If I could make a suggestion . . .' and then follow this advance label with their proposal. Average negotiators are significantly less likely to **label their behaviour** in this way — with one exception: the only behaviour that the average negotiator is more likely to label in advance is disagreement.

Carlisle's research also revealed that two behaviours with a similar function, **testing understanding** and **summarising**, are used significantly more often by the skilled negotiator. Testing understanding is a behaviour which checks to establish whether a previous contribution or statement in the negotiation has been understood. Summarising is a compact restatement of previous points in the discussion. Both behaviours sort out misunderstandings and reduce misconceptions.

Carlisle also found that, consistent with our previous discussion, that skilled negotiators seek significantly more **information** during negotiations than do average negotiators.

The skilled negotiator seems to believe in the use of **questions**. Carlisle believes that questions:

❑ help the negotiator to obtain the necessary information with which to bargain;

❑ can be used as a deliberate strategy;

❑ give control over the discussion;

❑ are more acceptable responses to direct disagreement;

❑ keep the other party active and reduce that party's thinking
    time;
❑ can give negotiators a breathing space to allow them to marshal
    their thoughts.

Skilled negotiators **appear to reveal** what is going on in their
minds. This revelation may or may not be genuine, but it gives the
other party a feeling of security because their motives appear to be
explicit and above board. For example, average negotiators, hear-
ing a point from the other party which they would like to accept
but doubt the accuracy of, are likely to receive the point in an
uncomfortable silence. Skilled negotiators are more likely to com-
ment on their own **feelings**, saying something like 'I'm uncertain
of how to react to what you have just said. If the information you
have given me is true, then I would like to accept it, yet I feel some
doubts about its accuracy. So part of me feels happy and part feels
rather suspicious. Can you help me resolve this?'

   This kind of response can also be used instead of bluntly
disagreeing. For example, if a price quoted seems high, the skilled
negotiator would say: 'I'm very worried that we seem to be so far
apart on this particular point . . .', instead of disagreeing flatly with
it.

The effect of personality

As was stated earlier, one of the most straightforward and reliable
findings in studies on attitude change, is that the higher a person's
evaluation of the communicator, the more apt he is to change his
attitude when influenced by the communicator. The more favour-
ably people evaluate the source of a discrepant communication,
the more likely they will be to change their attitudes. This is the
basis of the theory of cognitive dissonance discussed earlier. The
question arises as to whether personality factors within the communicator also are instrumental in causing major attitudinal shifts
during the negotiation of issues. The following personality factors
seem to be related to success in communications during negotiation.

Locus of control

The locus of control of individuals determines the degree to which they believe that their behaviour influences what happens to them. Some people believe that they are autonomous — that they are the masters of their own fate and bear personal responsibility for what happens to them. They see the control of their lives as coming from inside themselves. Rotter (1966) calls these people **internals**.

Rotter also holds that other people view themselves as helpless pawns of fate, controlled by outside forces over which they have little, if any, influence. In this case they see the locus of control as being external rather than internal. Rotter calls them **externals**.

Gibson et al (1991:84) cited studies in which the Rotter scale for the identification of 'locus of control' was used. A study of 900 employees in a public utility, for example, found that internally controlled employees were more content with their jobs; more likely to be in management positions; and more satisfied with a participative management style than were employees who perceived themselves to be externally controlled. In a further study amongst entrepreneurs it was indicated that internals were found to feel less stress and employ more task-centred coping behaviours and fewer emotion-centred coping behaviours compared to externals. In addition the task-orientated coping behaviours of internals were associated with better performance.

Negotiating against externals implies that they will be more inclined to be led by the decision of the other side or by the rest of their group. Internals will be more inclined to play an active role in changing and debating the issues on the table.

The Myers–Briggs types

Myers and Briggs developed a test (Gibson et al. 1991:82) to help respondents discover their 'personality' or cognitive type. The test identifies people as **extroverted** or **introverted**, **sensing** or **intuitive**, **thinking** or **feeling**, and **perceiving** or **judging**. The answers given to the test were divided and classified into 16 different personality types. Apparently this method is widely used by organisations in the Western world. The following types, taken from the list, are relevant to negotiation:

The sensation–thinking types

These people are thorough, logical, practical and application oriented. In a negotiating situation they will be sensitive to detailed information and will demand facts, sometimes in the finest detail, from the other side. They will, according to Myers and Briggs, most often be in auditing, quality control and engineering positions.

The intuitive–thinkingBriggs types

These people are creative, independent and critical. As negotiators they will question continuously, and could be overcritical of any agreements or decisions that have been made. In business life they are lawyers, systems analysts or college professors.

The sensation–feeling types

They are committed, responsible and conscientious individuals, according to Myers and Briggs. They will be union negotiators, social workers, or drug supervisors who will question the ethics and moral validity of any decision.

The intuitive–feeling types

These are charismatic, people oriented and sociable individuals. They are most often found as politicians, public relations specialists and human resource directors. They are excellent at establishing relationships in negotiation and act as socio-emotional leaders in negotiation sessions. Smoothing conflict and trying to maintain a good climate is their forte.

Creativity

In an overview of the literature on the creativity trait in individuals, Gibson et al. (1991:84) concluded that creative people have been found to have superior ego strengths and handle problems constructively. He believes that the creative person can be disconnected from the act of creativity. Research indicates that people can be intelligent but not necessarily creative. The ability to be creative is available to everyone as an expression of personality that can be developed. There is even a view that creativity can be taught. Creative people are self-confident and motivated to succeed; they approach life enthusiastically and they push on evenly when they must overcome obstacles. These characteristics are important and valuable in any negotiating situation.

Machiavellianism

This concept is derived from the writings of Niccolò Machiavelli, an Italian philosopher and statesman (1469–1527) who was concerned with the manipulation of people and with the orientations and tactics used by manipulators versus non-manipulators (Christie & Geis 1970). The term *machiavellianism* is associated with being a political manoeuvrer and power manipulator. The term has a negative connotation.

From anecdotes or descriptions of power tactics and the nature of influential people, various scales have been constructed to measure machiavellianism. In one scale, the questions are organised around a cluster of beliefs about tactics, people and morality. This particular MACH scale differentiates between high and low machiavellians on the basis of how closely people endorse Machiavelli's manipulative rules of conduct (Christie & Geis 1970). In a job situation, HIGH MACH scorers would probably be suited to activities such as selling, negotiating, and acquiring limited resources. LOW MACH scorers are better suited for structured, routine and non-emotional situations. Planning, conceptualising and working out details would probably be activities best suited to LOW MACH scorers in an organisation.

Lewicki and Litterer (1985:268–270) also discuss various experiments done on machiavellianism in negotiation situations. In comparing HIGH MACHs with LOW MACHs they commented that HIGH MACHs:

❑ Are able to **lie** with greater credibility.
❑ Seem to **confess** less.
❑ Are able to maintain more direct, convincing **eye contact** with experimenters while lying.

❏ Attempted significantly more **manipulative** actions.

❏ Told **bigger lies**.

❏ Were more **verbally distracting** in their behaviour.

❏ Were far more **innovative** in the use of manipulative techniques.

❏ Seem to enjoy being in a **high power role**.

❏ Seem to **enjoy being manipulative**.

❏ Seem to be more **proactive** in their strategy.

❏ Seem to be more **opportunistic** in their sense of timing with regard to making or breaking coalitions.

❏ Seem to enjoy **winning**.

❏ Were less concerned with the **ethical** concerns of others in a situation.

Lewicki and Litterer (1985) also discuss an experiment where the *Prisoner's Dilemma* (a game of tactics between two teams) was used to analyse the differences between HIGH MACHs and LOW MACHs. In this game HIGH MACHs did not perform significantly better than LOW MACHs, although they tended to become more exploitative over time.

In conclusion, it would seem that people with high traits of machiavellianism are better in any intermediate negotiation that is distributive in character than are low machiavellians. LOW MACHs are more suited to negotiation where morality and long-term relationships are of more concern.

Killman–Thomas conflict orientations

Thomas (1977) has proposed that two personality dimensions best represent the ability of negotiators to act either according to rational criteria or according to the dictates of their own personality:

❏ the degree of **assertiveness** that a conflicting party maintains for his own preferred solutions or outcomes; and

❏ the degree of **co-operation** a party shows in working with the other party to achieve goals for both parties.

Thomas believes that five identifiable styles exist within these trait dimensions:

- ❏ **A competing style** — High on assertiveness and low on co-operation
- ❏ **An accommodating style** — Low on assertiveness and high on co-operation
- ❏ **An avoiding style** — Low on both assertiveness and co-operation
- ❏ **A collaborative style** — High on both assertiveness and co-operation
- ❏ **A compromising style** — Moderate on both assertiveness and co-operation

It can be concluded from the above discussion on personality that those who believe that there is a '**negotiating type**' may be misjudging the impact of their own personality on the attainment of the desired outcomes. Indeed, research has shown that most of the factors that affect the outcome of a negotiation are behavioural, and are under the negotiator's control. The art of negotiation may well be a 'learned' set of skills and behaviours, rather than qualities people are born with. Hence, individuals can practise and develop these skills and behaviours to improve their own effectiveness as negotiators.

There are some people, though, who have a better potential for success in certain, very specific situations. Thus, if a negotiator has a good understanding of the issues at stake; understands the dynamics of distributive and integrative bargaining; knows the effect of power differences; knows the principles of influence, changing opinions and attitudes; and knows the principles of common ground and those factors that will affect climate, then the negotiator's personality may do no more than give the negotiation a particular 'flavour' while the remaining elements are likely to have the major impact on the results obtained.

The role of needs

Nierenberg (1973) explains the negotiation process on the basis of needs and need differences that exist between negotiating parties. What is the role of individual and group needs in this regard?

Human needs are varied and complex. Nierenberg (1973:89) is of the opinion that an analysis of the needs of the negotiator and the target could be a worthwhile prenegotiation exercise. Individual needs could in some cases supersede the needs of the organisation being represented around the table. An example of this could be pursuing the need for status as a negotiator rather than the need for an immediate agreement.

Maslow (Gibson 1991:102) has proposed the existence of a so-called Needs Hierarchy (figure 5.3).

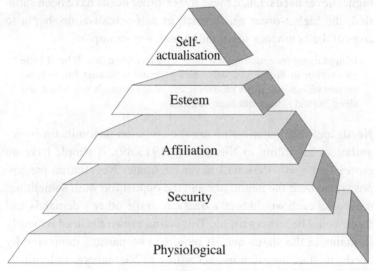

Figure 5.3
MASLOW'S NEEDS HIERARCHY

This is one of the most well-known theories of needs (and the motivation to fulfil them) that exists in literature today. According to Maslow, human beings have 'low level' needs that are physiological, and 'high level' needs that are needs for self-actualisation. Maslow ranked human needs as:

❑ **physiological** — the need for food, drink, shelter and freedom from pain;
❑ **safety and security** — the freedom from threat; that is, security from threatening events or surroundings;

❏ **belonging, social contact and love** — the need for friendship, affiliation, interaction and love;
❏ **esteem** — the need for self-esteem and for esteem from others; and
❏ **self-actualisation** — the need to fulfil oneself by maximising one's abilities, skills and potential.

Maslow's theory assumes that people have to satisfy their basic needs first, before directing their behaviour towards satisfying higher-level needs. Once these lower-order needs have been satisfied, the higher-order needs, such as self-actualisation, begin to control the behaviour of an individual. For example:

> In appraising (negotiating) a worker's performance, it will be of little motivation to him if you offer him promotion (status) for meeting certain objectives, if his physiological needs (enough pay to eat and sleep in safety) have not been satisfied.

Needs and their satisfaction are the common denominator in negotiation, according to Nierenberg (1973:89). If people have no unsatisfied needs they will never negotiate. Negotiation presupposes that both the negotiator and the opposition want something, otherwise each would turn a deaf ear to the other's demands and there would be no bargaining. This is true even if the need is merely to maintain the status quo. It requires two parties, motivated by needs, to start negotiating, according to Nierenberg. Individuals bickering over the purchase and sale of a piece of real estate; labour unions and management bargaining for a new contract; or the directors of two corporations discussing the terms of a proposed merger — all are seeking to satisfy needs.

Good negotiators will often probe relentlessly until they know exactly what the other party is **really** after. If the negotiators understand the problems and needs of the other side thoroughly, they could provide the means to resolve their frustration and leave the opposition highly satisfied. These methods of 'probing' are sometimes referred to as '**heat-seeking methods**' in the training material of salesmen. Negotiators must realise that they are seldom trying to reach an agreement; they are trying to solve a problem.

If negotiators are perceived to be able to solve the problems of the opposing side, they will have no problem reaching an agreement, regardless of the other offers received.

When one knows what needs and problems the opponent is experiencing, one can do one of the following:

❑ **Recognise** the need that is most important for him to satisfy at the present time and indicate to what extent that need could be satisfied if he would enter into a deal with you.

❑ Use the needs that are most apparent at a certain time as **'teasers'** to the other side, indicating that those needs will not be satisfied if the individual does not enter into the agreement.

Case 5.2
THE ROLE OF NEEDS

Pinetown 'The Bright Spot'

Pinetown is a bright spot in a rather dull office-letting market, says Ron Thackwell of estate agents JH Isaacs.

JH Isaacs's Pinetown office has arranged commercial leases valued at more than R4 million during the past three months.

Included in these deals is the renovation of Petronet from the Bayhead area to a high quality, three-storey building in Pinetown's Kings Road.

The first twenty months of the five-year lease, which was concluded by Kevyn Botes and Ron Thackwell, is in the form of a sublease from Industrial Investment Company, who occupied the entire building and have now moved to the ground floor.

The balance of the lease was negotiated directly with the landlord.

'Petronet's new premises are typical of the types of properties which are now in high demand,' said Mr Thackwell.

'Tenants are looking for smaller, quality suites and are not prepared to accept inferior finishes or rundown accommodation.

'It is opportune for landlords to look to upgrading and refurbishing in order to cater for the increasing demand from smaller tenants in the Pinetown CBD,' he said.

The Daily News, 31 July 1991.

It is important to realise that at any time there could be parallel needs operating. Apart from the fact that individuals and organisations try to fulfil more complex patterns of needs, there could also be a subtle needs conflict existing within the opponent's mind. For example:

> The great majority of people in most nations do not want war, but the individuals that represent them in international negotiation often permit themselves to be persuaded and propagandised into conflicts through their own needs for status and international esteem, thereby putting the safety of their countries in jeopardy.

Motivational orientation (MO)

Rubin and Brown (1975) used people's needs (their 'motivational orientation', or MO) to group individuals into three general types:

❑ **individualistic MO**;
❑ **co-operative MO**; and
❑ **competitive MO**.

These orientations may be briefly summarised as follows:

❑ A negotiator with an **individualistic MO** is predisposed to maximise his outcomes without regard to how the other bargainer fares. He is not interested in how the other party does, whether the other wins or loses in relative or absolute terms; he is concerned only about **maximising** his own individual outcome.

❑ A negotiator with a **co-operative MO** is predisposed to want to work with the other negotiator towards maximising their **joint** outcome. Each party is concerned with the other's welfare; whether the other wins or loses; and whether the negotiator achieves his own outcomes. The negotiator wants to win as much as he can, but, addition, he wants the other negotiator to win as much as he can.

❑ A negotiator with a **competitive MO** is predisposed to want to do better than his opponent. This party is concerned with his opponent's welfare and outcome to determine how well he himself is doing; the primary motivation is to win as much as possible and to **do better** than the other.

Negotiation will therefore take on a distributive or integrative character, based upon the **motivation** of the negotiators. MO thus becomes a very important 'intangible' that will shape the course of negotiations. A motivational orientation will be affected by individual differences in personality, situational factors such as constituency pressures, and by the economic reward available for co-operative or competitive behaviour.

Lewicki and Litterer (1985:134) have identified other 'needs' that play a very important role in the negotiation of various agreements.

The need for rationality

Rational behaviour in negotiation is usually defined as economic rationality. Economists traditionally presume that people are capable of determining which outcomes are more valuable or worthwhile than others, and are motivated to maximise their value or utility. Rational behaviour is defined as behaviour which is consistently directed towards maximising this utility. The need therefore exists to move away from each side's perception of 'irrationality' towards 'rationality'. Irrationality could include behaviour such as unpredictability and inconsistency, loss of control, 'tantrums' or inappropriate social behaviour.

The need for fairness and justice

This will include what is perceived as being fair in terms of the procedure being used during the negotiation, and what is fair in terms of the distribution within the final agreement. These are sometimes referred to as **distributive justice** (whether the outcome is fair in terms of what each party 'won' at the end), and **procedural justice** (whether the procedures did not favour one party at the expense of the other).

The need for equity

Each party has a perception of what he 'deserves' because of effort or time he has devoted towards the outcome of the negotiation.

The need for equality

Although this is very close to the need for equity, it is the need for equality of rights of both parties in the negotiation that is important.

All the above needs relate to what parties perceive as being 'just'. Their concept of what is right and wrong is often based on their value system, but also sometimes on the fulfilment of their needs relative to the fulfilment of the needs of others:

❏ Their needs could be **legitimate needs**, such as the need for housing in a community where everyone else has a house.

❏ Their perception of what is just will be influenced by the extent to which they can make use of **opportunities** that result from an agreement, compared to the other party's ability to make use of those opportunities.

❏ **Historical precedent**—their perception of justice will also be based on what they feel they should be entitled to in relation to the past. The statement 'It's always been done this way . . .' reflects this kind of thinking and is a very strong 'real base' in many negotiating situations.

Case 5.3

PERSUASION

Convincing the group

' . . . How could we start marketing Calps, guys?' John asks, in a much more low-keyed way. 'Shall we go for a national campaign, or do we start small? I believe, give them a great big bang and then supply the stuff in the key areas.'

'Would you clarify that please?' Peter responds.

'Well, we create a need, people will go and look for Calps and then try it out,' John explains.

'So, you think they will be happy not finding any?'

'We have to supply the basic volumes in key areas, of course.' Peter sits forward, and looks around (obviously he is doing some thinking) . . . 'Well, I studied what a few other guys did in this kind of situation. If we can start in a small yet very influential area such as Stellenbosch, and capture the market there, students who travel all over the country will spread the news. I suggest we won't need much advertising after that, don't you agree?'

John and the others nod. 'Gee, I like that. In this way we get an influential foot in the door.'

'We could invite the students to try samples, we could have campus parties, we could go flat-out there . . .'

'Imagine the guys at Tuks envying the Maties if the word starts to spread. That is creating a need, not so?'

Peter really has made a point . . . or so it seems.

CONCLUSION

Managers, marketers, preachers, teachers and parents are all in the persuading 'game'. Negotiators often have to do the persuasion over the table in limited time and in such a way that both sides find satisfaction when they review the agreement later. Negotiators will therefore have to realise that they are dealing with individuals who differ from them in many respects. They have different opinions, attitudes and needs, and sometimes conditioned ways of thinking and behaving. Once they understand their 'opponents' and have sufficient information on the causes of their actions, they should be able to convince the other side of the mutual value to be gained from the deal. It is also important to realise that, apart from the highly influential techniques described in this chapter, there are still many other elements in communication that affect negotiation. These have a lot to do with personality and lie within the domain of each negotiator's individual style, experience and 'tricks of the trade'.

CONCLUSION

CHAPTER 6

Handling Conflict and Aggression

In this Chapter

❏ The nature of *Conflict* and *Aggression*
❏ Methods and techniques that could help resolve conflict and win over the opposition
❏ Measures and techniques to overcome aggression
❏ *Overpowering Tactics:* The positive use thereof
❏ *Distributive Methods:* Plans and strategies for their prevention or use to facilitate reaching and maintaining constructive agreements
❏ The handling of co-operation and conflict through *Network Negotiation*

INTRODUCTION

During the course of the negotiation process, behaviour often occurs that can be labelled 'distributive' since it has the overpowering of the opposition as its primary objective. It can occur at any time during the negotiations, including before and after direct contact between the parties. Some of these behaviours could be planned and others could be more spontaneous due to frustrations that may occur during the bargaining process.

Distributive tactics and behaviours possess elements of manipulative, win–lose and competitive actions. During this phase or event, the goals and attainment of goals of one party are in fundamental and often direct **conflict** with the goals of the other party. Resources are fixed and limited, and each party wants to maximise its share of the resources. As a result, each party will resort to a set of strategies and tactics in order to maximise its share of the outcomes that are attained. For example:

> A labour union wants to negotiate an increase of at least 20 % in salaries (similar to the inflation rate of a particular year) so as to maintain minimum living standards, while the other party, management, cannot afford to give any increase because this could cause unacceptable losses for the company. For the workers, not getting this minimum increase would be totally unacceptable and make it impossible for them to continue working for the organisation. On the other side, management also feels that any increase above 5 % would make it impossible for them to continue operating on a profitable basis.

Distributive situations also occur in buying/selling situations such as buying a house or motor car.

During the Vietnam war, President Johnson believed that the military presence of the USA in Vietnam would ensure the viability of democratic institutions in South-East Asia and was determined to **win** that objective through a policy of negotiation backed by force. He therefore employed 'talk/fight' tactics consistent with enemy pressures and his strategic decision. As in some of the previous examples, there was no indication of an overlap in the aspiration and bargaining bases of the two parties in the Vietnam war.

In a similar fashion Admiral C Turner sat opposite the communists for ten months in Korea in the early '50s. Afterwards, in his book *How Communists Negotiate*, he made a number of recommendations, some of which were employed by ambassadors Harryman and Lodge during the Vietnam negotiations. These recommendations are typical of the gain–lose or distributive tactics typically employed during this period in international politics. The Americans wanted, at the very least, to gain certain concessions and were not willing to concede on them:

❏ No American concession should be made without an equivalent communist response.
❏ The communists should not be permitted to unilaterally choose the conference site, nor should it be in their area of control.
❏ The American team should be staffed with clear and rapid-thinking negotiators of the highest quality.
❏ America should be prepared to use the threat of force and be committed to implementation if necessary.
❏ Integrity on the part of the communists should not be assumed.
❏ Conferences should be brief and conducted within previously established time limits.

A conflict of needs and objectives of the negotiating parties often lies at the basis of all negotiation. In distributive negotiation there is a wide **gap** between the objectives of **opposing** parties. Those objectives could even be dichotomous and oppositional. An example of this is:

> The position of a team of negotiators representing an organisation that wants to procure a piece of land that lies within the boundaries of the Kruger National Park would be in direct conflict with the interests of nature conservationists and the Parks Board. The one party's gain is the other party's loss.

On the other hand, without conflict there will be no negotiation. Conflict is a prerequisite for negotiation. It is the way people deal with conflict that causes them to fall into the win–lose trap.

Let us consider the basis of **dysfunctional conflict** (any confrontation or interaction between groups that harms the negotiation process or hinders the achievement of the goals of both parties) and the ways in which that type of conflict can be dealt with.

THE CAUSES AND CONSEQUENCES OF DYSFUNCTIONAL CONFLICT

A dysfunctional conflict is any confrontation or interaction between individuals or groups that harms the negotiation or hinders the achievement of goals. Negotiators should seek to eliminate dysfunctional conflicts. Beneficial conflicts can often turn or be turned into harmful ones. In most cases, the point at which functional conflict becomes dysfunctional is impossible to identify precisely. It is generally defined as the point at which there is a breakdown of co-operation and the elimination of the generation of alternatives. The very same level of stress and conflict that may create a healthy and positive movement towards goals in one session, may prove extremely disruptive and dysfunctional in another session (or at a different time for the same group). A group's tolerance for frustration, stress and conflict can also depend on its constituencies and the objectives it serves. It could also depend on loss potential and issues at stake.

Gibson (1991:299) differentiates between conflict that could be:

❏ **too low**, impacting on group performance because of a lack of motivation to adhere to agreements;
❏ **too high**, resulting in chaos and breakdown of negotiations; or
❏ **optimal**, resulting in a positive, functional agreement that will hold for both parties.

As was said before, frustration lies at the core of most conflicts that occur in negotiation. When individuals in a win–lose mode feel that movement towards their objectives is being blocked or hindered, they can become self-centred and disruptive. Thompson identifies a number of causes for intergroup conflict (1967).

Causes of intergroup conflict

Work interdependence

Work interdependence happens when two or more parties must depend on one another to complete their tasks. The potential for conflict in such situations is high.

Pooled interdependence

Pooled interdependence requires no interaction between groups because each group, in effect, performs separately. However, the pooled performance of all the groups determines how successful the organisation will be. For example:

> The staff of an IBM sales office of one region may have no interaction with their peers in another region. Similarly, two bank branches have little or no interaction. In both cases, however, the groups are interdependent because the performance of each must be adequate if the total organisation is to thrive. The conflict potential is relatively low.

Sequential interdependence

Sequential interdependence requires one group to do its task before the next group can complete its task. Tasks are performed in a sequential fashion. In a manufacturing plant, for example, the product must be assembled before it can be painted. The output of one group serves as the input of another and conflict potential is relatively high.

Reciprocal interdependence

Reciprocal interdependence occurs when multiple groups provide input for a single group in the organisation. This occurs when expert teams from different departments are required to give their input at the same time. For example:

> In an operating theatre, the different skills of such experts as anaesthetists, nurses, technicians and surgeons are all required to function optimally at the same time. Because of the high degree of reciprocal interdependence, the potential for conflict is relatively high.

Differences in goals

Widely divergent goals could be the cause of frequent conflict during negotiations. Parties will have to move considerably more, relative to one another, before they can come to an agreement. For example:

> Labour union needs versus the needs of management, the need for more land by one country versus the protective interests of the neighbouring country, the need of one party to be independent versus the need of the other party for obedience to its authority are all examples of very divergent needs and will require substantial movement from both sides before an agreement can be reached.

Limited resources

If money, space, labour and materials are unlimited, each group could pursue (at least to a relative degree) its own goals. But in virtually all cases, resources must be allocated or shared. What often occurs in limited resource situations is a win–lose competition that can easily result in dysfunctional conflict.

Reward structures

Intergroup conflict is more likely to occur when the reward system is related to individual group performance rather than to combined group performance. When rewards are aimed at individual groups, performance is viewed as an independent variable even while the performance is, in reality, very interdependent. For example:

> In the marketing versus credit situation, the marketing group could be rewarded for sales produced and the credit department rewarded for minimising credit losses. In such a situation competition is directly reinforced and dysfunctional conflict inadvertently rewarded.

Differences in perception

As was discussed in the previous chapter, there could be many differences in perception that cause dysfunctional conflict. For example:

❏ There could be different **time horizons** between parties. For the one party it could be important to reach an agreement within a deadline, while others are much less concerned with the constraints of time.

❏ There could be large differences in **status** between the two parties around the negotiating table, with the result that the parties will be at different levels of satisfaction in terms of their esteem needs, causing them to have totally different objectives.

❏ There could be differences in information and **expertise,** causing conflict about the accuracy of information. In the same fashion the **credibility** of some of the experts in the negotiation could be doubtful and in competition with the opposition.

❏ **Cultural differences**, which result in a lack of understanding of language, habits, attitudes and education, could lead to misunderstanding that could cause dysfunctional conflict.

❏ **Constituents** that support negotiating teams could inadvertently be the cause of conflict. The teams may be perceived to be acting in the interests of certain parties and not in the interests of the negotiation itself. Personal differences, the playing of political games, and misunderstandings may also cause conflict.

Social/psychological causes of conflict

Robert A Baron, in his book *Human Aggression* (1980), studied the causes of conflict where aggression is a major determinant. He concluded that aggressive conflict could be caused singly or in combination by:

❏ Instinctive **frustrations**.

❏ **Social learning**. Because people identify from an early age with behaviour they see as effective, and because the adults in their environment could be solving their problems by means of aggressive behaviour, it could result in a social learning pattern that is followed by the child in later years.

❏ An unconscious **need to harm** or injure another psychologically in a social interaction can exist due to a sadistic personality trait, according to Baron.

❏ The **'training'** of members of a community for violent behaviour could result in aggression being instigated and expected by support groups and peers.

In South Africa this can sometimes be seen in the public statements of semipolitical organisations in which violence and the talk of violence is an everyday occurrence. Violence and aggression could be seen as an acceptable form of behaviour as a consequence of filmed or televised violence to which people are continiously subjected.

❑ **Crowding, noise** and **heat**.

❑ A **territorial 'war'** where the territory or space of one person is threatened by another.

❑ People being influenced by **non-verbal** and **molecular** cues from outsiders, causing an aggressive response.

❑ The inclination to aggression that exists in some personalities labelled as **'violence prone'**.

❑ The belief held by some people that **'letting it out'** is a much more acceptable form of dealing with aggression and conflict, than restraint. They therefore justify their violent and aggressive actions in this way.

❑ Various aspects of **attitude** such as prejudice, interracial aggression, gender differences, status differences, differences in expertise, and other differences in social evaluation are some of the main causes of conflict and aggression in interpersonal situations.

Case 6.1

SOCIAL LEARNING: 1991

Everyday violence

'. . . The jokes mask more serious fears: of whether there will be decent schools for their children, decent hospitals to soften their old age. Most serious of all is the violence, which spills from the townships more and more. Whites talk fearfully of Lebanon. They defend their gardens with big fences and rottweilers. Security firms multiply; the manager of one established outfit complains that "any fool with a gun and a dog can set himself up".

The vice chancellor of the University of the Witwatersrand, Johannesburg's English-speaking university, recently felt obliged to rule that guns should not be carried on campus. Restaurants get held up: the guests surrender watches, wallets, occasionally their shoes. The violence breathes truth into Archbishop Desmond Tutu's jibe: "In this country we have so many people who want to change so long as things remain the same."

Racial conflict and the violence that comes with it has another, more insidious effect. In a curious way, English-speaking whites suffer from the same denigration of self-improvement that affects black South

Africans. They feel they have to apologise if they are not engaged in the struggle. Many who leave the country do so at least partly in search of uncomplicated yuppiedom.'

A Survey in South Africa, *The Economist*, 1991.

Consequences of conflict

In negotiations there are many different consequences of conflict and aggression. Some of these were identified by Sherif and Sherif (1953) who claimed, in many studies, that the following tendencies could arise within and between parties as a result of heightening tension, stress, conflict and/or aggression:

Increased group cohesiveness

Competition, conflict or external threat often results in group members putting aside individual differences and closing ranks. Members become more loyal to the group with the result that even groupthink or risky shift decisions could occur. Due to these emotional factors, the group will stick together closely (the **'laager'** tendency), back each other up to a larger degree, and take decisions that are based on emotion rather than facts.

Rise in autocratic leadership

In extreme conflict situations, where threats are possible, democratic methods of leadership are likely to become less popular because members of the negotiating team need strong leadership. According to Sherif and Sherif, the team is likely to become more **autocratic**.

In the same way, when there is an undesirably high incidence of conflict between children in a family, parents tend to become more autocratic in the methods they use to smooth out or stop the conflict from recurring.

In contrast to this, it has been found that tribal and political violence in South Africa has been curbed to some extent, because leaders of the affected people were granted more authority and encouraged more democratic participation by their followers in the development of anti-violence strategies.

Departments within an organisation are often given the chance to negotiate and solve some of their interdepartmental problems. If this does not happen, the managing director, in many instances, will make a statement to the effect that he will personally take charge and decide how things will be done. Agreements are reached in this way, yet it is doubtful whether people really adhere to them while the underlying sources of conflict persist.

Deadlock

Conflict and aggression could easily cause a party to walk away from the negotiating table. Steers (1991:524) believes that inaction and the removal of an individual or party from an interaction is one of the most common reactions to conflict and aggression. Deadlock could take many forms (Wall 1985:60).

- ❏ Parties could officially declare a **deadlock** towards each other.
- ❏ They could **boycott** negotiation sessions.
- ❏ They could **ignore** opponents or mediators.
- ❏ They could **ignore deadlines** although they might have initially agreed on these deadlines.
- ❏ They could just **walk out** of any interaction.

Escalation of conflict

As was discussed earlier, there seems to be a tendency in humans to counter any action with a similar action. When aggression and conflict are countered in an 'eye-for-an-eye' fashion, this could lead to an escalation of conflict that could become very difficult to control in the long term.

In a situation where high levels of aggression are already present, the levels may be further escalated by the following reactions:

- ❏ An open counterstatement of aggression.
- ❏ Character assassination, or office gossip.
- ❏ Shouting at the opposition (emotional outburst).
- ❏ Violent arm movements (hostile gestures).
- ❏ Staring down opponents.

❏ Banging on the table with clenched fists.

❏ Extreme sarcasm in the face of aggressive statements from the other side.

❏ Making fun of a serious statement.

Wall (1985:65) refers to the role of irrational tactics in negotiation and indicates that irrational behaviour could sometimes be used very effectively in distributive negotiation. It could encourage the opposition to make concessions because they see the other party as being **irrational** and therefore do not know whether they will really execute their threat or not. For Wall, irrational tactics include:

❏ **Bluffing** — This could include inviting the other party to retaliate. It would constitute a challenge for them to execute their threat.

❏ The use of **illogical** and ridiculous arguments.

❏ **Abrupt changing** of the mind.

❏ **Impulsive** or careless speech.

❏ An **emotional** outburst.

❏ An **attack** on the competence and intellectual ability of the individual members of the other team.

Adherence

Of course, one of the outcomes of aggression and conflict could be that the opposition adheres to the request of the aggressor out of **fear** or their inability to cope with the conflict itself. This could aid the aggressive party to reach its objectives in the negotiation. It is doubtful, however, to what extent there will be any real commitment or change in attitudes due to the 'forced adherence' that took place because of the irrational or aggressive behaviour of the opposition. An agreement thus established could become complicated due to elements of **guilt** and **sympathy** creeping into the process. Apart from this, such a situation could leave **victims** who may present a problem at a later stage.

For negotiators it is therefore important to have some guidelines to follow and to develop some skills in the handling of aggression, conflict and irrational actions.

HANDLING CONFLICT AND AGGRESSION

There are many ways of handling conflict and aggression, depending on the cause of the conflict at the negotiation table. It is therefore important for negotiators to understand the underlying reason for their opponent's aggressive behaviour, irrational acts and ultimately, the reason for the escalation of the conflict situation. There are many approaches to this problem.

Separation

Breaking off face-to-face relationships is the most common approach to aid the cooling of inflamed tempers. Lewicki (1985:283) is of the opinion that the declaration of a **recess** or the calling of a **caucus** could serve a useful purpose in this regard. When conflict becomes unbearable it is an acceptable tactic to agree with the other side to adjourn the meeting and to meet again at a later stage, when the parties have had a chance to unwind. If, at the same time, an agreement could be reached that the purpose of the caucus will be for tempers to cool down and for the dialogue to become less emotional, it could serve as a form of **common ground** that could facilitate the negotiations to follow.

During this recess parties should focus their attention on finding **alternatives** that could break the deadlock in the talks and turn the discussion into a more positive one.

Separation of the parties may occur for short periods of time, such as a few minutes to a few hours, or may be planned to last for several days or weeks. Parties may use the time to evaluate their position with constituencies, gather new information, reassess their positions and commitments and consult with other interests.

Identifying a common enemy

In some respects, identifying a common enemy could help groups to resolve their differences temporarily. It would also unite them on some form of **common ground**: the common enemy. The common enemy may be a competitor who has just introduced a clearly superior product, it may be the receiver of revenue, the government, unemployment, or bankruptcy.

The common enemy phenomenon is often evident in domestic conflicts. According to Gibson et al. (1991:312) many police officers prefer not to become involved in heated domestic conflicts. This is true because, in far too many cases, the combatants close ranks and turn on the police officer whom they see not as an arbitrator, but as the common enemy.

The GRIT strategy

The 'Graduated Reduction Intention Technique' (GRIT) strategy is a mixed strategy — one in which the negotiator's concession-making shifts over the course of the negotiation. It was proposed by Charles Osgood (1962) during the early '60s as a method for **reducing tensions** between the Soviet Union and the United States. Osgood was alarmed by the reciprocal exchanges of the two superpowers in their cold, but belligerent, contest. One side would take an action that was intended or perceived to be threatening to the other side. In turn, the other side reciprocated with a belligerent act, and the counterpart again responded, causing a highly **tense escalation** of conflict.

This mutually amplifying process continued, with both sides becoming more hostile, more threatening, less trusting and less trustworthy. This process made it difficult for either side to institute a de-escalation process. Even when it announced its desire and intention to reduce tension or to take some co-operative step, its behaviour was seen as suspect or was perceived as a **competitive ploy**.

To **defuse** this costly, dangerous cycle (similar to the situation in which the former South African government and the ANC found themselves before Mr F W De Klerk's reforms in 1990), Osgood suggested that one side should undertake a number of small, unilateral, announced, conciliatory initiatives (concessions). In so doing, however, they should not reduce their capability to retaliate against the opponent. Additionally, the initiating side should invite, but not demand, reciprocity from the opponent. Especially for high-level and international negotiations, this seems to be a fairly effective measure which has been reviewed and tested by many authors (Wall 1985:100). Osgood summarised his conflict reduction strategy in **ten** detailed points:

❏ The strategy must be designed and communicated in a manner that emphasises the initiator's **intent** to **reduce tension**.

❏ The initiator must **publicly announce** each initiative, indicating **what** it is, **when** it will take place and **where** it will take place.

❏ Each initiative must be carried out **on schedule**.

❏ The opponents should be invited to **reciprocate**, but **no demand** for reciprocation should be made.

❏ Initiatives must be **continued** over time, even in the absence of reciprocation.

❏ Initiatives must be **unambiguous** and **verifiable**.

❏ The initiative should not impair the initiator's capability to **retaliate** against the opponent.

❏ Likewise, the initiatives should not **constrain** the initiator from responding with graded responses to the opponent's escalation.

❏ Initiatives should be **diversified**.

❏ When reciprocation is obtained the initiator should take subsequent steps that provide slightly **less conciliation**.

It is interesting that the South African government's strategy to defuse the conflict with the ANC during the De Klerk era corresponded (unintentionally or intentionally) to a large degree with the Osgood strategy.

Role reversal

When conflict becomes more heated, communication efforts concentrate on managing emotions and directing the next assault at the opponent. **Effective listening** declines. Parties think they know what the other side is going to say, and therefore they do not listen carefully. Often, thinking capacity is reduced in inverse proportion to loudness of voice. In intense conflict, listening becomes so diminished that the parties are frequently unaware that their positions may have much in common. Rappoport (1964) has termed this syndrome the **'blindness of involvement'**, since it inhibits the development of trust and the problem-solving process.

Role reversal is one way of helping each side to see things from the other's perspective. In the case of conflict, one party will then invite the other **to put themselves in the opposition's shoes**, looking at the issue from that perspective.

> For example, a member of management can put him or herself in the position of a union negotiator; a salesman can take the position of a customer; and vice versa.

Both parties can agree to exchange roles in a simulated negotiating session. If that is not possible, one side could pursue this strategy unilaterally, inviting the other to see matters from its perspective by asking question such as: 'What would you do in these situations? What strategy would you employ under these conditions? What would you do if your business was threatened in this way? What would you do if you went bankrupt as a result of increasing salaries? What would you do if you had an ultraconservative worker group which was pressurising you in this way?'

Role reversal could result in parties softening their stances on issues and could even lead to attitude change, according to Lewicki and Litterer (1985:286).

The 'declare' approach

Statements made during conflict in negotiating can be classified according to type. Pienaar (1991) distinguished between demand, defer, defect and declare statements during a conflict. When one party **demands**, the other party could respond by either demanding as well, or by **deferring**, **defecting**, or **declaring**. The following combinations could result:

Demand–demand reaction

'I want to use the fax machine' *versus* 'No, I want to use it.'
Result: Almost certainly an escalation of conflict and heightened tension.

Demand–defer responses

'We *must* decide now' *versus* 'No, let's postpone until next week.'
Result: Causes frustration and anger.

Demand–defect reactions

'You must attend the meeting on Saturday' *versus* 'If that is required I don't want to have anything to do with this committee.'
Result: Could cause anger, autocratic behaviour and feelings of hopelessness.

Demand–declare reactions

These reactions tend to deflate tension.
'I'll walk out of these talks if you keep on trying to manipulate us' *versus* 'You possibly feel angry and betrayed because you think that we are bringing issues to the table that don't belong here, not so?'
Result: To **declare** means to 'open up' feelings, distrust, and concerns that may be the cause of the increased tension. Declaring could, according to Pienaar, be instrumental in defusing this potential conflict. Two examples of **declare** statements are:

❏ 'For us, your approach seems to be extremely aggressive. We believe the source of this is the incident during the previous meeting. Could you clarify your feelings in this regard?'

❏ 'If you negotiate in this way, you make us feel inferior. We don't want to feel that way since we want to feel that we enter this agreement because of the merit of the case and not because you are forcing us.'

Creative alternatives

Many disputes reach an impasse, not because the parties' positions are so far apart, but because neither wants to discuss alternatives. For Nierenberg (1973:189), being able to come up with creative alternatives is one of the basic requirements of successful conflict resolution in negotiation. Creating alternatives for mutual accommodation allows all parties to become winners regardless of tension and conflict during the earlier stages of the process.

A good creative alternative is one that satisfies some needs of each participant in a negotiation. A creative alternative will allow the parties more time during the negotiation, the chance to consider the new alternatives and the prospect of another meeting. Opposing parties are less immune to **novel alternatives** that are brought to the table. If the alternative is brought to the table during a very tense period it could serve as a concession to the other side. Certain levels of conflict can, according to Nierenberg, also be useful in facilitating the creation of new alternatives.

Too often, negotiators do not exercise their mental capabilities to generate creative alternatives. Instead, they openly discourage the search for new methods of resolving differences. Some become locked in by the dispute or conflict and refuse to test other approaches. The ability to think or say 'What else?' can help parties consider other possibilities. It can unplug otherwise closed channels of investigation and conversation, whereas arbitrarily saying 'I don't like it' or 'It won't work' can be defeating for all concerned. The 'not invented here' or 'not thought out here' syndrome is a major obstacle towards reaching settlements or agreements in principle and to the establishment of a base for a possible compromise. Looking back on some of the less successful negotiations, Nierenberg believes that the inability to create and listen to new alternatives is often the principal reason for not reaching a settlement.

It has been reported that General Jan Smuts, at the time prime minister of South Africa, when faced with thousands of strikers at a British coal mine, started off by asking them to sing him a song. He told them that he had heard, while in South Africa, about their famous ability to sing beautiful songs, but had never had the opportunity to hear them personally. They started singing and soon their aggression and conflict were rechannelled into their singing. The use of this **'creative' alternative** to aggression helped the General to defuse the conflict effectively.

Subtle movements

When one team attempts to overpower the other by exerting a disproportionate amount of power or aggression, it is necessary to 'defuse' this disparity in power, sometimes by subtly changing perceptions. Pienaar (1991) postulates that distraction, the causing of uncertainty, and the causing of **personal doubt**, could in fact achieve these objectives. To achieve these ends, the following body movements could be used in close interpersonal encounters:

❑ **Eye movements** towards a sensitive body area ('zapping') causes self-doubt and lack of concentration regarding the issues or facts on the table.

❑ **Small movements,** imitating the movements (even the blinking of eyes) of the 'aggressor' amongst opponents, causes tension, lack of concentration and uncertainty.

❑ **Glaring** at molecular movements of an opponent such as hand and lip movements will cause introspection and a loss of concentration.

❑ Movements within the private **body zones** of the opponents will cause distraction and defensiveness instead of offensiveness.

❑ **Territorial 'games'** through slight touching and extension of legs, arms and body to occupy the space of opponents causes defensiveness and uncertainty.

Care must be taken in the use of these techniques, according to Pienaar, since they could cause an escalation (rather than de-escalation) of the conflict and power. They should only be attempted when a team or individual is confronted with unduly aggressive conflicting parties or persons.

Wall (1985:40) expanded on the above approach by listing several direct and indirect strategies for the purpose of either increasing the negotiator's 'strength', decreasing the 'strength' of the opponent or altering the power relationship between the parties (table 6.1).

Aggression modification responses

In the 5 600 years of recorded human history, there have been more than 14 600 wars — a rate of approximately 2,6 per year. Further, of the roughly 185 generations of human beings who have been born, only ten generations have known the blessings of uninterrupted peace. Faced with this disheartening record of continued violence, one may well wonder whether it is, in fact, possible to prevent or control aggressive behaviour.

Baron (1977), in an influential study on the prevention and control of human aggression, is of the opinion that the answer is a definite 'Yes!' Baron, in an overview of the literature and a summary of various experiments by himself and others on aggression, came to the conclusion that, contrary to the views espoused by Freud, Lorenz, Ardrey and others, **aggression** is not essentially innate. Rather, it seems to be a **learned** form of **social behaviour**, acquired in the same manner as other types of activity and influenced by many of the same social, situational and environmental factors. Aggression, in short, is not genetically or instinctively preordained; it arises, instead, from a complex set of conditions that encourage and stimulate its occurrence.

Baron (1977:269) believes that aggression, as an acquired form of behaviour, is readily open to modification. Just as individuals can learn to behave aggressively and can be encouraged to do so by external (or even internal) conditions, they can be taught to behave in a **non-aggressive** manner and to refrain from harming others. During negotiations individuals and parties can be expected to act in a way that they have been taught is right or wrong.

Table 6.1

THE WALL STRATEGY FOR ALTERING PERCEPTION
OF POWER AND OVERPOWERING TACTICS

Increase negotiator's strength	Reduce opponent's strength	Alter relationships of strength (leverage)
Acquire status	Close opponent's outside options	Move to address opponent's weak points
Develop abilities and skills	Prevent opponent's coalitions, alliances and support	Protect negotiator's weak points
Voice disclaimers	Weaken opponent's stand with his or her constituency	Wait until opponent is vulnerable
Strengthen logic	Disorganise opponent's constituency	Make end run
Increase size of bargaining team	Reduce opponent's status or expertise	Flank the opponent
Go on record	Prevent opponent from establishing commitments	
Stockpile	Recruit opponent's associates	
Strengthen stand with constituency	Utilise informant	
Make co-operative arrangements with third party		
Develop outside options		

JA Wall (1985).

Needless to say, it is one thing to proclaim the possibility of controlling human violence, and quite another to indicate practical steps that might be taken to accomplish this end. Aggression and conflict are highly complex phenomena, influenced in many ways by a wide range of factors. Thus it would be naive to assume that they can be controlled in a simple or straightforward manner at all times. Yet, despite this complexity, there seem to be many **practical** steps that, if taken, might prove to be of considerable value in **reducing** the prevalence or intensity of human aggression or violence in interpersonal situations.

For Baron, behaviour modification should start at a very young age. Individuals' reactions in a negotiating situation will be influenced to a large extent by what they were taught while they were children. At the present time youngsters are exposed to what might reasonably be termed 'systematic **training for violence**' (Baron 1977:270). Through television and other mass media, they witness countless incidents of violence and in this manner are equipped with a wide range of techniques for harming others. Even worse, these episodes are presented in a context that often seems to imply that aggression is a perfectly acceptable and appropriate technique for handling relations with others. When it is realised that such beliefs are being strengthened and reinforced by peer groups, society at large, work environments, and even parents, it is not surprising that the incidence of aggression and overt violence in many societies has risen sharply in recent years.

Firstly, as a measure to reduce aggression, the content of television shows, movies, comic books and other widely distributed items could be changed. It is certainly a difficult task and one that raises many complex ethical and legal issues; yet, evidence seems to suggest that such changes, if carried out in a consistent manner, would be well worth the effort.

As a **second** measure, according to Baron, **society should seek to eliminate social conditions** that both encourage and reward the performance of overt aggression. Such behaviour is currently rewarded in a number of different contexts. For example:

❏ Young children (especially boys) are frequently praised by both their peers and parents for behaving in a tough, and **'macho'** manner.

❏ Similarly, adults are **rewarded** in various ways for acting aggressively in settings ranging from the athletic playing field to the executive boardroom.

❏ The inefficiency in the existing system of criminal **justice** often ensures that criminals who transgress against others (and in this manner gain important material rewards) only rarely 'pay' for their offenses.

Thirdly, Baron believes that society should seek to eliminate as many of the antecedents of aggression as possible from the environment. Many of these, of course, are not under our direct control (uncomfortable heat, traffic problems and so on). Many others, however, are under our control (unpleasant noise, crowding, the presence of weapons and other aggressive cues). Thus, active steps to eliminate, or at least reduce, the prevalence of such **conditions** may succeed in moving us closer to the goal of a humane society without overt aggression.

Finally, Baron believes that even in cases in which aggressive responses have already been acquired and where such behaviour has been instigated, techniques for preventing the occurrence of overt harmful actions do exist. There are many responses that can be taught to children from childhood onwards on how to control and reduce aggression of individuals and groups in society. Some of these techniques that have application in close interpersonal and group settings are the following.

Punishment

What would be the reaction if the opponent is punished during the negotiation through verbal means (reprimanded), punished through subtle means (such as zapping) or through walkouts and/or similar responses? According to Baron (1977:277) punishment and threats of punishment are effective in reducing aggression only under conditions in which:

❏ the aggressor is not very angry;
❏ the magnitude of punishment anticipated is great;
❏ the probability that such punishment will actually be delivered is high; or
❏ they have little to gain from their initial plans.

When such conditions do not prevail, threat and punishment may totally **fail** to inhibit overt aggression.

The actual delivery of punishment, too, seems to be effective, according to Baron, only under certain conditions. In particular, it is successful in inhibiting later aggression only where the punishment is viewed as **legitimate** by its recipients, where it follows aggressive actions quite **swiftly**, and where it is administered in a sure and **predictable** manner. When such conditions do not prevail, punishment often 'backfires' and actually enhances the occurrence of aggressive behaviour.

Therefore we can **conclude** that, if a threat of punishment, or punishment itself, is administered during negotiations it will only be effective if:

❏ it is delivered by someone who is very influential;
❏ this person is perceived to have the ability (and the will) to execute the punishment;
❏ those punished have too much at stake in the process; and
❏ the punishment is deemed to be a fair response.

Catharsis

The suggestion that providing angry individuals with the opportunity to 'let off steam' in some safe manner will cause them to feel better and weaken their tendencies to engage in more dangerous forms of behaviour, is the basis of the famous **catharsis hypothesis**.

Existing evidence lends support to the first of these proposals. According to Baron, participation in various forms of aggression may indeed cause angry individuals to experience sharply reduced emotional arousal. Negotiators asking for a recess at a time of an emotional outburst and inviting the other side to **let off steam** and then return, could indeed be helpful.

Evidence regarding the second suggestion — that present aggression reduces the likelihood of future assaults — is less consistent. Apparently, only direct attacks against the source of one's anger or annoyance can produce such an effect — a fact that reduces the usefulness of catharsis as a means of controlling overt aggression. Further, the duration of such an effect, once produced, is as yet unknown. Thus it seems reasonable to conclude that the benefits of catharsis, as a technique for preventing violence, have been somewhat overstated in the past.

> Therefore, if a labour union is negotiating with representatives of management, such as the personnel officer and a consultant, acts of aggression towards them during negotiation are not likely to cause a reduction of future aggression. If the source of the aggression is present (one supervisor who has treated a group of workers in an inhumane way), the chances of future reduction of aggression may diminish to some extent. If management, in this case, asked the person who caused the aggression to be present at a meeting, it could be helpful, but it is not always practical to expose negotiating parties to the source of their frustration.

Empathy and humour

Baron reported highly successful experiments where empathy and feelings of amusement and humour were used to reduce aggression in interpersonal situations. He based the reason for this success on the well-established principle that all organisms — including human beings — are incapable of being engaged with two **incompatible responses** at the same time. In accordance with this principle it would be expected that the introduction of responses incompatible with anger or aggression will be highly effective in inhibiting conflict and verbal assaults against aggressors.

Therefore, if opposing parties respond to an aggressive outburst with either **empathy** or **humour** or another response that is incompatible with the expression of anger, it will be highly effective.

Nierenberg (1973:193) also emphasises the importance and use of humour in the control of highly conflicting and difficult situations.

He referred to an incident in 1967 when police in West Berlin, who had to handle a demonstration with the minimum of violence, used humour to gain their objective. The following report of this incident was published in the *New York Times* of November 6, 1967:

'Ladies and gentlemen, please move on or be prepared to get your bath robes and towels ready. We are going to have to stage some unusual aquatics.'

The voice that boomed the message from the loudspeaker belonged to Vernor Texter, a policeman. The crowd laughed and the people cheered. This took place during a student demonstration in the heart of West Berlin. By the time the water cannon was turned on a minute later (against the sit-down demonstrators), in the middle of the street, most of the spectators and the protesting students had left. 'There are always those without a sense of humour,' Mr Texter remarked of the few that remained to get drenched.

Nierenberg believes that negotiators who have the ability to use humour are never at a loss for a strategy.

He cited a further example from 1930 when Huey Long, who was a master of humour, achieved yet another one of his objectives through the use of humour. One year the opening game of the Louisiana State University Football Team was marred by poor advance sales. To his horror, Long found that the circus was opening the same night. To prevent the unfair competition against his beloved team, Long searched in the law books. There he found a Louisiana law, enacted but never enforced, providing for the compulsory dipping of animals to prevent the spread of ticks. He then called John Ringling North, the circus owner and politely asked him to change the opening date. Mr North would not. 'Well,' said Long, 'Louisiana has a dip law. As I interpret it, your animals will have to be dipped. Have you ever dipped a tiger? Or how about an elephant?' North did not open in Baton Rouge that day.

The majority of Baron's studies on humour proved that 'laughter is the best medicine' for anger. There are some exceptions: exposure to **hostile humour** — in which some target is harmed, attacked or made to look foolish — could enhance, rather than inhibit, aggressive actions.

Negotiating parties should therefore be careful about the kind of humour used in the presence of others and should be careful with any material that is insulting or **derogatory** to the other side, or that refers to **sensitive** political, sexual or religious matters.

Visible suffering

When aggressors verbally attack other people in face-to-face confrontations, they are often exposed to signs of **pain** and **suffering** on the part of their 'victims'. For example, the 'victim party' may show its distress by pleading, asking for help, covering the eyes or mouth or making other movements that would indicate emotional suffering. What, then, are the effects of such feedback on the further behaviour of the aggressor?

The findings of a number of different experiments cited by Baron (1977:261) suggest that under some conditions those actions sharply reduce the strength or the frequency of further attacks upon the victim, especially in a face-to-face situation. The feedback from the suffering side tends to elicit feelings of **empathy** in the aggressors and this, in turn, causes them to lower the strength of their verbal attacks.

Pienaar (1991) refers to this reaction as **collapsing power**, and believes this to be a highly effective response if one party tries to overpower the other by means of overtly aggressive behaviour at the negotiating table. The 'collapse of power' will imply that a team under attack will show signs of asking, even pleading, for help in some cases, and apologising to the other side. He is of the opinion that it is often used as a highly effective measure to counter conflict and aggression by trained negotiators worldwide. Collapsing power by one side would mean that the other side cannot escalate its power any further in the face of the 'collapse' by the one side. The reason for this is the fact that most people will feel empathy with a 'collapsed' side, and also the fact that an incompatibility of responses has been created by this 'collapse'.

The fractionating approach

As was noted earlier, a major difficulty in the resolution of conflict is that, as a conflict intensifies, the size and **number of the issues** involved expand. As a conflict escalates it 'snowballs': bits and pieces of other issues are accumulated, resulting in a large, unmanageable mass. While small conflicts can be managed one at a time, larger conflicts become unwieldy and less susceptible to any easy resolution. The problem for negotiators, therefore, is to develop strategies to contain **issue proliferation** and reduce the dispute to manageable proportions.

Fisher and Ury (1981) have advocated a method of **issue control** in negotiation. In a well-known article on fractionating conflict, Fisher (1964) suggested three major ways of reducing a large conflict into smaller parts:

❏ **Reduce** the number of parties on each side. Since the sheer number of parties at the table can make negotiations considerably more complex — more time is needed to hear each side, more opportunities for disagreement can occur — it is found that ground rules are needed for ways in which to limit the number of parties involved. The fewer the actors present, and the more the conflict can be limited to two individuals, the more likely the parties are to reach a mutually favourable settlement.

❏ **Control** the number of **issues** involved. A second way to control the size of a conflict situation is to keep the number of issues manageable, according to Fisher. He believes, however, that only one issue at a time could easily cause win–lose strategies to develop, because one issue at a time is too limited. He believes that coupling the issue with another, so that two issues are involved, and then defining the issue more broadly so that resolution can benefit both sides, could defuse conflict and enable the parties to reach an agreement. Small packages of two or three issues are frequently easier to resolve because multiple issues facilitate packaging and trading of concessions.

❏ State issues in **concrete terms** rather than as principles. A third way a conflict becomes difficult to control is when events are treated as 'matters of principle', according to Fisher. Small conflicts can rapidly become intractable disputes when their resolution is not treated as an isolated event, but instead must be consistent with the broader 'policy' or 'principle'. Resorting to argument about policies or principles is often a strategic defence by high-powered parties against any change of the status quo. Fisher believes that parties should question whether the issues ought to be addressed at the principle or policy level. If need be, the parties can agree that the concrete issues should be settled, with no expectation as to how the policy will later be established.

Fisher believes that it should be pointed out that **exceptions** can be made to all policies and that principles and policies can be maintained, even if minor deviations are permitted to exist. For example, while honesty is the best 'policy', there are times when deviation from the truth may be necessary. The parties may be willing to agree that this may be one of those times.

HANDLING CONFLICT AND CO-OPERATION THROUGH NETWORKING

It is often said that it is not what you know in life that counts but who you know. The control of information is what networking is all about. The access to a mailing list, the list of clients, the knowledge of who will be included in someone's entourage are things that cannot be priced, only valued. But even that would render networking a commodity and not the subject of an empirical investigation, which it merits. Networking has become a concept used at all levels, by many, from media magnates to insurance salesmen.

Network negotiation

It is important for the negotiator to realise that he does not nego-tiate with only one party at any one time. In fact, a much larger scenario should be considered: Negotiations take place either directly or indirectly, both with highly visible as well as obscure or even 'silent' parties. Thus, for example, some insurance companies attempt to increase their profitability by saving on consultants' fees. By negotiating with consultants or representatives to form an independent 'business unit' and later a totally independent organisation, they no longer have to foot the bill for office space and cars, or pay allowances, etc. However, they also realise that affirmative action requires a symbiotic relationship between representatives and less sophisticated clients. They are therefore not only increasing their profits in the short term, but financing the cost of affirmative action in the long term. The representative who is negotiating his own package does not realise that he is merely a small part of the whole equation. However, if he realises the process and knows who is involved and then collectively involves the media, his own power base vis-à-vis the insurance company changes vastly. Clearly, **networking is the basis of intraorganisational and interorganisational politics**. It must be realised that power, in and around organisations, is a very negotiable and volatile variable.

The politics of networking

It is imperative that when a negotiator deals with power as a 'currency', the nature of the power relationships is understood. In biology, one can identify various types of power relationships: symbiotic, parasitic, commensal, allotropic, predatory, amensal, and mutual antagonism. These biotic relationships also occur between parties involved in business and negotiation.

❑ **'Symbiotic'** relationships are intimate, direct, mutually beneficial and co-operative. This kind of relationship is evident in co-operative political networking. In the example above, it could be evident in the interaction between representatives themselves that it is important to maintain a relationship of concensus, cohesion, and conjoint action.

❑ The **'parasitic'** relationship is one in which one party benefits but the other, by definition, loses. Normally when this type of relationship prevails, the benefit is obtained by the weaker or smaller party and the losses are accrued by the larger or more powerful party. The ever-present foreign aid packages which are exchanged between the wealthy and the economically weak countries, globally, are an expression of this type of relationship. The weak gain at the expense of the rich.

❑ A '**commensal**' relationship exists when one party gains but the other party does not really suffer loss.

❑ Instances where the small and weak are unaffected, whilst the larger and stronger party benefits, are often referred to as '**allotropic**'.

❑ A '**predatory**' relationship is in evidence when the large and/or strong exploit or even destroy the weak and small.

❑ '**Amensal**' describes the nature of the power relationship where one party loses without the other being affected. An example would be where the wealthy are being taxed disproportionately, without the poor benefiting. Or, in the example of the insurance industry described above, where the representatives are deprived of the benefits they enjoyed before, as ordinary employees, without the insurance company being affected at all by the creation of independent business units.

❑ In '**mutual antagonism**' parties are competitors and both sides try to maximise gain and minimise loss, but in fact both parties are harmed and suffer loss. A price war is a good example.

❑ '**Neutralism**' is an association where one party is not really affected by the other, but aware of its existence.

For negotiating networks to facilitate growth and maintain consensus, rather than enhance conflict and exploitation, is obviously a very difficult, time-consuming and sensitive process. Every negotiator must identify the prevalent **power** relationships. Not only must these relationships be identified: they must also be controlled, since they are obviously dynamic and not static. The effective negotiator consolidates relationships with his followers and tries to win his adversaries over to his side—but that is often wishful thinking. Conflict and co-operation are always in a state of flux. The successful negotiator, therefore, views his domain as a chessboard and realises that every piece is crucial. To be outnumbered, outsized, or different is nothing new; but to be outwitted will always remain totally unacceptable.

The negotiator must be aware of his relative power and negotiate a network that could allow him to change his power position at any time. Negotiation needs a strategy but it is in reality more of a continuous, adaptive process. Therefore, the successful negotiator carefully nourishes relationships, guards them jealously and secures their permanence through careful aftercare.

Networking within organisations

Establishing a sound network within a company has recently become easier, basically because of two variables: organisational size and technology. Because organisations worldwide have designed flatter structures, the key players within specific areas are more visible. Fundamental business science teaches that organisations are basically **political machines**, with those in control of the budget and structure probably the most potent political sources. Furthermore, technology has had a major impact. New technology not only speeds up processes, but it also renders companies more penetrable. It is therefore easier to make contact with key personnel due to the lack of 'buffer' personnel who kept them inaccessible in the past. Now one can gain access to such people more readily because of technology. Conference lines, cellular telephones and fax machines put any key decision maker within easy reach of outsiders, and also make for more personalised contact within the company. An intimate knowledge of the interpersonal power relationships between key players has led to an increase of political activity within companies.

Boundary spanning networking

Boundary spanning negotiation requires contact across boundaries. It requires high levels of trust, flexibility and visibility. More importantly, however, it requires a willingness to accept other people's perceptions and their relationships, and the ability to create order through the process of negotiation. The negotiator who works with key personnel from different companies must anticipate that there are also other stake holders. He must identify these interorganisational people of influence, as well as their motivations and attitudes. But above all else, interpersonal relationships are critical for effective networking.

This might imply that the effective network negotiator can identify, contact and secure the help of others for his own objectives. Since the present authors stress the role of ethics as the so-called 'politics of survival', it will be necessary to explain what is meant. This does not imply that we do not perceive the successful negotiator to be a soft target or without the will and means to realise his own objectives. It merely implies that a good negotiator never lies or uses undue coercion. The effective negotiator must realise that he can bring together two people who perceive their relationship to be mutually antagonistic, by making them aware of a greater mutual enemy, who could destroy them both. He could turn an adversary into a friend by making him aware of a dangerous parasitic party, or even make a small company aware that it may be the target of predation. However, the scrupulous negotiator realises the value of his privileged position and, whilst boundary spanning, he should never violate the relationship of **trust** at stake between himself and the relevant parties. A conflict of interest should always be declared.

A negotiation network is like a company — it should be expanded and used for the creation of wealth and order. It is not the shady world of espionage or a licence to spread discontent and malice. Any negotiator who does the latter, will soon lose the trust of others, and by definition his network. Maintaining a negotiation network requires hard work and diligence, drive and planning.

The process of negotiating a network
Establishing the network

Networking can be done on various levels within an organisation. It seems surprising to the present authors that so few companies have included it in their strategic planning. However, many organisations rely on external consultants or organisations to provide them with such strategic information.

The networking system starts with individuals whose boundaries span external information networks. Very few representatives in fact record what interpersonal contacts they have had, or accumulate data about those people and their products as well as their preferences and dislikes. This kind of information should be stored and centralised or disseminated as with any other strategic variable. However, since the process of negotiation for a corporation is a multiple impact process, i.e. many people on **multiple** occasions make **contact** on numerous issues and in many currencies, it is imperative that all information be assimilated in such a way that people have access to it and that it is transformed to suit the level at which it is required.

An example of data accumulation would be a retail representative recording all information elicited, on an electronic device, as soon as possible after a negotiation. Information would include details such as the name of the person contacted, his position in the channel of command, his personal preferences and dislikes, the success variables of the contact, the agreement detail, the grievances reported, the other people encountered, the time frames negotiated, financial aspects of the negotiation, and other people to whom he would like to introduce the contact, etc. This information can be disseminated to other representatives dealing with the same company and should be shared in matters of transfer, promotion, new appointments, etc.

On the operational or marketing level the information can be used for planning, timing and for focusing on strategic activity of a comparative nature: how do representatives compare on a visibility level; who needs what training; what are the critical success factors and problem areas of each product, etc. At top managerial level the information is vital for planning, trend analyses, and strategic, personal and corporate growth requirements.

Obviously this will require a corporate dedication to automate information management and to maximise its benefits at every level.

Establishing a network and technology

Computerisation has already been introduced into some sectors of the economy, like financial institutions, retail companies and outlets, dispatch and distribution. This tendency has developed to the point where products are electronically marked, priced, purchased and traded; in fact some sectors of the economy have moved into an almost perfect market where all information is shared. For example, insurance brokers have almost total access to personal files across companies. Thus the efficiency levels of companies are virtually identical but since no computers can replace **personal contact** for maximising effectiveness, that aspect should never be disregarded. Computerisation allows paperwork relating to facts and figures to be reduced, but the quality of personal services must be maintained.

Computers allow new forms of corporate control on virtually every level: location, time spent, volumes achieved, transfers assured and deliveries monitored from the point of ordering to the provision of requirements. Minimal training is required to utilise small portable computers, which are user friendly and buffered by a main computer. The risk for any company lies with its main computer: the shell is difficult to penetrate, but once inside, the rest is easily transferred and accessed from the outside. This book is not directed at computer risk management, but suffice it to say that any company which does not address the issue of electronic sabotage and risk, is naive. (See *Time Magazine,* August 21, 1995.)

Co-operation and networking

The whole aim of networking, both electronically and interpersonally, is to maximise co-operation and to turn potential critical conflict situations into situations of mutual benefit, efficiently and effectively. However, the strategic nature of all information should be scrutinised to assess risk.

Co-operation or helping behaviour is aimed at establishing mutually beneficial and comfortable relationships between companies and their employees, so that together they can create unexplored alternatives for growth. The existence of conflict and helping behaviour stimulate the creation of alternatives or new data and ideas. In the process, conflict is encouraged and turned into co-operative behaviour.

A strategy of co-operation is always best for continued growth, but it needs maintenance. Internationally, businesses explore activities such as co-operation with greater vigour than issues such as exploitation, or even competition. The main focus of strategic co-operation in business is for companies to find common ground, i.e. become more unified. Hence co-operation on economic, social, business, scientific and other levels provides the greatest and fastest means of growth. Networking has become an essential strategic planning tool — in traditional strategic formulations too much time was wasted in attempts to outdo competitors, as opposed to seeking **conjoint benefits** and growth.

Moreover, aggression is often encountered and one cannot wish it away. It merely promotes conflict without creating alternatives. When aggression is socialised, it becomes assertiveness, but within the context of co-operation. Again, one would be naive to assume that everyone can turn conflict into co-operation. Some will attempt to misuse the positive approach advocated by the present authors, and one will have to deal with this in the old, conventional way. But it should be quite evident that aggression cannot extract the positive elements of conflict in the long term. The truly effective negotiator will realise that ethics are vital to survival and growth.

Case 6.2

CONFLICT AND HUMOUR

John's anger

. . . John obviously doesn't like the attention and approval Peter enjoys. I can sense his restlessness. He is becoming fidgety and he is not listening at all when Jim asks him to pass the ashtray. He is quite alone in his opinion that the campaign should be countrywide.

'Sorry guys,' John begins, his voice on edge. 'If you carry on with this ridiculous proposal I'll report you to the boss. I know what David wants; it is not this!' He violently pushes his chair back and gets up as though he is about to leave.

I notice Jim's irritation with John. 'What a creep!' I wonder whether John overhears the whisper.

'David is crazy about Western Province rugby, John, he'll love the suggestion,' I quip. Everyone, except John, laughs in relief. Even John has to smile.

'Come on, John, you've got to help us with this, we need your input. The boss is sold on Maties and you know it.'

'I suppose you're right, but we have to include a six-month strategy in our proposal at least.'

'Yes, John, I believe that is a valid point . . .'

CONCLUSION

A negotiator should understand why conflict, aggression and escalating oppositional spirals occur. He should understand the frustration people suffer as a consequence of their individual needs, backgrounds and company position.

Negotiators should realise that dysfunctional conflict and aggressive behaviour could have a negative effect on reaching agreements and could unnecessarily cause groups to move further apart.

If negotiators understand the methods and skills they need to be effective and if they have the ability to counter conflict and aggression, they are more likely to achieve creative agreements of benefit to their organisation, their constituents, their families, their 'opponents', and themselves.

CHAPTER 7
Specialised Negotiation Areas

In this Chapter

❑ *Different kinds of negotiating situations*:
- The crisis situation
- Labour union negotiation
- International negotiation
- Intercultural negotiation

❑ Requirements and problems of specialised negotiations
❑ Strategies for dealing with specialised negotiations
❑ *Negotiation in South Africa:* Requirements and future developments

INTRODUCTION

No negotiating situation will be exactly like the previous one. An industrial manager will encounter many different negotiating situations in each day, week or month of his working life. Negotiating with an employee about arriving late at work could be followed by negotiation with an existing overseas supplier about possible expansion of the business. This could be succeeded by a small committee meeting where it may be of crucial importance to 'negotiate' about the approval of a new incentive bonus scheme for the organisation. Later during the day, managers may be faced with lawyers, departmental heads, bosses, environmental or welfare groups and/or government agents about various objectives.

After work, 'negotiation' could continue with children at home about their mediocre marks at school, their non-adherence to house rules or about their church attendance. With his wife he could be negotiating holiday plans or a family crisis. With the local garage he could be negotiating about the servicing of his car.

Many rules for achieving success could be applied to all of these situations. Some of these rules were discussed in the preceding chapters. Various negotiation situations place different demands on the negotiator and some could be extremely stressful and nerve-wracking. The following paragraphs will be devoted to the discussion of some 'unique' situations and could help negotiators when they approach similar scenarios in the future.

CRISIS BARGAINING

When reflecting on the history of South Africa since the early 1970s, it becomes apparent that a lot of movement has been achieved by the forces opposing the South African government through what can be described as methods related to **crisis bargaining**. Although it could be possible that, in future, crisis bargaining situations will occur less frequently in southern Africa, this method will, no doubt, still be used many times in the future due to the effectiveness thereof and the fact that people opposing the strategies of the crisis bargainer are often ill-equipped to handle the situation.

On studying the actions of 'expert' crisis bargainers from history dating back to Che Guevara and including Fidel Castro, Lenin, Stalin and the ANC, one can conclude that, from the position of the crisis bargainers, a certain pattern emerges:

❑ **The establishment of legitimacy**. For example: 'Why do we have to learn Afrikaans?' or 'Why should the land of the Boerevolk be given to the blacks?'

❑ **The polarisation of opposition**. For example: 'It is only the Afrikaner who wants us to learn Afrikaans at school', or 'It is only the National Party minority government that wants to give our land away.'

❑ **The expression of 'overkill' strategies**. For example: 'We will burn the school and kill the people', or 'We will leave no stone unturned, go to whatever length, including violence, to stop this fraudulent act by the government.'

❑ **Actions are chosen that are within the experience of the constituencies** of the bargainers. For example: The burning of their own schools, the destruction of symbols close to them, or: the detonation of a bomb at a school in a conservative area of Pretoria.

❑ **Actions are chosen that go outside the experience of the adversaries**. For example: Actions take place in the townships, or the main forces of action are concentrated in the conservative areas of the country, in towns such as Ventersdorp, Pretoria, and Pietersburg.

❑ **The maintenance of pressure on own constituencies**. For example: Threatening of own people, necklacing those who deviate from the main objectives, or character assassination of people who were seen as conservative and later change to become more liberal.

❑ **The selection of a target, the polarisation of it and the freezing of the target**. For example: Some years ago only Wimpy bars were selected for attacks and not any of the other fast-food chains; only Mr F W de Klerk is singled out for attacks and labelled a 'sell-out'.

❏ **The formation of a small-group defence line**. For example: The well-known Group of Ten in the townships in the early '70s; a small group of relative unknowns who were behind the conservative crisis actions of the early '90s.

❏ **Indirect negotiation amidst the maximum exposure of adversaries**. For example: When hostages are exposed, necklace murders televised, mass funerals staged while the individuals behind these events are not exposed themselves; infrequent deeds of terrorist action that are publicised widely.

❏ **Geographic, political and economic diversification**. For example: When actions are also taken to Sebokeng and other black townships; when the farmers 'revolt'; when bombs are detonated in places where no such action has taken place before, so as to give the impression of widespread action; and more 'organisations' are formed that are supposed to act on behalf of the conservative Afrikaner.

❏ **The emphasis on a symbolic martyrdom**. For example: Constant reference to the suffering of Sharpeville; the hunger strike of Mr Piet Rudolph in jail while ANC detainees are all freed.

❏ **A disorientation of constituencies to avoid fragmentation**. For example: Radio silence, no response to government challenges or questions from the press; when statements such as 'An injury to one is an injury to all' are made.

The question now arises as to how to **counter** these actions. Although there are many ways to counter the above, the following are some of the more important strategies. They are discussed in the same order as the above:

❏ **Delegitimisation (or delinking) of issues**. For example: When the government states: 'Afrikaans has never been a compulsory subject', or 'blacks have been given farms dating back to the times of President Paul Kruger and Dr Verwoerd.'

❏ **Integration of issues**. For example: Referring to 'we' constantly; referring to debates in parliament, with the opposition, about the issues at stake.

❏ **Expose overkill strategies for what they are**. For example: Publicise to the people why the schools are burned, why bombs are detonated and who is responsible.

❏ **Responses to actions within and outside the experience of the constituents**. Inform everyone in the country, keep within the experience range of all the citizens.

❏ **The affirmation of security**. For example: The relieving of pressure, the making of small political concessions.

❏ **The declaration of a willingness to negotiate and to generate alternatives**. When negotiation takes place, the ideal set-up would be to choose a **small group versus a small group** situation.

❏ An effort is made to **build relationships** while the **effective use of the media** should be investigated and **flexibility** should be demonstrated.

Hostage negotiation

Hostage negotiation is one specialised area of crisis bargaining where it is important to solve the crisis quickly (often within hours). Many articles have appeared on the problems of handling hostage negotiations, and a number of general rules on negotiating the release of hostages can be deduced. Abbott (1986:34–35) discussed the so-called **time-phase** model for hostage negotiation, based on a 'simple' kidnap operation. This model could be a yardstick for measuring the progress of negotiation or act as a guideline to negotiators on the handling of similar and more intricate hostage negotiations. The time-phase model emerged after Abbott studied the recurring pattern and sequences in thirteen successive operations by one hostage negotiating team. The sequential phases and their percentage of total operation time are as follows:

❏ Introduction — 15 %
❏ Demands — 50 %
❏ Impasse — 10 %
❏ Suicide — 10 %
❏ Surrender — 15 %

He divides crisis negotiation into the above five phases and concluded the following:

The introductory phase

This is a 'getting to know each other' process. Not much negotiation work is done during this period, according to Abbott. Considerable effort is also expended by the negotiator to find common ground with the suspect after a brief introduction of names and roles. The **common ground** can include things like both of them having dogs, both being married (or divorced), a shared dislike of certain people, and so on. Apart from the fact that it provides a wealth of useful information about the suspect that can be used later, it sometimes does help to establish a more comfortable and co-operative atmosphere. Then the next phase can begin.

The demand phase

This is, according to Abbott (1986:34), where most of the negotiating work is done. This phase is composed of two distinct parts: demands **made** and demands **met** or **refused**.

Demands made could be things like: 'Just go away', which is disregarded by most negotiators and could be followed by: 'Go to the boss about it'. Demands could include an escape vehicle, food, liquor, rifles, the presence of a friend or a loved one. It seems wise to compile a complete list of demands that are made in this regard. Abbott feels that the more demands, the more flexible the negotiating team's basis for negotiation, since a lot of time could be spent on each of the demands and variations thereof.

Abbott found that 60 % of the total demand phase is spent on **demands met or demands refused**. This is a very crucial stage of any hostage negotiation since, for the first time, a suspect could be given a 'no' answer. His frustration level and anger could easily begin to escalate at this point. The anger tends to be directed at both the situation in general and at the negotiator in particular. Negotiators can use the increased tension in many ways. By continuously 'going back to the boss' and having to return empty-handed on most of the demands, several things tend to happen:

❑ The suspect could start distrusting the negotiator.
❑ He could become more upset.
❑ He could start threatening absurd actions, with injury to the hostage or injury to anyone else within reach.
❑ There could be a breakdown of communication and a refusal to talk further.

The impasse phase

This phase refers to a long period of silence that is usually an extremely tense period following the previous phase. According to Abbott, the negotiators have a difficult decision to make at this stage. They could try to regain the attention of the suspect by shouting to him, calling him continuously, throwing stones at windows and so on. Much of the literature seems to favour keeping the suspect awake and agitated. It could be important for negotiators to consult experienced and more senior negotiators when deciding what to do. Abbott found, in most cases, that the suspect realises at this stage that his situation is hopeless and that there are no further demands to be made or compromises to be gained. This causes him to become depressed and to feel hopeless.

The suicide phase

According to Abbott, this phase has occurred in virtually every negotiation studied. Sometimes it is only a half-hearted threat on the part of the suspect, lasting only a few minutes; but more often it becomes a very serious, overriding issue. Skilful handling by the negotiator of the suspect at this point is imperative. There is a lot of material on the handling of suicidal patients and it could be useful to study some of these so as to be able to handle this stage with greater confidence. In summary, the negotiator could:

❏ Give the suspect some reason for hope.
❏ Suggest alternative actions that could help him get out of his predicament with the least damage to himself or his family.
❏ Talk about long-term future 'great' things that he could still achieve, if he could just overcome this 'temporary' setback.

The surrender phase

Abbott believes that the work of the negotiator usually becomes fairly straightforward in this phase. Yet time should be spent during the final stages of the 'deal', making sure that the suspect understands all the steps involved in the actual surrender process. Often suspects are calm and more positive during this stage. They are even relieved. On the side of the negotiators, there could still be a lot of anxiety for the tactical officer or police. The situation could still be highly explosive and should be handled with the greatest of care.

The phases almost always occur in the order presented. Rarely does an operation move from the introductory phase directly to the suicidal phase with nothing in between. Similarly, the impasse phase rarely comes before the demand phase. However, according to Abbott (1986 :35), not all the phases described in the model need to be present in a particular operation. One or more of them may be absent — except for the first and the last.

LABOUR UNION NEGOTIATION

The labour union movement differs substantially from country to country. In the last decade, since the legal recognition of labour unions in South Africa, management has had to face a revolution in collective bargaining.

Bargaining for wages

Initially the labour unions' priority was merely to bargain for better wages. Today their ambitions concern not only wages, but a far greater area, ranging from traditional wage benefits to maternity leave and pension participation.

However, it seems likely that **wages** will be the item of first and foremost priority in collective bargaining for some time to come. The inflation rate in South Africa has outstripped wage increases in recent years, with the result that real wages have fallen and that South African wage earners are now worse off than three years ago. Pressure on wages will probably remain high in the foreseeable future. Management will therefore have to face unions on a regular basis for many years to come.

Labour union negotiation is often seen as one of the most difficult types of negotiation that anyone could encounter.

The negotiation procedure

Piron (1988:77) believes that the first and foremost agreement that management should negotiate with labour unions should be the **negotiation procedure**. This procedure is one that sets out the way in which the negotiations should proceed to achieve a substantive agreement, or the renegotiation of the recognition agreement between management and the union, or both. In many ways the negotiation procedure can also be termed the **formalisation of the common ground** that exists between the parties at ground level; the common ground in this case being the way the parties are going to deal with each other in the future.

Because of the frequency with which both management and the union could in future refer to the negotiation procedure, it is imperative that it should be carefully designed, since loopholes in this agreement could have a huge financial impact on future agreements. The procedure referred to above will obviously be part of the recognition agreement between management and the union, and in many ways the most important part of that agreement. Piron (1988:77) believes that a procedural agreement should at least include the following:

❏ Management and union should preferably agree that they will negotiate on wages and conditions of employment on an **an-**

nual basis. It could be wise to include the month of the year in which the negotiation will take place, and how long it will last.

❏ The negotiation procedure can set out the specific **subjects** on which the company and the union will bargain. Taking into account industrial council limitations in this regard, parties could agree to bargain on:

- real as opposed to minimum wages, and
- minimum conditions of employment.

The disadvantage of having such a closed list is that it can easily lead to a dispute as to what is or is not a bargaining subject.

Where works councils or other bodies are involved in wage bargaining for employees who are **non-unionised**, provision must be made for the relationship between the unions and this representative body (or works council) in bargaining with management. For example, it could be agreed that the works council will be notified of all the demands made by the union during negotiation.

The nature of representation

The **number of negotiators** who will represent either side can be determined in the negotiation procedure. The number varies but, according to Piron, the limit is usually ten to twelve negotiators. From the management point of view, irrespective of the number of management representatives sitting at the bargaining table, an effective team of a maximum of three negotiators is often preferable. The number around the negotiation table is often one of the most complicated issues for the negotiators to handle.

From the union point of view, the **choice of negotiators** can present a problem, since many recognition agreements provide for wage bargaining by the shop stewards assisted by up to two full-time union officials, who are also often the chief spokesmen. When there are more shop stewards at the plant than can be accommodated in the negotiating team, it creates more problems for the union than for management, because the opportunity for disagreement within the union team is that much greater.

At the same time, if management bargains with the union team who frame themselves as **spokesmen** and not as **mandated representatives**, it can cause grave difficulties if the workforce later decides to dishonour the agreement after signing, by striking in support of new wage demands. Piron (1988:78) is of the opinion that it could be useful to record all bargaining on tape and to play the tape back to the workforce in the canteen at a later stage. The negotiators are sometimes left with no option but to negotiate in a room that is big enough to accommodate all the shop stewards. Frequent caucusing of spokesmen with the shop stewards could also, to some extent, help to overcome the problem of **mandate**. The problem of spokesmen is also aggravated if a number of plants in the company bargain with the management at the same time.

Dispute procedure

The agreement can also provide that, before either party can declare a dispute, three or even four bargaining meetings must be held, and no two of these meetings can, for example, be held on the same day. They can also state that, should no agreement be reached through these meetings, either party may declare a **dispute**, in which case the matter would be referred to whatever form of dispute settlement the parties have agreed upon. This could be:

❑ mediation,
❑ arbitration, or
❑ arbitration with mediation.

Should no agreement on wages and conditions of employment be reached at negotiation meetings with unions, the dispute arising out of these negotiations can be referred to the dispute procedure. The negotiation of a dispute procedure is one of the most important parts of the recognition agreement. In this section, agreement is reached on the mechanisms that are available for the settlement of disputes. The dispute procedure could involve a series of processes that are agreed upon and are designed to resolve all types of disputes between the parties.

Legalising agreements

Should **agreements** be reached at any of the collective bargaining meetings, provision should be made to reduce the agreement to **writing**. These agreements can then become binding on the parties. The fact that the agreement becomes binding on the parties does not mean, however, that it automatically becomes binding on the employees. Piron (1988:80) believes that it is safer, from a legal point of view, for management to undertake to incorporate the terms of the collective agreement into the contract of employment of each individual union member.

Management–worker relationships

Negotiation largely depends for its effectiveness on the good faith of both parties. If parties come to the bargaining table with the intention of not reaching an agreement, the negotiating procedure will become an empty shell. It is, therefore, important for management to realise that negotiation with unions does not start at the negotiating table, but starts long before within the company, every day of the year where management deals with workers and a **relationship** is established and 'negotiated'.

Management attitude

Piron (1988:128) believes that one of the major problems that has confronted recognition relationships is one that is almost absurd in its simplicity but which creates a vast number of problems in practice, namely the meaning of the word **negotiation**. He believes that in the negotiation of a recognition relationship, the parties undertake to negotiate not only the relationship, but many substantive matters. The result has been that, whilst a number of management teams have negotiated recognition relationships in good faith, they have not really appreciated the meaning of the term **negotiate**. The attitude of some management teams towards substantive negotiation has been one of **consultation** rather than negotiation. Some managers have felt that if they explain the economic climate in the country and the economic position of the company, this explanation justifies an acceptance by the union of management's proposals. Union officials often find themselves having to listen to 'lectures' from management around the table. Management has then sometimes been bewildered by the union's response which has generally been one of distrust, disappointment and frustration.

The problem of a lack of understanding amongst managers of the true meaning of the term 'to negotiate' has been compounded by the fact that a number of unions have made demands for very significant wage increases; so much so that demands for increases of 60 % or more across the board have not been infrequent (Piron 1988:129). One result of these high demands has been that some managements have not taken them seriously, thinking them too preposterous for serious consideration. Consequently management commitment to the negotiation process has declined.

Decision making versus negotiation

The lack of understanding of the term 'to negotiate' extends to the side of emergent union members and especially shop stewards. They seem to confuse the concepts of negotiation and **decision making**. For example, although the line between negotiation and consultation is thinly drawn, it would appear that a number of shop stewards overemphasise the role of negotiation in the implementation of, for example, disciplinary procedures, and do not take into account the differences between negotiation, consultation and representation of a union member in a disciplinary enquiry.

Relationships and agreements

It is also felt by some authors (Nierenberg 1973:228) that some negotiators do not understand the fact that the **relationship** of the parties should almost always be superior to the agreement. Management/labour problems often stem from the literal interpretation of a **contract**. The spirit of the agreement is often much more important than the agreement itself. When a satisfactory relationship has been established, the written contract is merely incidental.

The written contract is there only to prevent memory from failing and confusion from occurring.

In labour union negotiation, possibly more than in any other area of negotiation, it is of the utmost importance that the relationship between parties is given primary attention. Management should refrain in all instances from indulging in actions that could sever this relationship. The most important virtues, when negotiating with unions, seem to be **patience**, **empathy** and real **concern** for the wellbeing of individuals and the organisation. Besides this, those who negotiate with labour unions should especially refrain from using the word 'I' instead of 'us', and they should have excellent information on the personal and financial needs of their party and their opposition. They should understand the 'small politics' in their own and the other side. They should, most importantly, have total control over their emotions and, regardless of any utterance or actions by the union, should remain calm and never lose control of themselves.

Case 7.1

CRISIS WITH THE UNION

Mercedes dispute: a case of 'factory tribalism'?

On August 16, about 200 workers occupied the plant, without following procedures, over demands that the company pull out of the car industry's national bargaining forum (NBF) and bargain inhouse.

The plant remains closed, despite the dismissal and subsequent eviction of the workers in a police raid last weekend, and the company says it will not reopen until certain key concerns have been addressed in negotiation with NUMSA.

Management wants the union's assurances that the 'problem relating to Mercedes's participation in the NBF' has been resolved. But it is also looking for an agreement on a 'practical process to remove the problems impacting on the growth and viability of the company'.

Alleging that the dispute is costing it R13 million a day, management has bluntly warned that its future in South Africa is at stake . . .

... As a condition for joining the NBF, employers stipulated that they would bargain centrally for real wages and that plant negotiations would only take place by agreement. The union agreed because single-tier bargaining made sense where real, rather than minimum pay, was at issue, and in an industry comprising a handful of large employers with similar resources.

But the Mercedes rebels believe they can clinch a more favourable deal for themselves — a R3,50 an hour figure has been mentioned — in talks with their own management.

NUMSA accepts that plant bargaining can bring short-term gains. 'But we explained to members that a national forum is a more stable floor for wages. If there is only bargaining at the plant, levels can fluctuate substantially,' said Fanaroff ...

Drew Forrest, *Weekly Mail*, 13 September 1990.

INTERNATIONAL NEGOTIATIONS

Negotiating has a basic structure the world over, but the practical principles — how and when things should be done — vary from business culture to business culture. What might be regarded as a necessary display of aggressive pricing in the United States could be viewed as the ultimate in bad manners in Saudi Arabia, while the Japanese may react to your personal manner and its associated mannerisms in an entirely different way than would Russian trade officials. What is good for business and the country in Britain might be regarded as the height of inefficiency in Germany. Let us consider some elements of negotiation in some of the more important trading centres of the world today.

Negotiating in the United States of America

Americans are often known as the world's **fastest** dealers. They operate as if there were no tomorrow and very little left of today. They rush in and out where angels have not even thought about treading (Kennedy 1987:83).

Americans move fast ...

This makes for a major adjustment crisis when a negotiator from Chicago meets a negotiator from almost anywhere else. In dealings with Americans you most certainly must speed up, if only a little — how much depends on which of you wants the deal the most. Two Americans making a deal are a picture of haste — their language reflects their moves: 'Make it snappy', 'Jump to it', 'What are we waiting for?', 'Have we got a deal, or don't we have a deal?'

So, being in a hurry seems to impress peers in the United States of America. Success is synonymous with **pace**. The entire nation seems to be extremely **time conscious**, and, in America, wasting time is viewed as wasting life itself.

Americans think big . . .

Because of the very size of the United States market, people seem to think big and solve things in big ways. For negotiators from small countries it is often difficult to prove to Americans that they could supply the quantities and volumes expected by their American partners.

On the critical side one should state that, although they seem to like to get involved in 'big' deals, **quality** sometimes suffers in the process. There are often huge delays and sometimes a lack of attention to detail is evident.

Americans and the law . . .

Any individual or company that has the intention of negotiating in America should be aware of the importance of the **legal profession** in the USA. Handling grievances, complaining, getting refunds, **suing** the suppliers and generally fighting for your rights are all par for the course in American negotiating. The expectation is that sooner or later deals will go wrong in some way, because making deals faster means making more mistakes.

The American negotiator operates in a world of prepared contracts or established systems of doing business. They tend to protect themselves via many **legal ploys**. A plethora of preprinted forms exist that require your signature to get things done. It's a protective device to make sure that you have signed away your rights (or, at least have had them severely curtailed). For this reason negotiators should read paperwork very carefully — and take their time about it. If there is any disagreement about anything, the negotiators should refuse to sign until it is changed. According to Kennedy (1987:89) the impression that you cannot change a printed form, is in fact a form of American intimidation. Therefore they will tell you that this or that 'rule' applies to delivery, minimum orders, payments and so on. They have the biggest and most prosperous legal system in the world.

Americans and power . . .

Americans seem to love to impress their foreign counterparts with just how powerful they are. They do this by emphasising the size of their company — 'the biggest in California' — in terms of **market share**, billion-dollar sales or numbers of employees. Because of the size of the American market they also tend to have a monopolistic attitude to doing business; they believe, and get you to believe, that you need them more than they need you.

Americans and CVs . . .

It could be important for individuals travelling in the United States of America to keep master copies of their curricula vitae (CV) ready in their briefcases. Americans like to know with whom they are dealing. The role of **testimonials** seems to be important in the United States. These testimonials are often inflated pictures of themselves. When one enters an American's office, one is often struck by how many certificates, letters of recommendation, pictures in the presence of top politicians and suchlike are displayed. It could therefore be to the benefit of the negotiator to have similar testimonials at hand.

Americans and competitiveness . . .

Even in their approach to negotiating, Americans are obsessed with 'winning'. Theirs is a land of **winners** and **losers**. For the winners, nothing is too good; for the losers, there is nothing. Success breeds success, they believe. Tough language and tough modes of expression represent that **competitive** edge which seems to characterise all Americans. Therefore (according to Kennedy 1987:94), you will get the business if you can bring professionalism into your presentation. It is very important to have an effective presentation of your case ready at all times. This must reflect the sheer excellence of your quality control, realistic prices that suit their market philosophy, and the proven ability to deliver the quantities you promised.

Negotiating in Japan

Japanese businessmen have a well-earned reputation for being formidable negotiators. The fact that Japanese business has expanded worldwide in the last forty years to the extent that they have become one of the world's major exporting countries, is sufficient proof of their ability to establish themselves and their products.

Perhaps the most noticeable characteristic of Japanese negotiation is the tendency to **personalise** business relationships. They want to get to know the representative of the other company before agreeing to do business with him. This personalising takes many forms:

❏ The overseas agent may have to find a **go-between** who can vouch for his integrity.

❏ Endless preliminary get-togethers, spanning many months, may take place before substantive exchanges get underway. During these early meetings, the Japanese are known to ask innumerable **questions** that appear to have little or no relevance to the business at hand.

The foreign businessperson must remember that in Japan, time spent cultivating a **relationship** is not wasted; it may well yield rich dividends. Indeed, developing a personal relationship may well be more important than the terms being negotiated.

The Japanese personalise their business dealings in part because they view an impersonal relationship as almost **sordid**. They do not feel comfortable dwelling on the profits to be made. They shun any overt displays of a mercenary spirit.

The Japanese develop their personalised relationships with business partners as a way of making sure they will meet their **obligations**. Japanese relationships, in business and elsewhere, are usually not compartmentalised but widely encompassing. Their managers, for example, often display an interest in their workers' private lives that goes far beyond anything comparable in South Africa. While this concern may be sincere, it is at the same time an attempt to obtain the worker's loyalty, co-operation and diligence.

Spoelstra (1981) classified a number of important variables relating to negotiation in Japan. These should at least be considered by foreigners on their visits to that country.

Nemawashi

The initial concern for all negotiators visiting Japan should be to establish a **relationship**. This would involve many hours of ground work (*nemawashi*) and repetitive meetings through which trust, essential in a long-term relationship, will be established.

Honne to tatemae

Honne refers to the 'real' us, the 'real' truth. *Tatemae* refers to the **face** we show to the outside world, the one we would like them to believe to be representative of us. Negotiators will have to accept that they will have to face the *tatemae* side of the Japanese, and only after a long build-up and *nemawashi* (ground work) will they be able to break through to the *honne* of Japanese corporate and individual behaviour.

Osaeru

This refers to the ability to control yourself at all times. For many religious, cultural and educational reasons the Japanese have a high regard for **emotional self-control**, thus foreigners often complain that they cannot understand Japanese facial expressions and body movements. The Japanese seem to be totally without emotion around the negotiating table. This is, however, the attempt of an individual, who is possibly as emotional as anyone else, to control his emotions at all times on behalf of the organisation that he represents. The foreigner must remember that the Japanese have had training in emotional control since childhood and are possibly much better at this than their foreign counterparts.

Ringi

Foreigners visiting Japan would be well advised to read more on the operation of a Japanese organisation and the way that decisions are made. The *ringi* system refers to the **decision-making** system that is used within Japanese organisations. Because of the concept of employee ownership that is much more encompassing than is found in the West, Japanese will have to **consult** many more people before a decision is made. This system, in fact, means that no decision can be made without the consent of a large number of individuals. So, when they are pushed for a decision around the negotiating table, the Japanese cannot, even if they would like to, announce certain decisions and agreements without due consultation with every single other employee that is affected in the process.

Nintai

Because of the above, and for many other reasons, it is imperative that foreigners use the utmost **patience** (*nintai*) when they are in Japan — patience in waiting for reactions when Japanese negotiators have to go back to their respective organisations to reach decisions; patience in waiting for answers; patience in establishing long-term relationships. Patience is often said to be the most valued virtue that any individual could possess in Japanese society.

Politeness

There are certain minimum rules of politeness that foreigners should adhere to at all times. They could include the following:

❑ *Meishi* (business cards). No foreigner can visit Japan without an ample stock of business cards that have a description of his role and identity, company and basic company information. At each first meeting with a Japanese person it will be expected that business cards will be exchanged. If these business cards could be printed in Japanese on the one side, it would smooth relationships even further.

❑ *Ojigi* (the bow). Japanese have a 'no-touch' culture. Individuals seldom touch each other in greeting. Yet when foreign businessmen visit Japan, local businessmen will probably not mind shaking hands with them. When observing the Japanese team it could be of value for negotiators to watch the depth of the bow, which will indicate the **seniority** of the individual in the team. Another variable that indicates seniority is age. Although Japanese ages are difficult to guess, one can accept that, because of the seniority promotion system that is still used in most Japanese companies, the oldest person will also be the most senior in the group and will possibly have to be addressed first.

❑ *Omiyage* (presents). Japanese are keen givers of presents. Foreigners are well advised to take many small presents with them. The wrapping of the presents is possibly of more importance than the present itself, so care should be taken that they are perfectly wrapped. **Presents** are normally always handed out at the beginning of luncheons or meetings with the Japanese and not at the end, as is sometimes the practice in Western countries.

It should be stated that no individual visiting a foreign country is supposed to become exactly like the people of the country. It is accepted in all countries that **foreigners will behave slightly differently**. Yet there are limits to the extent to which these differences will be accepted. The same goes for Japan. If you are the visitor you should be sensitive to your host's needs and wishes. Sensitivity to the rules of politeness is always important in negotiation. In cross-cultural negotiation this can be the cause of many misunderstandings and even the break-off of relationships.

Verbosity versus listening
Japanese culture seems to tend to favour silence. Listening behaviour and the asking of questions rather than the making of many

statements is favoured. Being verbose and frequently interrupting the speaker is not highly regarded.

Collapsing power

As was stated in previous chapters, the Japanese tend always to approach negotiation from an **inferior** power base. They will often use apology, statements of weakness and suffering, since these seem to be virtues in Japanese culture.

Information

Good information on both yourself and the other side is one of the core elements of successful negotiation in Japan. Smith (1989) refers to the value of information in his many dealings with Japan. Whilst representing companies in the South African coal industry, he observed that Japanese negotiators, in an initial negotiation, often had more information on the costing and financial affairs of South African mines than the South African representatives themselves. One can imagine what a tremendous advantage the Japanese negotiators had around the negotiating table under those circumstances.

Lawyers and contracts

In Japan, going to court is usually not a realistic alternative when conflict develops between two companies. Moreover, the Japanese do not have a history of looking to the law for a solution to their differences. Japanese companies prefer contracts that are short and vague. As conditions change the terms are altered accordingly. In the West, contractual obligations are precisely spelt out. Although Western companies renegotiate agreements with one another, this practice is not common. The Japanese seem to accept that international business contracts will have to be long and detailed, but they feel more comfortable with a **flexible** arrangement. Too much emphasis on legal matters, contracts, or lawyers could even be regarded as an **insult** in Japan.

Subtlety

The Japanese often like to use **indirect** negotiation rather than a direct approach. It could, in some cases, even be regarded as impolite to bring up some issues directly at the negotiation table.

> A good example was when Mr Nelson Mandela visited Japan a few years ago and, without the Japanese expecting it, requested from the Japanese parliament a donation of R25 million to the ANC. In many other countries Mr Mandela had uttered similar requests in public and this had been acceptable, but in Japan it was virtually regarded as an 'insult' and it generated a lot of unfortunate publicity for Mr Mandela and the ANC.

Body language

Foreigners must accept that Japanese body movements are different from those they themselves use. They should be careful not to draw undue conclusions from any movements made by the Japanese. During negotiations, the Japanese tend to keep their hands totally **still**, do not stare or make direct eye contact with individuals on the other side of the table, and many possibly even take up much less **space** at the table than their Western counterparts. The Japanese buffer zones are smaller than those of most Westerners, but at the same time they believe that staring into the eyes of the opposition is impolite. Then again, large movements with the hands could be regarded as hostile.

Interpreters

In Japan it could be wise to bring and pay for your own interpreters during negotiations, since there could otherwise be many misunderstandings. It is important to set out detailed points and clear objectives that are to be discussed when visiting Japan, and to give them to your Japanese counterparts so that they can be well prepared. They do not seem to like surprises when negotiating.

The absence of 'no'

A long-term and usually 'win–win' approach to virtually all negotiation is emphasised by the fact that the Japanese rarely come out with a straight 'no' answer. When a Japanese businessman deliberates by drawing breath through his teeth and saying: *'Saa'* or

'Muzukashii da na . . .' ('It's difficult') one can usually interpret it as a negative answer. When the Japanese say: *'Hai'* ('Yes') the foreigner should never accept that the 'Hai', which according to the dictionary means 'Yes', actually means 'Yes' in the Western sense. It possibly only means 'Yes, I have heard you', and not that it is acceptable in terms of an agreement.

Short-term visitors are often misled in Japan. They will present their ideas, and assuming an agreement has been reached, return home. The local representative will then have to find out whether an agreement was in fact reached, or whether it was just an **impression** given by the Japanese firm to avoid embarrassment and to retain **face**. In effect, the Japanese tell people what they want to hear, and few foreigners are able to discern their true reactions to a proposal.

Entertainment

The Japanese like to entertain their visitors. Sometimes it is suspected that they prolong the entertainment and will only negotiate on the last day of the foreigner's visit so that he has to lower his bases to at least take some form of agreement back home. Yet entertainment in itself is an important feature of Japanese negotiation. The Japanese are extremely proud of their whole service and entertainment industry, and the restaurants are one of the most outstanding features of a visit to Japan. Foreigners should, as far as possible, try to refrain at all times, from criticising the food. The best policy is to compliment Japanese food when necessary and to avoid expressing any criticism of Japanese society, culture, food or environment. This will help to establish a healthy relationship.

It is quite possible that the above characteristics, and some others that the Japanese possess, have so adequately equipped them that they have been able to establish themselves firmly in the international market.

Case 7.2

INTERNATIONAL 'GOOD FAITH'

TOKYO — Chrysler Corp is to become the first of the US Big Three car manufacturers to take control of its distributor in Japan, a company spokesman said yesterday.

The announcement that Chrysler will take over Seibu Motor Sales Co. Ltd., a dealership belonging to the Seibu-Saison group, came as a trade war with the United States loomed over access to Japan's car market.

The United States and Japan are holding talks in Geneva and have set a deadline of midnight tonight for an agreement on access to US cars and spare parts to the Japanese market.

The US industry maintains that unfair barriers are hurting foreign autos and auto parts sales in the Japanese market, and thus threatens 100 % tariffs against 13 models of Japanese luxury cars. The main issue in the talks revolve around the question of dealerships for US models in Japan, as well as increased purchase of parts by Japanese manufacturers, and the replacement parts market.

'Yes, Japan is largely a closed and protected market, but we see this transaction as a "good faith" step in the light of the trade issues facing Japan and the United States,' said Denis Root, vice president of Chrysler International Corporation, and general manager for its Asian-Pacific operation.

Mr Root said the timing of the announcement and the Geneva car talks, at which neither side has expressed optimism, was coincidental 'even if it may seem hard to believe'.

Chrysler's scheme for increasing its share in the world's second largest market will see the company first increase its stake in Chrysler Japan Sales Ltd., its importing firm, from 15 % to 70 %. 'It will then buy Seibu Motor Sales, which will have merged with the importer, currently controlled by J Osawa and Co. Ltd., another Seibu-Saison group company,' the spokesman said.

Chrysler estimates that the plan will cost more than $100 million. It will then control 10 car showrooms and 108 franchise dealers, as well as technical installations. The American concern also plans to set up a spare parts centre that will work closely with Chrysler's new regional logistics centre in Singapore.

Mr Root said Chrysler 'intends to start knocking on doors' in coming days to further increase its commercial network. He said the aim was to have 500 concessions by the year 2000 and to have sales of 100 000 units a year. Chrysler, which also distributes its cars in Japan through some Honda dealers, sold 13 600 vehicles last year.

Daily Dispatch, 28 June 1995.

Negotiating in Europe

Many changes are occurring in Europe. From 1992, through the expansion of the EEC (European Economic Community), many previous difficulties in terms of borders and control disappeared for foreigners doing business in Europe. However, there will still be many features that are unique to each of the cultures present in Europe that will not change that quickly or even at all. In Europe the negotiator should always be aware of the history of each of the countries and also its likes and dislikes in terms of the other nationalities in that part of the world.

The Germans

With the disappearance of the border between East and West Germany there are many new challenges in both these parts of Germany. Business negotiation can possibly be expected to be slightly different depending on which part of Germany the negotiator finds himself in. In most parts of Germany the negotiator can expect efficiency in the technical sphere and also in all the aspects related to the arrangements of a foreigner visiting that country.

The Germans have a sense of **superior quality**, so you will have to convince them that you are able to meet the standards that they require. It is not unnatural to expect them to insist on detailed information about the organisation that you represent. They will want to know, for example, just how financially sound your company is and how your proposal affects that soundness.

In financial matters they are extremely **conservative** and are risk-averse. The Germans can, therefore, be expected to be extremely cautious about propositions that leave them exposed to high risk of loss.

The Germans seem to invest in sound projects, using sound finance, with **sound prospects** of getting a profitable return, and they choose to work with companies abroad if those companies have something to offer which cannot be acquired locally and are unlikely to jeopardise the commercial strengths of their company. During negotiations the Germans will normally insist on strict adherence to delivery promises to meet their own highly disciplined production schedules. They will insist that you agree to tight penalty clauses on top of even tighter delivery promises in order to get the business. To cover themselves they may even demand a generous warranty period for your product, plus extensive credit in anticipated compensation for failure to meet them on this.

They are seen as **hard bargainers**, yet they are able to create extremely pleasant surroundings, with beautiful rooms and beautiful scenery in which to negotiate. The Germans are normally extremely formal and professional in their relationships and expect the same from you. They prefer not to be called by their first names, but rather as 'Herr Schmidt' or 'Dr Schmidt'. They are conservative in terms of dress (similar to the Japanese).

The one thing negotiators do not have to worry about in Germany is getting paid, provided that the terms of the contract are met. Germans are **punctilious** in their business affairs, formal in their relationships and generally very competitive in their outlook.

The French

If you negotiate with the French it is likely that the negotiation will take place in the French language, even if the French negotiator speaks perfect English. They seldom make any concession on this, unless they happen to be abroad or need your business badly. So, if the French negotiator speaks to you in English, you have probably received the biggest concession you are likely to get that day (Kennedy 1987:142).

The French are not known for being very punctual. They do not always turn up at the agreed time. In social matters, such as a formal dinner, there is an informal convention that the more important the chief guest, the later he or she will turn up — so if you are invited to dinner with the company president you can expect to start eating about thirty minutes late.

According to Kennedy, the French have no compunction about taking advantage of you in the negotiation if they have the economic leverage to do so. They will hold you strictly to the deal and nothing but the deal, as long as it suits them. If it does not, they will breach the deal and defy you to stop them. Therefore you must examine the contract carefully.

Relationships with the French must be entered into on a long-term basis before you get the 'normal' amount of goodwill common to relationships with others. If you can establish a good rapport with a French company over many years and can trade to mutual advantage without the blessing of accidental upsets, then you will find an extremely compatible partner. They might even warm to you socially and the pay-off that follows in terms of good food, great wine and lovely weather will make the 'atrocities' of the past well worth enduring (Kennedy 1987:143).

The Italians

If the French can be exasperating with their lack of punctuality at formal dinners, the Italians are even worse. They are by far the least punctual people in Europe, that is, assuming they turn up at all.

Italian business leaders are frightfully autocratic when it comes to dealing with subordinates within their own organisation and not much more democratic when dealing with outsiders. Their organisations relish protocol and status and they never accept an insult lying down. They are, however, always extremely charming about everything they do, even when telling you 'no'.

The Italians have a **volatile** temperament. They will, however, accept that you could also lose your temper for a short period of time. Business negotiators tend to dress smartly, groom themselves neatly and occupy modern, well-equipped offices. They make entrances and exits with a flourish, eat and drink well (but not excessively) and talk about their families with pride (Kennedy 1987:144).

The Dutch

The Dutch, especially the older generation, are ultraclean and orderly and they like everything in business to be the same. Because nobody else speaks their language, the Dutch speak many other languages and are very good **linguists**. Almost everybody

you meet will speak English and/or German, which makes negotiation much easier.

In some respects the Dutch are regarded as a little bit hard-
headed and sometimes even a trifle ruthless when given their way.

The British

The British have a wholly justified reputation for one business trait
above all others: they have a bad record for **late delivery** of almost
every product they produce. This is the single most consistent
complaint of foreign importers of British goods and it is heard right
across the world, according to Kennedy.

The English have a reputation for being gentlemen (generally
very honest in their dealings, even when things go against them),
though for the most part they are said to be merely amateurs. More
than 80 % of British managers, for instance, are totally unqualified
— only 7 % have university degrees. Their approach to business
is well short of professional standards and they compare badly with
overseas executives. This means that they appear at negotiations
poorly prepared, can be inflexible in the critical phases and do not
exert much energy. Many of the high-profile, successful English
entrepreneurs are not native-born (Robert Maxwell, Tiny Row-
lands, Charles Forte, Rupert Murdoch, to name a few).

Amateurism in business management is seen in the stubborn-
ness of British negotiators — an almost 'take it or leave it' attitude.
No wonder so many traditional businesses have succumbed to
takeovers and reorganisation from entrepreneurs who have understood the changing markets of Europe and are ready to try something new.

The Russians

Although Russia is not really part of Europe, it has, of late, moved
much closer to Europe after its policy of liberalising its markets.
Soviet trade negotiators are **professionals**, not enthusiastic amateurs. They prepare thoroughly, are well briefed, and their internal
systems compel them to act in ways that force you to disclose a

great deal more than is normal in Western negotiations, especially about the technical aspects of the products involved.

The Russian negotiator's obsession with **technical data** is not surprising if the industrial and political structure of his society is taken into account.

Many Russian officials are charged with checking the suitability, reliability and quality of purchases, and they take full responsibility for their decisions. Hence, they are careful; they work not according to hunches and entrepreneurial initiative but are risk-averse and routine-minded. In other words, they check everything and require evidence of this for their records. These records can be used by other committees whose sole job it is to see that everything has been checked.

Negotiations are likely to be divided into two stages: First, an assessment of the level of **technical** advancement of the product you are selling and what commitments they can extract from you in these qualifying negotiations, and second, the negotiation of the **terms** under which you will trade (Kennedy 1987:34).

With the liberalisation and the opening of markets that used to be closed to the Western world, such as those in the CIS, China and Korea, many more opportunities for business negotiations have arisen worldwide. There are hundreds of cultures and nations around the world, each with its own value system, attitudes and negotiating behaviour. Each has its own language and different ideas on what is good or bad, and what is polite and impolite. The discussion of the few countries and peoples above is just a small indication of some of the differences that could be encountered in those countries. There are many more. The professional negotiator will, before visiting any new country or culture, equip himself with sufficient knowledge of his opponents so that he can deal with them with insight, sensitivity and confidence.

INTERCULTURAL NEGOTIATION IN SOUTHERN AFRICA

South Africa is a multicultural community. More than ten different home languages are used within the boundaries of South Africa.

Many different cultures with varying values and attitudes live side by side in this part of the world.

After the dismantling of apartheid there are more opportunities to meet, to deal and to negotiate with people from different cultures. One can expect that the business and organisational world will, to a larger extent, become **multicultural** in its make-up. This requires that individuals become much more sensitive to the needs, habits, value systems and lifestyles of peoples from different cultures. The old 'colonial' attitudes are changing drastically in this process.

Many misunderstandings occur due to misinterpreted actions of people from other cultures. There are a number of postulates regarding cultural differences in southern Africa. Let us consider some of them and their possible impact on a negotiation strategy.

It is often stated that people of Africa have a different attitude to **time** and the use of time than those of European descent. The phrase 'African time' is often used in day-to-day discussions, possibly referring to a tendency of some individuals to be less constrained by deadlines and appointments. Those who negotiate with labour unions have also reported that managers will have to get used to long time delays and drawn out discussions about trivial topics in labour union negotiations, due to a lack of urgency on the part of African workers. Negotiators will possibly have to adapt by becoming much more patient in situations where there could be a difference in time perspective.

It has been postulated that some groups in South Africa have a much shorter time-frame than others. They tend to think only a few days or weeks ahead in time, where Europeans have a much longer time perspective and can plan years ahead with ease. This postulate may be devoid of any truth and may, in fact, be related to personal wealth and other factors. Yet, if there is a huge difference in the personal incomes of individuals around the table, it is possible that those with lower incomes will have a shorter time perspective than those with higher incomes.

There seems to be a tendency for more **consultation** in decision making amongst some cultures in southern Africa. Spoelstra

(1981) found differences (between two worker groups, close to Pretoria) in their tendency to consult others in decision making. Some writers refer to the well-known *kgotla* system amongst some southern African indigenous groups where, for example, decisions are not made until all the members of the 'extended family' have been consulted. The same attitude extends to business and this system contrasts with 'American-based' management styles which tend to display much more centralised and individualised decision making.

Some cultures in Africa will **behave differently** to European and Indian cultures. For example, some groups totally avoid eye contact during interpersonal talks with individuals from other cultures. They believe that direct eye contact, or staring into the eyes of other parties in close interpersonal encounters, is impolite. Some individuals, not understanding this, could feel that an individual who avoids eye contact is behaving suspiciously, is lying or cannot be trusted.

Similar to the above postulate on **eye contact**, some cultures believe that it is polite for a man to **enter a door** before a woman or before a guest. This apparently comes from the tradition that the man walks into danger first to protect those who follow. It is a sign of politeness amongst some South African cultures. Many individuals have misconstrued this behaviour because they have not understood the underlying reason for it. They have seen it as impolite, whilst it is in fact the opposite.

Handshaking is also seen differently by some African cultures. To some, it is advantageous to have a firm handshake, while to others, the handshake must be 'soft'. Recently it has even become fashionable amongst certain urban Africans to use three repetitive handshakes when greeting another. The touching of hands is therefore prolonged much longer than it used to be. For some it is an unsettling experience to be touched for that long and also with a hand that is not firm. Some groups seem to think that this is the polite way of shaking hands, since it is an indication of empathy and a lack of aggression. For some it also indicates a social closeness to the party that is greeted in this way.

Some southern African cultures often approach negotiation from an **inferior status position**, addressing the other side in an extremely polite manner. This could be a result of the suppression experienced during the colonial era of South Africa. Yet, regardless of the reason, negotiators sometimes have difficulty coping with this inferior status position and tend to make larger concessions than normal when faced with such a situation.

It is postulated that rural people especially have a higher regard for age than Europeans do. This **respect for age** could also be the result of the social make-up of some cultures in South Africa. Some individuals seem to be much less concerned with age differences around a table. It could, therefore, be regarded as highly impolite if someone from a different language group addresses an older man from another group in a derogatory way. Extreme politeness to an older person by someone from another culture could be construed by some as the keeping of **distance**, while in fact it might be showing respect for his age.

It is sometimes believed that a similar value system such as the *'honne to tatemae'* of the Japanese culture exists amongst some South African cultures; in other words, that it is acceptable to have a **face** that you show to the **outside world** (that could even be construed as lying) and another **true face** which you do not normally show to the outside world. If this postulate is true, it would, in fact, mean that Africans could sometimes be expected to 'lie' at the negotiating table as long as it is acceptable to the group they represent. It could even be regarded as polite and the right thing to do regardless of whether it may, in fact, be 'illegal' in terms of some Western laws.

Because of years of discrimination, it could be that some South African cultures are extremely conscious of being regarded as 'second class citizens'. Negotiators should be sensitive to this feeling so as to be able to establish a sound common ground with the 'other side' of the table. This will include the way that individuals are addressed during negotiation. In the past managers were addressed as 'Mr' or 'Mrs', or even 'Baas' (Afrikaans for 'Master') or 'Sir', but seldom by their first names, while black workers, on the other hand, were commonly addressed by their first names. It could be important for negotiators to make sure that individuals are addressed in exactly the same way during any intercultural interpersonal discussion. It could be important, in terms of the rules of parity, to insist that exactly the same address system is used by everyone. In the case of names that are difficult to pronounce, those who are to use them should prepare themselves in advance, before the negotiation, so that they can pronounce and remember them well.

The **legal contract** is a Western vehicle that was largely brought to this country by the British. One can expect that local cultures will not regard contracts with the same amount of trust as European companies dealing with other European companies. It is therefore postulated that the establishment of relationships is often much more important than what is stated in the **contract**, when dealing with 'local' cultures in southern Africa.

Because of many years of separation between cultural groups, negotiators must be aware of many **stereotypes** that exist. Since most stereotypes are incorrect, teams should evaluate their own stereotypes about the other side and determine whether there is any truth in them at all. Stereotypes prevent individuals from listening to the other side properly and could cause undue and undesirable aggressive reactions.

One can also expect that the **'body language'** of different cultures, although their members all live in the same country, could be quite different. Some groups touch their faces with greater frequency than others, they cover their eyes or mouths more frequently, have different eating habits, express different likes and dislikes, and are sometimes less direct in the expression of their wishes. Negotiators should be aware of some of these differences and it could be of value to acquire some information from anthropological sources on the cultures and individuals they are about to face.

It is accepted that a lot of changes have taken place in recent years in southern Africa. There are even some who believe that people from different cultures have moved much closer together and are, to a large extent (especially in the case of urbanised people), accepting value systems that are much closer to 'American values' than to their traditional values. Some urbanised Africans would like to be, and even insist on being treated in exactly the same way as Europeans (or Americans) are treated. By having information on culture and having an open mind, the negotiator can be prepared at all times and will not react in a surprised or inappropriate way to differences in behaviour.

CONCLUSION

Different negotiation situations could require different strategies. There could be a danger in overemphasising differences, especially in culture. Commonalities are probably more prolific and more important than any differences that may exist. Negotiators should search rather for what is common than what is unique in other individuals.

When a negotiator is confronted with a highly complicated situation such as a crisis, a hijack, a strike at the plant or a tense meeting of international politicians, he may find that the skills and approaches that were discussed in earlier chapters are quite sufficient. However, he may have to bear certain minimum requirements of politeness and behaviour in mind. In South Africa, a more sensitive approach to cultural differences could become increasingly important. Many of the postulates of this chapter on intercultural negotiation could soon change drastically. Hopefully, though, they will serve to make negotiators somewhat more careful because of the gradual growth in importance of continuous and ongoing relationships that will be to the benefit of all future agreements.

References

Abbott, T.E. 1986. Time-phase model for hostage negotiation. *Police Chief.* Vol. 53 (4), pp 34–36.

Arenson, E. and Linder, D. 1965. Gain and loss of esteem as determinants of interpersonal attractiveness. *Journal of Experimental Social Psychology.* Vol. 1, pp 156–171.

Argyle, M. 1975. *Bodily Communication.* London: Methuen.

Bales, R.F. 1950. *Interaction Process Analysis: A Method for the Study of Small Groups.* Cambridge, Massachusetts: Addison-Wesley.

Baron, R.A. 1980. *Human Aggression.* New York: Plenum Press.

Bettinghaus, E.P. 1966. *Message Preparation: The Nature of Proof.* Indianapolis: Bobbs-Merrill.

Bostrom, R.N. 1983. *Persuasion.* Englewood Cliffs, New Jersey: Prentice-Hall.

Carlisle, J. 1978. Successful negotiators. *Journal of Consumer and Industrial Trading.* Vol 2 (6), pp 7–11.

Christie, R. and Geis, F.L. (Eds.) 1971. *Studies in Machiavellianism.* New York: Academic Press.

Cialdini, R.B., Cacioppo, J.T., Bassett, B. and Miller, J.A. 1978. Low-ball procedure for producing compliance: Commitment then cost. *Journal of Personality and Social Psychology.* Vol. 36, pp 463–478.

Cialdini, R.B., Vincent, J.E., Lewis, S.K., Catalan, J., Wheeler, D. and Darby, B.L. 1975. Reciprocal concessions procedure for inducing compliance: The door-in-the-face technique. *Journal of Personality and Social Psychology.* Vol. 31, pp 206–215.

Dahl, R. 1957. The concept of power. *Behavioural Science.* Vol. [no not given], pp 202–203.

Delport, P. 1990. General principles of the law of contract. *Negotiation Skills Workshop.* Midrand, South Africa: Eskom Training Centre.

Feigenbaum, C. 1975. Final-offer arbitration. Better theory than practice. *Industrial Relations.* Vol. 14, pp 311–317.

Fisher R. and Ury, W. 1981. *Getting to Yes: Negotiating Agreements Without Giving In.* Boston: Houghton Mifflin.

Fisher, R. 1964. Fractionating conflict. In Fisher, R. (Ed.) *International Conflict and Behavioural Science.* New York: The Craigville Papers, New York Basic Books.

French, J.R.P. and Raven B. 1959. The basis of social power. In: Cartwright, D. (Ed.) *Studies in Social Power.* University of Michigan: Ann Arbor Institute of Social Research, pp 150–167.

Friedman, J.C. and Fraser, S.C. 1966. Compliance without pressure. The foot-in-the-door technique. *Journal of Personality and Social Psychology.* Vol. 4, pp 195–202.

Friedman, J.L., Carlsmith, J.M. and Sears, D.O. 1974. *Social Psychology.* Englewood Cliffs, New Jersey: Prentice-Hall.

Friedman, J.L., Carlsmith, J.M. and Sears, D.O. 1981. *Social Psychology.* Englewood Cliffs, New Jersey: Prentice-Hall.

Gibson, J.L., Ivancevich, J.M. and Donnolly, J.H. 1991. *Organisations: Behaviour, Structure, Processes.* 7th ed. Boston: Irwin.

Haber, R.N. and Fried, A.H. 1975. *An Introduction to Psychology.* New York: Holt, Rinehart and Winston Inc.

Hall, E. 1966. *The Hidden Dimension.* New York: Doubleday.

Henderson, P.E. 1989. Communication without words. *Personnel Journal.* Vol. 1, pp 22–29 (January).

Jacques, E. 1982. *The Form of Time.* New York: Crane Russell.

Janis, I. 1973. *Victims of Groupthink: A Psychological Study of Foreign Policy Decisions and Fiascos*. Boston: Houghton Mifflin.

Janis, I.L. and Mann, L. 1965. Effectiveness of emotional role playing in modifying smoking habits and attitudes. *Journal of Experimental Research in Personality*. Vol. 1, pp 84–90.

Kennedy, G. 1987. *Negotiate Anywhere!* London: Arrow Books.

Kipnis, D. 1976. *The Power Holders*. Chicago: University of Chicago Press.

Knapp, M. 1978. *Non-Verbal Communication in Human Interaction*. 2nd ed. New York: Rinehart and Winston.

Kraut, R.E. 1973. Effects of social labelling on giving to charity. *Journal of Experimental Social Psychology*. Vol. 9, pp 551–562.

Lakoff, G. and Johnson, M. 1980. *Metaphors we live by*. Chicago: University of Chicago Press.

Lewicki, R.J. and Litterer, J.A. 1985. *Negotiation*. Homewood, Illinois: Richard D Irwin.

MacMillan, I.C. 1974. *Aspects of Manipulative and Accommodating Behaviour by Graduate Middle Managers*. Unpublished Doctoral Thesis. Pretoria: University of South Africa.

Madriakis, S.G. 1990. *Forecasting, Planning and Strategy for the 21st Century*. New York: Free Press.

Marsh, P.D.V. 1988. *Contract Negotiation Handbook*. Essex: Gower Press.

McGuire, W.J. 1973. Persuasion, resistance and attitude change. In Poole, I.S., Frey, F.W., Schramm, W., Macoby, N. and Parker, G.B. (Eds.) *Handbook of Communication*. Skokie, Illinois: Rand McNally.

Mehrabian, A. 1971. *Silent Messages*. Belmont, California: Wadsworth.

Miles, R.E. and Snow, C.C. 1978. *Organisational Strategy, Structure and Process*. New York: McGraw-Hill.

Milgram, S. 1963. Behavioural study of obedience. *Journal of Abnormal and Social Psychology.* Vol. [no not given], pp 371–378 (October).

Mintzberg, H. 1984. Power and organisation life cycles. *Academy of Management Review.* Vol. [no not given], pp 207–224 (April).

Neale, M.A. and Bazerman, M.H. 1985. The effects of framing and negotiation overconfidence on bargaining behaviours and outcomes. *Academy of Management Journal.* Vol 28, pp 34–49.

Neale, M.A., Huber, V.L. and Northcraft, G.B. 1987. The framing of negotiations: Contextual versus task frames. *Organisational Behaviour and Human Decision Processes.* Vol. 39 (2), pp 228–241.

Nierenberg, G.I. 1973. *Fundamentals of Negotiating.* New York: Hawthorn Books.

Nieumeijer, L. 1988. *Negotiation — Methodology and Training.* Pinetown: Owen Burgess Publishers.

Osgood, C.E. 1962. *An Alternative to War or Surrender.* Urbana: University of Illinois Press.

Palland, B.G. and Jonges, P. 1966. *Beknopt Leerboek der Psychologie.* 9th ed. Groningen: J.P. Walters.

Pease, A. 1981. *Body Language.* London: Sheldon Press.

Peters, C. 1983. *How Washington Really Works.* Massachusetts: Addison-Wesley.

Pienaar, W.D. 1991. *Negotiation Skills Workshop Handout Module 1.* Seminar Series. Pretoria: School of Business Leadership, University of South Africa.

Pienaar, W.D. 1995. *Time and Timing—Hidden Dimensions of Strategic Adaptation under Conditions of Uncertainty.* Proceedings of the Annual Conference of Banque de Insinger Beauvour, Nijenrode University, Maarsden, Holland.

Pienaar, W.D. and Robinson, C.G. 1983. *Bargaining and Negotiation.* Four-day workshop. Seminar Series 8. Pretoria: School of Business Leadership, University of South Africa, Pretoria.

Piron, J. 1988. *Recognition or Rejection: Trade Union Recognition in South Africa.* 2nd ed. Johannesburg: Southern Book Publishers.

Rappoport, A. 1964. *Strategy and Conscience.* New York: Harper and Row.

Reader's Digest. 1984. *Great Illustrated Dictionary.* London: Reader's Digest.

Ridley, M. 1994. *The Red Queen—On the Nature of Human Sexuality.* London: Penguin.

Robinson, C.G. 1977. Bargaining and Negotiation Strategy. In Nasser M., Schmikl, G., Van Veijeren, G.J., Venter, J. *Readings in Organisational Behaviour.* Johannesburg: McGraw-Hill.

Rotter, J.B. 1966. Generalised expectations for internal versus external control of reinforcement. *Psychological Monographs.* Vol. 1, No. 609, pp 80.

Rubin, J.Z. and Brown, B.R. 1975. *The Social Psychology of Bargaining and Negotiation.* New York: Academic Press.

Schelling, T.C. 1960. *The Strategy of Conflict.* New York: Oxford University Press.

Schiffman, L.G. and Kanuk L.L. 1983. *Consumer Behaviour.* 2nd ed. New Jersey: Prentice-Hall.

Scott, B. 1988. *Negotiating.* London: Paradigm.

Sherif, M. and Sherif, C. 1953. *Groups in Harmony and Tension.* New York: Harper and Row.

Smith, G.H. 1989. *The Study of Business Negotiation in Japan.* Unpublished AEP Script. Pretoria: School of Business Leadership, University of South Africa.

Sperber, J. 1984. *Fail-Safe Negotiation.* New York: Free Press.

Spoelstra, H.I.J. 1981. *Kulturele Determinante van Organisatoriese Doeltreffendheid in Suid-Afrika en Japan.* Unpublished D. Comm. Thesis. Johannesburg: Rand Afrikaans University.

Spoelstra, H.I.J. 1990. Consumer perceptions and motivation. In Du Plessis, P.J., Rousseau, G.G and Blum N.H. 1990.

Consumer Behaviour. Johannesburg: Southern Book Publishers.

Spoelstra, H.I.J. 1991. *Negotiation Skills Workshop Handout, Module 3.* Four-day workshop. Pretoria: School of Business Leadership, University of South Africa.

Steele, C.M. 1975. Name calling and compliance. *Journal of Personality and Social Psychology.* Vol. 31, pp 361–369.

Steers, R.M. 1991. *Organisational Behaviour.* 4th ed. New York: Harper Collins Publishers.

Strauss, A. 1978. *Negotiation: Varieties, Contents, Processes and Social Order.* San Francisco: Jossey-Bass.

Thomas, K.W. 1977. Towards multidimensional values in teaching: The example of conflict behaviour. *Academy of Management Review.* Vol. 2, pp 484–490.

Thompson, J. 1967. *Organisations in Action.* New York: McGraw-Hill.

Tregoe, B.B. and Zimmerman, J.W. 1989. *Top Management Structure: What it is and how to make it work.* New York: Simon and Schuster.

Tuckman, B.W. 1965. Development sequences in small groups. *Psychological Bulletin.* Vol. [no not given], pp 384–399 (November).

Tzu, S. 1988. *The Art of War.* Clavell J (Ed). London: Hodder & Stoughton.

Wall, J.A. 1985. *Negotiation: Theory and Practice.* Glenview, Illinois: Prentice, Scott, Foresman and Co.

Weber, M. 1947. *Theory of Social and Economic Organisation.* New York: Free Press.

Wilkinson, M. Moral laws of the selfish gene. *Financial Times.* April 23, 1995.

Wilson, E.O. 1975. *Sociobiology.* Cambridge, Massachusetts: Harvard University Press.

Wright, R. 1995. *The Moral Animal.* London: Little Brown.

Index